The Literary Traveller
in
Edinburgh

For Chris

THE LITERARY TRAVELLER IN EDINBURGH

A Book Lover's Guide to the World's First City of Literature

Allan Foster

MAINSTREAM
PUBLISHING
EDINBURGH AND LONDON

First published in Great Britain in 2005 by
MAINSTREAM PUBLISHING COMPANY
(EDINBURGH) LTD
7 Albany Street
Edinburgh EH1 3UG

ISBN 1 84018 998 3

A catalogue record for this book is available
from the British Library

Typeset in Apollo, Univers and Zapf Chancery

Printed in Great Britain by
Scotprint, Haddington

Take not my hand as mine alone –
You do not trust to me –
I hold the hand of greater men
Too far before to see.

Follow not me, who only trace
Stoop-head the prints of those
Our mighty predecessors, whom
The darknesses enclose.

I cannot lead who follow – I
Who learn, am dumb to teach;
I can but indicate the goals
That greater men shall reach.

Robert Louis Stevenson,
Recruiting Songs (1872)

ACKNOWLEDGEMENTS

This book could not have been written without the help of those below. Thank you to you all:

Chris Foster, Noël Donoghue, Kevin O'Brien and Becky Pickard at Mainstream, Maureen Still, Arthur Still, Fred O'Brien and the staff of the Northern Design Unit, Robin Smith and the staff of the National Library of Scotland, Helen Osmani and the staff of the National Museum of Scotland, the staff of the Central Library's Edinburgh Room, Elaine Greig and the staff of The Writers' Museum, Nik and Nancy Phelps, Larry the O, Alan Marchbank, Ian Nimmo, Ron Macintosh, David Ross, Susannah Honeyman, Joy Fraser, Harry Winslow, June Clark, Lis Lee, Tom Bryan, Alistair Pattullo, Ken Bogle and the staff of Loanhead Library, Ray Harris, Walter Elliot, Jennie Renton, Richard Browne, Charlie Woolley and all at Sandy Bell's, Robert Turnbull and all at Rutherford's, Lizzie MacGregor and the staff of the Scottish Poetry Library, the staff of Kelso Library, John Hay and the staff of the Museum of Childhood, Kath McDonald, Bob Watt, Stewart Conn, Joan Lingard, Ewen MacCaig, Quintin Jardine, Jason Patient, Fiona Hooper, Dawn and Tony Greaves, Lucy Foster, Jack Foster, Chloe Foster, Kit Foster, Leah Wilkinson, Cissie Riddles, Ainslie Thin, George Fraser, Kate Love, Lord Tweedsmuir, Ann Macmillan, Andrei Dolnitski, Rob Gray, Sophy Dale and UNESCO City of Literature, John and Felicitas MacFie, Gordon Innes, Catherine Walker and the staff of Napier University Library, Neil Cape, Jim Wilkie, Peter Bell, Bill Smith, Morris Paton, Tim Bell, John Skinner, Jan Rutherford, Borders Books, Susan Pettigrew and the staff of Edinburgh University Library, Barbara Lamont, Jane Kenneway, Dougie Telfer, Derek Bolton, Karen Soutar, Christina Cran, Blackwell's, Hannah Smith, Rick and Ann Till, Andrew Pringle, Tom Chambers, Gordon J. Thomson, Ottakar's, Elizabeth Strong, Peter Galinsky, Stephanie Pickering, Donald Grant, William Lytle, David Govan, Gordon Martin, Jo Christison, Audrey Walker, Eddie Fenwick, Bert Barrott, Eric Dickson, George Watson's College.

Contents

Introduction

Treat this book like a treasure map that tells ye whaur tae howk. Then tak yer hurdies on a puckle dander roond this windflaucht city. Sometimes yer shovel will turn up gold, occasionally a wee bit shite, but when yer lookin for literati, who knows whaur yer finger-nebbs will alight. A guid guidebook shouldnae tell ye ony mair than ye want tae know or huv time tae absorb, so I hope this book leaves ye gaggin fur a wee keek mair. And mony a keek lasted mony a man a' his days. The journey, of course, never ends, but the treasure is there for the taking.

Allan Foster

Old Town

EDINBURGH CASTLE

> It is hardly necessary to say much about this Castle,
> which everybody has seen; on which account,
> doubtless, nobody has ever yet thought fit to describe it
> – at least that I am aware. Be this as it may, I have no
> intention of describing it . . .
>
> George Borrow, *Lavengro* (1851)

It may project a Colditz-like visage, but history has proved
Edinburgh Castle about as impregnable as a child's piggy-bank.
It never controlled any strategic north–south route and
invading armies often just gave it a wide berth, fighting
Scotland's decisive battles under the shadow of the much more
tactically positioned Stirling Castle, 30 miles to the north-west.
Much of the Scottish nobility shunned its refuge, preferring the
delights of Holyrood, and according to Midlothian-born
novelist Margaret Oliphant (1828–97), the room where Mary,
Queen of Scots gave birth to the future James VI and I 'would
scarcely be occupied, save under protest, by a housemaid in our
days'. Today, the Castle is one of the UK's most visited
attractions, but if it's just the spectacular view you're after,
nearby Calton Hill offers similar vistas at no charge.

The old Parliament Hall, on the south side of the Grand
Parade, was used for royal banquets as well as for meetings of
Parliament. It was here in 1440 that the Earl of Douglas and his
younger brother were invited to dine as guests of the King,

ten-year-old James II, by his Regents Sir Alexander Livingstone and Sir William Crichton. The House of Douglas was seen as a threat to the Regency and the invitation was a trap, described dramatically by Sir Walter Scott in *Tales of a Grandfather* (1828–30):

> Of a sudden, the scene began to change. At an entertainment which was served up to the Earl and his brother, the head of a black bull was placed on the table. The Douglases knew this, according to a custom which prevailed in Scotland, to be the sign of death, and leaped from the table in great dismay. But they were seized by armed men who entered the apartment. They underwent a mock trial, in which all the insolences of their ancestors were charged against them, and were condemned to immediate execution. The young King wept and implored Livingstone and Crichton to show mercy to the young noblemen, but in vain. These cruel men only reproved him for weeping at the death of those whom they called his enemies. The brothers were led out to the court of the Castle, and beheaded without delay.

'The Vaults' were used as a prison for French soldiers during the Napoleonic Wars, a period which Robert Louis Stevenson used as the setting for *St Ives* (1897), in which he relates the adventures of the Vicomte de Saint-Yves:

> It was in the month of May 1813 that I was so unlucky as to fall at last into the hands of the enemy . . . Into the Castle of Edinburgh, standing in the midst of that city on the summit of an extraordinary rock, I was cast with several hundred fellow-sufferers . . .

English writer George Borrow (1803–81) lived within the Castle walls as a boy when his soldier father was posted there, and the famous landmark duly features in his autobiographical novel *Lavengro* (1851). 'To scale the rock was merely child's play for the Edinbro' callants [young boys],' he recalled. Once, he casually remarked to a friend while seated at the rock's summit that the story of William Wallace was 'full of lies'. To this, his friend retorted, 'Ye had better sae naething agin Willie Wallace, Geordie, for if ye do, De'il hae me, if I dinna tumble ye doon the craig.'

Novelist Eric Linklater (1899–1974) was billeted at the Castle during the

William Wallace impersonator Adam Watters regularly guards the entrance to the Castle esplanade, and thou shalt not pass until you've donated some spare change to the Anthony Nolan Bone Marrow Trust.

First World War after he was badly wounded at Ypres. He featured Edinburgh Castle in *The Impregnable Women* (1938), his modern version of Aristophanes' *Lysistrata*, and describes it in his 1934 novel, *Magnus Merriman*, as 'Scotland's castle, Queen Mary's castle and the castle of fifty thousand annual visitors who walk through it with rain on their boots and bewilderment in their hearts'.

SEE ALSO: Sir Walter Scott, Swanston Cottage, Margaret Oliphant.

FURTHER READING: M.D. Armstrong, *George Borrow* (Haskell House, 1982); M. Parnell, *Eric Linklater: A Critical Biography* (John Murray, 1984).

(RAMSAY GARDEN)

Ramsay Lodge
Home of Allan Ramsay (1686–1758), poet, bookseller, publisher and creator of Britain's first lending library

> When these good old Bards wrote, we had not yet made Use of imported Trimming.
>
> Allan Ramsay, from the preface of *The Evergreen* (1724), a collection of Scots poems written before 1600

Allan Ramsay was the precursor of Robert Fergusson and Robert Burns in helping to reawaken and develop an interest in the vernacular tradition of Scottish song and verse, and, in so doing, inspired their genius. Like Fergusson and Burns, he enjoyed the camaraderie of the tavern, the bawdy song, the brothel and the language of the common people. He was a poet who became a bookseller and publisher, but, probably more importantly, he was also a great propagandist who did much to rejuvenate the Scots language.

He was born in the Leadhills, Lanarkshire, on 15 October 1686. His father, who died shortly after his birth, was factor to the Earl of Hopeton. In 1701, Ramsay was apprenticed to an Edinburgh wig-maker, and in 1710 opened his own premises in the Grassmarket. He was inspired to write verse when he became a member of the Easy Club, a literary and political drinking club he helped found in 1712. He became the Club Laureate in 1715 and began publishing his own work in broadsheets. His reputation as a poet began to grow and, in 1718, the master wig-maker metamorphosed into a bookseller and converted his premises into a bookshop. Four years

Allan Ramsay's statue at the corner of Princes Street and The Mound.

13

later, he moved from the Grassmarket to a shop in the Luckenbooths 'alongside St Giles Church', where his window looked onto the City Cross. It was from this building, in 1728, that Ramsay created the first lending library in Britain, wonderfully described by the God-fearing Reverend Robert Wodrow as a place where 'All the villainous, profane, and obscene books and plays, as printed in London, are got down by Allan Ramsay and lent out, for an easy price, to young boys, servant weemen of the better sort, and gentlemen.'

He published the first collection of his own poems in 1721, and, in 1723, he published *The Tea-Table Miscellany*, collections of eighteenth-century songs and ballads, and, in 1724, *The Evergreen*, containing the works of Scotland's late medieval poets, including Dunbar and Henryson. In 1725, while living and trading in Niddry's Wynd (now Niddry Street) he produced his dramatic pastoral *The Gentle Shepherd*. Ramsay founded Edinburgh's first theatre in 1736 in Carruber's Close, off the High Street, but this was soon closed down following the Licensing Act of 1737, which banned theatrical performances outside the City of London. Ramsay's wrath penned many a satirical verse to the Court of Session on this subject, which not only humiliated him, but 'cost him dearly':

> Shall London have its houses twa
> And we doomed to have nane ava?
> Is our metropolis, ance the place
> Where langsyne dwelt the royal race.

In 1755, he retired from his business to the house he had built on the slopes of Castle Hill. Known affectionately as 'the goose-pie' because of its octagonal shape, he lived out the rest of his life there with his 'burd' (wife). He died on 7 January 1758 and is buried in Greyfriars Kirkyard.

SEE ALSO: Greyfriars Kirkyard, Robert Fergusson, Robert Burns.

FURTHER INFORMATION: Ramsay Garden, Castle Hill, is situated near the top of the Royal Mile. On Ramsay's death, his house passed to his son Allan, the famous portrait painter. Other occupants over the years have included poet and essayist Anne Grant (1755–1838) and novelist John Galt (1779–1839).

FURTHER READING: J.B. Martin, *Allan Ramsay: A Study of his Life and Works* (Greenwood Press, 1973).

(JAMES COURT)

Site of the residence of James Boswell (1740–95), where Dr Johnson lodged prior to their tour of the Hebrides in 1773

Servile and impertinent, shallow and pedantic, a bigot and a sot, bloated with family pride, and eternally blustering about the dignity of a born gentleman, yet stooping to be a talebearer, and eavesdropper, a common butt in the taverns of London . . . Everything

which another man would have hidden, everything the
publication of which would have made another man
hang himself, was matter of exaltation to his weak and
diseased mind.
                                    Lord Macaulay (1800–59) on Boswell

The American literary critic Edmund Wilson (1895–1972) once
described Boswell as 'a vain and pushing artist', and he was
probably right. He certainly comes across as extremely
persistent and an ardent social climber. He also picked up
prostitutes, contracted gonorrhoea, was the father of an
illegitimate child, had prolonged bouts of drunkenness and was
unfaithful to his wife. In spite of these apparent shortcomings,
however, Boswell's inherently perspicacious nature and his
intimate knowledge of Johnson have clearly combined to
produce a biographical masterpiece which has never been
equalled.

Boswell was born in Edinburgh in 1740, the eldest son of
Lord Auchinleck, a lawyer who came from a family of wealthy
Ayrshire landowners. He was educated at a private academy in
Edinburgh and by private tutors, later studying law at
Edinburgh, Glasgow and Utrecht. His ambitions began leaning
towards literature, politics and the theatre, but it was as an
advocate that he practised for most of his life, which left him
feeling 'sadly low-spirited, indolent, listless and gloomy'. While
in Europe, he skilfully effected meetings with Voltaire, Rousseau
and the Corsican hero Pasquale Paoli, which inspired him to
write his *Account of Corsica* (1768), his first significant work. In
1769, he married his cousin, Margaret Montgomerie, a long-
suffering woman who endured his infidelities until her death,
leaving Boswell with six children and a guilt complex.

He first met Dr Johnson (1709–84) on his second visit to
London, on 16 May 1763 at Tom Davies' bookshop in Russell
Street, and from then on cemented his friendship with him on
his all-too-infrequent visits to London. On 14 August 1773, Dr
Johnson arrived in Edinburgh to begin his famous tour of the
Hebrides with Boswell, and it was at Boswell's townhouse at 501
on the western half of James Court (destroyed, unfortunately, by
fire in 1857, but later rebuilt) that he entertained Johnson that
Saturday evening:

> My wife had tea ready for him, which it is well known
> he delighted to drink at all hours, particularly when
> sitting up late. He shewed much complacency upon
> finding that the mistress of the house was so attentive
> to his singular habit; and as no man could be more
> polite when he chose to be so, his address to her was
> most courteous and engaging; and his conversation
> soon charmed her into a forgetfulness of his external
> appearance.
>
> We sat till near two in the morning, having chatted
> a good while after my wife left us. She had insisted, that
> to shew all respect to the Sage, she would give up her
> own bed-chamber to him, and take a worse. This I

> cannot but gratefully mention, as one of a thousand
> obligations which I owe her, since the great obligation
> of her being pleased to accept of me as her husband.

On Wednesday, 18 August 1773, Boswell and Johnson set out from James Court on their celebrated tour of Scotland and the Hebrides, returning to Edinburgh 83 days later on Tuesday, 9 November. Johnson was 63 years old and Boswell 32. 'I mentioned our design to Voltaire,' wrote Boswell. 'He looked at me as if I had talked of going to the North Pole . . .'

They each kept a journal, and while Johnson was busy cynically scrutinising Scotland, Boswell was busy scrutinising and recording Johnson. 'We came too late,' wrote Johnson, 'to see what we expected.'

In 1784, when Boswell was 44, Johnson died. Two years later, Boswell was called to the English Bar and moved to London with his wife and children, but his practice was unsuccessful. He was also unsuccessful in his pursuit of a political career, and he eventually began to write his *Life of Samuel Johnson*, 'perhaps now the only concern of any consequence' that he would 'ever have in this world'. While he was writing his *Life*, other biographies of Johnson were being published, and his greatest fear must have been that the public, having gorged on Johnson, would finally say enough was enough – and Boswell's was stretching to two volumes at a cost of two guineas. It was finally published in 1791, and its reception, recorded Boswell, was 'very favourable'. Forty years later, in 1831, Thomas Macaulay declared it the best biography ever written, and Thomas Carlyle, writing in *Fraser's* magazine in 1832, described it as a book 'beyond any other product of the eighteenth century . . . It was as if the curtains of the past were drawn aside, and we looked into a country . . . which had seemed forever hidden from our eyes . . . Wondrously given back to us, there once more it lay. There it still lies.'

Boswell, however, had always been well aware of his talents, writing in his journal for 20 January 1763, 'I think there is a blossom about me of something more distinguished than the generality of mankind.'

SEE ALSO: Dr Johnson, David Hume, St Giles.

FURTHER READING: I. Finlayson, *The Moth and the Candle: Life of James Boswell* (Constable, 1984); G. Turnbull (ed.), *The Yale Editions of the Private Papers of James Boswell* (Edinburgh Uni. Press, 2004); D. Hankins and J. Caudle (eds), *The General Correspondence of James Boswell, 1757–63* (Edinburgh Uni. Press, 2004).

RIDDLE'S COURT

Former home of David Hume (1711–76), Scottish philosopher, historian and political thinker

> A man who has so much conceit as to tell all mankind that they have bubbled for ages, and he is the wise man who sees better than they – a man who has so little scrupulosity as to venture to oppose those principles which have been thought necessary to human happiness – is he to be surprised if another man comes and laughs at him?
>
> Dr Johnson on David Hume

Dr Johnson's reaction to Hume was typical for his time. As a celebrated atheist, sceptic, believer in civil liberties, opponent of 'divine right' and a political thinker who greatly influenced European thought, it's not surprising that many thought that David Hume was in league with the Devil. Even the binge-drinking, whoring and gonorrhoea-ridden James Boswell thought his character might be besmirched by associating with Hume, commenting, 'I was not clear that it was right in me to keep company with him.' German philosopher Immanuel Kant, however, was not so blinkered, reporting in the *Prolegomena* that Hume 'first interrupted my dogmatic slumber', and Jeremy Bentham said Hume 'caused the scales to fall' from his eyes. Charles Darwin considered him a central influence, and history now rightfully ranks Hume as one of the great men of genius in eighteenth-century Edinburgh.

Born in Edinburgh in 1711, Hume spent his childhood at Ninewells, his family's estate near Chirnside in the Scottish Borders. When he was 12, he attended Edinburgh University but did not graduate. He later studied law and was briefly employed as a clerk for a Bristol sugar importer before entering the Jesuit College at La Flèche in 1734, where for three years he read French and other European literature. It was here, between 1734 and 1737, that he drafted his first and most important work, *A Treatise of Human Nature*, which he published anony-mously in 1739. Its hostile reception prompted Hume to describe it as falling 'dead-born from the press'. He produced two, more popular, volumes of *Essays Moral and Political* in 1741 and 1742. He applied for the chair of moral philosophy at Edinburgh in 1744, but his religious scepticism ruled

David Hume's statue on the corner of Bank Street and the Lawnmarket.

17

against him. For the next seven or eight years, he held various posts as tutor, secretary and minor diplomat, returning to Edinburgh in 1751 to take up a post as librarian to the faculty of advocates.

Hume's first permanent Edinburgh home was at Riddel's Land (now Riddle's Court), 322 High Street, 'in the first court reached on entering the close, and it is approached by a projecting turret stair'. Hume described his household as 'consisting of a head, viz. myself, and two inferior members – a maid and a cat. My sister has since joined me, and keeps me company.' It was in this house that Hume wrote his *Political Discourses* (1752) and started on his monumental *History of England* (5 volumes, 1754–62). In 1753, he moved to Jack's Land, now renumbered 229 Canongate, where he lived for nine years, and where he completed his *History*, a work which became a bestseller and at last made him financially independent. From 1763 to 1765 he acted as secretary to the British ambassador in Paris, where he was fêted by the French court. He befriended Rousseau and returned to London with him in 1766, but they later quarrelled bitterly. In 1767, he became undersecretary of state for the Northern Department, returning to Scotland in 1768, where he lived out the rest of his life as a man of letters at his house on a corner of St Andrew Square – a then-unnamed street. One day, his maid informed him that someone had chalked 'St David's Street' on the wall. 'Never mind, lassie, mony a waur man has been made a saint o' before.'

David Hume died aged 65 of intestinal cancer on 25 August 1776, and is buried in Old Calton Burial Ground, Waterloo Place.

SEE ALSO: Old Calton Burial Ground, Pilrig House, Dr Johnson, James Boswell.

FURTHER INFORMATION: From 1762 to 1770, Hume lived across the street from Riddle's Court in James Court, a flat he later leased to James Boswell. During the 1960s, the southern edge of George Square was demolished to make way for the new buildings of Edinburgh University. The tall tower built to the east of the library was named David Hume Tower, and a better example of an architectural monstrosity will not be found anywhere. Robert Garioch immortalised the tower in his poem 'A Wee Local Scandal'. A statue of David Hume was erected in 1997 on the corner of Bank Street and the Lawnmarket by the Saltire Society to mark its 60th anniversary. Due to the statue's low height, Hume's head can often be seen sporting a jaunty traffic cone.

FURTHER READING: R. Graham, *The Great Infidel* (Tuckwell Press, 2005); A.J. Ayer, *Hume* (Oxford, 1980); P. Jones, *Hume's Sentiments* (Edinburgh Uni. Press, 1982).

LADY STAIR'S CLOSE

Site of Baxter's Close (now demolished)
Lodgings of Robert Burns (1759–96) on his first visit to Edinburgh during the winter of 1786–7

> Men and women quite suddenly realised that here lay one who was the poet of the country – perhaps of mankind – as none had been before, because none before had combined so many human weaknesses with so great an ardour of living and so generous a warmth of admission. Certainly none had ever possessed a racier gift of expression for his own people.
>
> Catherine Carswell on the death of Burns,
> in *The Life of Robert Burns* (1930)

Robert Burns is without doubt the most celebrated of Scottish poets. He left for posterity a volume of work which, written in his native tongue and championing the common man, has

contributed significantly to Scottish cultural identity. Following the success of the first edition of his poems in July 1786, the famous Kilmarnock edition of *Poems, Chiefly in the Scottish Dialect*, Burns was eager to print a second edition as soon as possible, but the Kilmarnock printer insisted on full payment in advance. Unable to pay, he was persuaded to try for a second edition in Edinburgh.

And so the 'ploughman poet' set out from Ayrshire for his first visit to the metropolis on a borrowed horse, arriving on the evening of 28 November 1786. After stabling his horse in the Grassmarket, he made his way to nearby Baxter's Close, off the Lawnmarket, where he shared lodgings with his old friend John Richmond, from Mauchline, employed at this time as a clerk in a law office. Richmond's room, which he rented for three shillings a week, consisted of 'a deal table, a sanded floor and a chaff bed', and was conveniently situated below a brothel.

One of the first things Burns did after his arrival was to search out poet Robert Fergusson's neglected grave in Canongate Kirkyard and set the wheels in motion for a simple memorial stone to be erected over his unmarked grave. He also visited the Castle and the Palace, stood in reverence outside Allan Ramsay's house and climbed up Arthur's Seat with all the ardour of a typical tourist; but he had come to Edinburgh for much more than sightseeing.

In his pocket, he carried a sheaf of introductory letters from his Masonic brothers back in Ayrshire and, within a week, doors opened and his star began to rise. The Earl of Glencairn was particularly helpful, and Professor Dugald Stewart was instrumental in getting the Kilmarnock edition favourably reviewed by Henry Mackenzie in *The Lounger*, a magazine published by William Creech, who was to become the publisher of the second edition of Burns's poems, the Edinburgh edition, in April 1787. Glencairn took out a subscription of 24 copies and persuaded the Caledonian Hunt to take up 100 copies, which earned them the book's dedication. The Edinburgh edition was heavily oversubscribed, and, after a second and third print run, 3,000 copies were eventually printed. This edition had 22 new poems, including the 'Address to a Haggis', and the copyright was sold to Creech for 100 guineas.

Burns was 28 years old, just under 6 ft tall, well built with a slight stoop from years at the plough, and with the twinkle in his eyes of a Don Juan. Dressed in his famous blue coat, buff waistcoat, buckskin breeches and high boots, with neck and cuffs trimmed with lace, Robert Burns the ploughman poet had arrived.

Everybody who was anybody made a point of meeting this latest vogue of the city's salons and drawing rooms and Burns initially enjoyed being the focus of so much fame and attention. It wasn't long, however, before he began to feel like a prize pig brought from his pen for the amusement of the party guests. He wrote to a friend:

> I am willing to believe that my abilities deserved a better fate than the veriest shades of life; but to be dragged forth, with all my imperfections on my head, to the full glare of learned and polite observations, is what, I am afraid, I shall have bitter reason to repent.

Eventually, the novelty of the ploughman poet wore off for the city's literati and Burns became something of an embarrassment, with Dugald Stewart commenting, 'his conduct and manners had become so degraded that decent persons could hardly take any notice of him'. To be fair to Burns, he had probably had enough of the airs and graces of genteel Edinburgh and was reaching out for what he enjoyed best – drinking wine, wooing lassies and singing a bawdy song.

Although Burns had become disillusioned with the trappings of fame, he did achieve what he came to Edinburgh for: a second edition of his poems. He also befriended the printer of his book, William Smellie, who in turn introduced him to his famous drinking club, The Crochallan Fencibles. James Johnson approached Burns to help him with the lyrics of the second volume of his book *The Scots Musical Museum*, a collection of songs, many of which were eventually written by Burns and occupied him until the end of his life.

On 5 May 1787, Burns left Edinburgh on horseback for a tour of the Scottish Borders with his law-student friend and fellow Mason Bob Ainslie. One person Burns didn't meet in Edinburgh was James Boswell, who was visiting London at the time. History would have been the better for a description of the immortal bard from the pen of Boswell. One wonders what he would have made of Burns.

SEE ALSO: Anchor Close, St James Square, Buccleuch Street, Burns Monument, Canongate Kilwinning Lodge, White Hart Inn, St Giles, William Smellie, William Creech, The Writers' Museum, Sciennes Hill House, Robert Fergusson, Clarinda, Jean Lorimer, Henry Mackenzie, The Blind Poet pub.

FURTHER INFORMATION: Baxter's Close, which was demolished in 1798 during the construction of Bank Street, would have been on the east side of Lady Stair's Close.

FURTHER READING: D. Daiches, *Robert Burns* (Saltire, 1994); J.A. Mackay, *A Biography of Robert Burns* (Alloway, 2004); I. Grimble, *Robert Burns* (Hamlyn, 1986); Revd G. Gilfillan, *National Burns* (London, 1880).

The Writers' Museum
Dedicated to the life and works of Robert Burns, Sir Walter Scott and Robert Louis Stevenson

> There's muckle lyin yont the Tay that's mair to me nor life
> Violet Jacob (1863–1946). Quotation inscribed in stone in the Makars' Court

There is an argument for building a new and more spacious writers' museum for Edinburgh that would do full justice to its vast literary heritage, but trading the small and rather stuffy Lady Stair's House for a prizewinning architect's steel and glass vision would be literally losing the plot. Edinburgh's literary past is historically welded to the cramped, rabbit-warren ghetto of the Old Town, and it seems only fitting that a museum dedicated to

three of its biggest hitters should be located here. Lady Stair's Close was the chief thoroughfare for foot passengers from the Old Town to the New Town prior to the opening of Bank Street. Today it is a spacious square, but in the eighteenth century this area was packed cheek by jowl with tenements, including the adjacent Baxter's Close, where Robert Burns lodged in the winter of 1886–7. Outside the museum is the Makars' Court, where Scottish writers, from the fourteenth-century poet John Barbour to Sorley Maclean, are celebrated with inscriptions carved into stones. The house, which has had many owners, was built in 1622 for local merchant Sir William Grey, but its most memorable occupant was the Dowager Countess of Stair, who

Robert Burns in James Sibbald's Circulating Library, Parliament Square, **by William Borthwick Johnstone. The young Walter Scott is seated in the foreground.**

presided over Edinburgh's fashionable society and, as the Viscountess Primrose, inspired Scott's story 'My Aunt Margaret's Mirror'.

The museum is on three floors. The RLS room is in the basement, Scott's on the middle floor and Burns's on the top.

Artefacts connected to Stevenson on display include: various photographs and paintings; the 'Davos' printing press on which he and Lloyd Osbourne produced *Moral Emblems* and *The Graver and the Pen*; a first edition of *A Child's Garden of Verses* (1885); letters to W.E. Henley and Alison Cunningham; a 1908 edition of *An Inland Voyage*; a copy of George Borrow's *The Bible in Spain*, which Stevenson took with him on his *Travels with a Donkey*; a wineglass and plate used at Vailima, the Stevensons' home in Samoa; riding boots used in Samoa; and also a cabinet made by the infamous Deacon Brodie, which sat in young Louis's bedroom.

The Scott collection includes: his wallet; walking sticks; a brass face-plate and latch from 39 North Castle Street; a letter claiming exemption from the Army Reserve; a lock of Scott's hair; first editions of *Waverley*, *The Antiquary* and *The Vision of Don Roderick*; and a rocking horse with one foot-rest higher than the other to accommodate his right leg, disabled through poliomyelitis contracted when he was about 18 months old.

The Robert Burns collection includes: a lock of Jean Armour's hair; her gloves and umbrella; an account and receipt sent to Burns for the erection of a headstone on Robert Fergusson's unmarked grave; drawings and poetry by Clarinda; and a round carved oak table, made from the rafters of the Crochallan Fencibles' club rooms in Anchor Close.

SEE ALSO: Robert Burns, Sir Walter Scott, Robert Louis Stevenson, Clarinda, Robert Fergusson, William Smellie.

FURTHER INFORMATION: The Writers' Museum, Lady Stair's Close, Lawnmarket, Edinburgh EH1 2PA. Tel: 0131 529 4901. 10 a.m.–5 p.m., Monday to Saturday. Sundays during August, 12 p.m.–5 p.m. Admission free.

BRODIE'S CLOSE

Site of Deacon Brodie's house
A notorious burglar who fascinated and inspired Robert Louis Stevenson

> Do you see this table, Walter? He made it while he was yet a 'prentice. I remember how I used to sit and watch him at his work. It would be grand, I thought, to be able to do as he did, and handle edge-tools without cutting my fingers, and getting my ears pulled for a meddlesome minx!
>
> From *Deacon Brodie, or, The Double Life* (1880), by RLS and W.E. Henley

William Brodie entered Stevenson's imagination, and no doubt his nightmares, from a very early age. His bedroom at Heriot Row — which was furnished with items of furniture made by Brodie — was where his nurse Cummy, 'with her vivid Scotch imagination' (recalled Stevenson's wife), had told him endless tales about the rogue.

Brodie was a cabinet-maker and respected member of the Town Council, but after hours he whored, gambled, boozed and supported two mistresses and numerous children. He financed his expensive lifestyle with nocturnal robberies, often carried out on his customers using door keys copied while working in their houses. His last armed robbery was at the excise office in Chessel's Court, on the Canongate, where the authorities caught his gang in the act. Brodie escaped to Holland, but was later captured. He was hanged at the Tolbooth on a gallows of his own design in 1788, and is buried in an unmarked grave in the kirkyard of the former Buccleuch Parish Church.

Stevenson wrote a play about this unsavoury character with his friend W.E. Henley in 1880. They wrote three more plays together, but neither were dramatists, and the plays are rarely read, let alone performed, today.

To say that Deacon Brodie inspired *The Strange Case of Dr Jekyll and Mr Hyde* would be stretching it, but it was probably one of many ingredients which seeped into Stevenson's 'fine bogey tale' about the division of good and evil in man. Stevenson wrote the story, which came to him in a dream, when he was seriously ill with a 'hectic fever' at his house in Bournemouth in 1885. The first draft of the story was written in three days, but after Stevenson's wife criticised him for missing the point, i.e. missing the allegory, he

Deacon Brodie
by John Kay, 1788.

burned the manuscript and rewrote the story as we know it today. Although it is set in London, it was Edinburgh that inspired many of the landscapes. The story became a bestseller in Britain and America and the adjectival expression 'Jekyll and Hyde' is now part of the English language.

SEE ALSO: Howard Place, Inverleith Terrace, Heriot Row, Pilrig House, Colinton Manse, Swanston Cottage, Baxter's Place, Glencorse Kirk, Rutherford's Howff, New Calton Cemetery, Old Calton Burial Ground, St Giles, Hawes Inn, Rullion Green, W.E. Henley, Alison Cunningham, Henderson's School, *Kidnapped* Statue, RLS Club, Museum of Scotland, George Mackenzie, Martyrs' Monument, Edinburgh Castle, Old College, Parliament Hall, Holyrood Park, Royal College of Surgeons' Museum, R.M. Ballantyne, RLS Memorial, Writers' Corner.

FURTHER INFORMATION: A cabinet made by Deacon Brodie, which was in Stevenson's childhood bedroom, can be seen at The Writers' Museum, Lady Stair's Close. Brodie is buried in the graveyard of Buccleuch Church, on the west side of Chapel Street. Deacon Brodie's Tavern (0131 225 6531) is opposite Brodie's Close, and The Jekyll & Hyde pub is located at 112 Hanover Street (0131 225 2022).

FURTHER READING: W. Veeder and G. Hirsch (eds), *Dr Jekyll and Mr Hyde after One Hundred Years* (Uni. of Chicago Press, 1988); J. Herdman, *The Double in Nineteenth-Century Fiction* (Palgrave, 1990).

THE HEART OF MIDLOTHIAN

The Old Tolbooth Prison featured in Walter Scott's 1818 novel

The Heart of Midlothian was the nickname of the Old Tolbooth Prison, which was situated close to the north-west corner of St Giles. Built in the early fifteenth century, it served over the years as a town hall, a customs office, a Parliament and a Court of Session. An eighteenth-century visitor to the prison described it as having 'no ventilation, water nor privy: filth was thrown into a hole at the foot of the stair, leading to a drain so completely choked as to serve no other purpose but filling the gaol with a disagreeable stench'. The Heart of Midlothian was also the name of the prison's punishment cell: a 9-ft square, iron-plated oak chest, built into a stone wall and sealed by a heavy iron door. When the prison was demolished in 1817, Walter Scott acquired the door of the punishment cell and added it to his collection of relics at Abbotsford, his Border retreat.

Captain Porteous was imprisoned in the Old Tolbooth after he was sentenced to death for ordering the City Guard to open fire on a stone-throwing crowd after a public hanging in the Grassmarket in 1736. He was later reprieved, but an enraged Edinburgh mob dispensed their own justice, storming the Tolbooth and hanging him from a dyer's pole. Scott recounted the events of that night in his novel *The Heart of Midlothian* (for a full account, see Grave of Captain Porteous, Greyfriars Kirkyard).

The Old Tolbooth.

Dorothy Dunnett imprisoned her romantic hero, Francis Crawford of Lymond, in the Old Tolbooth in her very first historical novel, *Game of Kings*, published in 1961. The site of the prison today is marked by inlaid brass sets, and a heart-shaped motif sunk into the cobbles, near the statue of the Seventh Duke of Queensberry. As befits the memory of such an obnoxious place, the passing public traditionally embellish the cobbled motif with generous gobbets of spit, although the reasoning behind the gesture for most daily gob-droppers has long been forgotten.

SEE ALSO: Birthplace of W.S., childhood home of W.S., townhouse of W.S., Lasswade Cottage, Parliament Hall, Greyfriars Kirkyard, Scott Monument, Holyrood Park, St John's Churchyard, The Writers' Museum, High School, Old College, Sciennes Hill House, Assembly Rooms, J.G. Lockhart, Portobello Sands, Canongate Kirkyard, The Edinburgh Walter Scott Club, Dorothy Dunnett.

FURTHER INFORMATION: In 1813, an Act of Parliament proposed the building of a new prison, and Calton Jail opened in 1817 on Regent Road, the year the Old Tolbooth was demolished. Although the new prison had a modern interior, the exterior was in a fake-Gothic style inspired by the Waverley novels. The turrets of the old governor's house can still be seen in the south-east corner of the Old Calton Burial Ground, Waterloo Place.

PARLIAMENT SQUARE

Parliament Hall
Where advocates Walter Scott and Robert Louis Stevenson perambulated in conference with their clients

> I walk about Parliament House five forenoons a week, in wig and gown; I have either a five- or six-mile walk, or an hour or two hard skating on the rink, without fail; and – well, this is not so good perhaps but is part of my system – I sit up late at night and sometimes wet my whistle.
>
> RLS, letter to Sydney Colvin (1875)

Simon Crouch portraying Walter Scott, sheriff-deputy of Selkirkshire, at the Scott's Selkirk festival. (© Rob Gray/ digitalpic)

Although Scott and Stevenson both qualified as advocates, their law careers were very different. Stevenson passed his Bar exams in July 1875 and was given the enormous sum of £1,000 from his father to launch his legal career. He ceremoniously put up a brass plaque at 17 Heriot Row, but shortly afterwards he retired from the law, by which time the money was all spent. Financial insecurity never appeared on his horizon as his father bankrolled him well into his writing career. Earning a living as a lawyer was never seriously considered.

Scott remained a lawyer all his days. In 1792, he qualified as an advocate, became principal clerk to the Court of Session in 1806 and remained sheriff-deputy of Selkirkshire until his death in 1832. His first novel, *Waverley*, was published in 1814, but novel-writing at that time was viewed as a lowly form of literature – certainly not something a principal clerk to the Court of Session should be involved with – and Scott sensibly published anonymously. Also, Scott liked being a part of the Establishment, and a career in the legal world ensured he remained part of it.

The courts are housed in old Parliament House, a seventeenth-century building fronted by a nineteenth-century facade in Parliament Square, home of the Scottish Parliament between 1639 and the Act of Union in 1707 and now part of the High Court complex. The building comprises Parliament Hall and the Inner and Outer Houses. Advocates still promenade and strut around Parliament Hall just as Scott and Stevenson would have done, waiting to be hired, or in conference with their clients. Under the gilded oak hammerbeam roof of the Great Hall stands a statue of Scott, surrounded by portraits of legal worthies over the centuries, lit by the huge Great South Window depicting James V founding the College of Justice.

RLS in advocate's robes.

SEE ALSO: Sir Walter Scott, Robert Louis Stevenson, Quintin Jardine.

FURTHER INFORMATION: Parliament Hall is open to the public. RLS's advocate's thesis is in the National Library of Scotland. The courtroom Scott used in Selkirk when he was 'Shirra' is open to the public from April to October (tel: 01750 720761).

HIGH STREET

St Giles Cathedral
The High Kirk of Edinburgh

> Come, let me see what was once a church!
> Dr Johnson in Boswell's *Journal of a Tour to the Hebrides* (1785)

A church has stood on this site at the epicentre of the Old Town since before AD 854. Over 1,000 years later, St Giles, reputedly named after a French saint who supported the Auld Alliance between Scotland and France, still stands unyielding, having survived numerous reincarnations, renovations, burnings, riots, the doctrines of John Knox and the stinging criticisms of Dr Johnson and Robert Louis Stevenson, the latter remarking, in 1878, on its latest renovation in *Edinburgh: Picturesque Notes*:

> The church itself, if it were not for the spire, would be unrecognisable; the Krames are all gone, not a shop is left to shelter in its buttresses; and zealous magistrates and a misguided architect have shorn the design of manhood, and left it poor, naked, and pitifully pretentious.

Boswell thought it 'shamefully dirty' (an ironic comment coming from someone Dr Johnson could smell in the dark! – see Canongate, Boyd's Entry), but considering St Giles has been used over the years as a prison, police office and general storeroom, its past state of degradation is not surprising. Today it stands solitary and detached, but until fairly recently in history it was cramped by encroaching tenements, the Old Tolbooth Prison and the Luckenbooths shopping arcade – seven timber-fronted tenements of six storeys clamped to its north wall. The clutter and filth of its past have now disappeared, but even in the twentieth century, the haunting presence of 'its tattered bloodstained banners of the past' sent a chill through

27

Jean Brodie's pupil Sandy, who 'had not been there, and did not want to go'.

St Giles's first minister after the Reformation in 1560 was John Knox (c.1513–72), a theologian who has been branded by history as a joyless, narrow-minded bigot. Rightly or wrongly, anyone who writes a tract entitled 'The First Blast of the Trumpet Against the Monstrous Regiment of Women' has to take what's coming to them. Nobody, however, can deny Knox's place as the father of the Protestant Reformation in Scotland, which replaced the Catholic Church with the Presbyterian Church of Scotland, founded on Calvinist principles. His *Historie of the Reformation of the Church of Scotland* was first printed in 1587. The poet Edwin Muir wrote a biography of Knox, but when writing it came to dislike Knox intensely, understanding 'why every Scottish writer since the beginning of the eighteenth century had detested him: Hume, Boswell, Burns, Scott, Hogg, Stevenson; everyone except Carlyle, who, like Knox, admired power'. Dr Johnson described Knox as one of the 'ruffians of the Reformation' and Boswell relates in his *Journal of a Tour to the Hebrides* that he 'happened to ask where Knox was buried'. Dr Johnson burst out, 'I hope in the highway. I have been looking at his reformations.' Dr Johnson almost got his wish. Knox was buried in St Giles Churchyard, which once stretched from its southern wall down to the Cowgate. Today it has been completely built over, and John Knox now lies under asphalt, at the rear of St Giles, near the statue of Charles II, where a small yellow square on parking bay 23 marks the spot.

Sixteenth-century soldier of fortune Francis Crawford of Lymond fought a duel with the truly evil Sir Graham Reid Malett on the steps of St Giles's altar in Dorothy Dunnett's historical novel *The Disorderly Knights* (1966), where the Kirk's 'long, white tapers pricked to life with their small flame the dim treasures of jewels and paintings, of silver-gilt and delicate, hand-sewn fabric'.

Jenny Geddes, who kept a greengrocer's stall outside the Tron Kirk, is famous in the history of St Giles for chucking a stool at the Dean of Edinburgh when he began reading from an English prayer book in 1637 (part of Charles I's policy of imposing Episcopalianism in Scotland, which, for many, reeked of Catholicism). 'Villain! Dost thou say Mass at ma lug?', screamed Jenny at the pulpit. The Dean made a hasty retreat, followed by a volley of stones outside in the street, and the rioting that ensued led eventually to the signing of the National Covenant.

To view St Giles's many literary memorials, enter through the main west entrance and walk anticlockwise round its walls.

Robert Burns (1759–96)
On entering, turn full circle to view the centre stained-glass window installed in the west gable celebrating 'Robert Burns, poet of humanity'.

Robert Louis Stevenson (1850–94)

About 20 paces from the entrance, over on the right, is the Moray Aisle, where a memorial to Robert Louis Stevenson can be seen. In 1887, RLS and his family were in New York, where the American sculptor Augustus Saint-Gaudens started work on a medallion of RLS, sculpted from sittings at St Stephen's Hotel from 23 September. The medallion was not completed until five years later, and ended up on display in the hall at Vailima, the Stevensons' home in Samoa.

In a letter to Saint-Gaudens, written in July 1894, RLS describes the medallion's arrival at Vailima:

> This is to tell you that the medallion has been at last triumphantly transported up the hill and placed over my smoking-room mantelpiece. It is considered by everyone a first-rate but flattering portrait. We have it in a very good light which brings out the artistic merits of the god-like sculptor to great advantage. As for my opinion, I believe it to be a speaking likeness and not flattering at all, possibly a little the reverse.

Stevenson was ill at the time of the first sittings and in bed draped with blankets, as early sketches revealed, but when Saint-Gaudens was working on the finer details in the spring of 1888, when RLS's health had much improved, the sculptor transformed the sickbed to a couch and the blankets to a travelling rug.

An enlarged copy was erected at St Giles in 1904 based on the original medallion, which featured RLS with newspaper, cigarette and ivy border. For the enlarged memorial, however, what was considered a more 'timeless' image was created: the cigarette became a pen and a decorative border of heather and hibiscus, intertwining Scotland and Samoa, was included. Personally, I can't think of a more representative image of RLS than of his lying in bed covered in blankets smoking endless fags. Why the substituted pen should make him more 'timeless' is beyond me, and I can't help feeling he's been sanitised for posterity. 'It's no like him!' commented his old nurse Cummy; but his wife, Fanny, claimed it was her favourite image of her husband.

The Robert Louis Stevenson Memorial.

Margaret Oliphant (1828–97)

Along the wall from RLS, beneath the window, to the right of a door, is a gold-reliefed plaque in memory of Margaret Oliphant. Novelist, essayist, biographer and historian, Oliphant wrote over 100 books, but is best remembered for her *Chronicles of Carlingford* series (1863–76), which earned her the sobriquet 'a feminist Trollope'. Born in Wallyford, she married her artist cousin Francis Oliphant and was early widowed. Left with debts and three young children to bring up, she was forced to write for an income. From her house in Fettes Row, her pen poured out a prolific flow of work, distinguishing her as Edinburgh's first full-time woman of letters. She formed a close relationship with Edinburgh publisher Blackwood and *Blackwood's Magazine*, writing their history in *Annals of a Publishing House* (1897). A memorial service was held for her in 1908 at St Giles, during which she was described in an address as 'the greatest Scottish female writer since Mrs Ferrier'.

Robert Fergusson (1750–74)

To Oliphant's left is a memorial plaque to the witty and earthy poetic genius Robert Fergusson, whom Burns acknowledged as his 'elder brother in misfortune, by far my elder brother in the muse'. Fergusson died aged only 24, in the public asylum which stood behind the building which is now the Bedlam Theatre in Forrest Road.

Gavin Douglas (c.1474–1522)

Opposite the organ gallery, to the right of the green choir stalls, is a memorial plaque to Scottish poet and prelate Gavin Douglas, who, from 1501 to 1514, was Provost of St Giles. He is best remembered for his Scottish vernacular translation of the *Aeneid* (*Eneados*, with prologues, 1553) and his allegorical poem *The Palice of Honour* (c.1501). Through the influence of Queen Margaret Tudor, he became Bishop of Dunkeld in 1515, an affiliation which later caused him to be imprisoned in Edinburgh Castle. In 1521, he was found guilty of treason and exiled to England, where he died of the plague.

Walter Chepman (1473–1538)

To the left of the organ gallery is the Chepman Aisle, last resting place of Walter Chepman, who, with master printer Andro Myllar, set up Edinburgh's first printing press in 1507. Chepman was a local merchant and clerk to the King's secretary, who was granted a Royal patent to procure a printing press. They operated from the Cowgate, at the foot of Blackfriars Wynd, with equipment imported from France, where Myllar had trained as a printer. Little of their work survives today, although four copies of their original *Aberdeen Breviary* still exist.

Marquess of Montrose (1612–50)

Also in the Chepman Aisle lies one of the great romantic figures of Scottish history, James Graham, Marquess of Montrose: poet, soldier, Calvinist, Royalist and one of the first to put his name to

The tomb of the Marquess of Montrose.

the National Covenant in support of Presbyterianism in 1638. He later defected to the King, but was eventually betrayed and hanged at the Cross in the High Street on 21 May 1650. His body was quartered and displayed at the gates of Stirling, Glasgow, Perth and Aberdeen. His trunk was buried on the Burgh Muir and his head fixed to a spike on the Tolbooth. Eleven years later, Charles II ordered that his remains be gathered and buried in St Giles Cathedral. On the anniversary of his death, his tomb is often bedecked with flowers from admirers around the world. During his imprisonment, he wrote the following poem:

> Let them bestow on ev'ry airt a limb;
> Open all my veins, that I may swim
> To thee my Saviour, in that crimson lake;
> Then place my pur-boil'd head upon a stake;
> Scatter my ashes, throw them in the air;
> Lord (since Thou know'st where all these atoms are)
> I'm hopeful, once Thou'lt recollect my dust,
> And confident Thou'lt raise me with the just.

Robert Stevenson Memorial Window

A stained-glass window in memory of RLS's grandfather, Robert Stevenson (1772–1850), by James Ballantyne, 1873, can be seen at the north-east corner (top left) of the Cathedral.

William Chambers (1800–83)

In the first aisle after the gift shop lies the tomb of William Chambers. The brothers William and Robert Chambers (1802–71) were born into a mill-owning family in Peebles who hit hard times after their charitable father reputedly issued cloth on credit to French prisoners of war to make themselves clothes during the war with Napoleon. After the war, they returned to France promising to repay their benefactor, but they never did, and the family was ruined. William became apprenticed to an Edinburgh bookseller, and shortly afterwards his younger brother Robert set up as a bookseller on Leith Walk. When William's apprenticeship came to an end, he went into partnership with his brother. They purchased a small hand-press and in 1824 printed and published Robert's *Traditions of Edinburgh*. In 1832, they began publishing *The Chambers' Journal*, a weekly magazine, the circulation of which reached 84,000 copies within a few years. *Chambers' Encyclopaedia* followed in 1859, published in 520 parts between 1859 and

1868. Educational publishing made both brothers extremely wealthy and their many philanthropic gestures included funding the restoration of St Giles. William was Lord Provost of Edinburgh twice. Chambers merged with Harrap and is now known as Chambers Harrap Publishers Ltd. The company is based in Edinburgh.

James Dalrymple, 1st Viscount Stair (1619–95)

On the archway of the next aisle, the St Eloi Aisle, is a plaque to the memory of Viscount Stair, whose place in Scottish literary history was secured when the marriage of his daughter, Janet Dalrymple, inspired Sir Walter Scott's *The Bride of Lammermoor* (1819), a love story set against political intrigues following the aftermath of the Civil War. Scott wrote the novel during a period of illness when he was heavily drugged, and reputedly had no recollection of writing it, describing it as 'monstrous, gross and grotesque'.

SEE ALSO: Robert Louis Stevenson, Sir Walter Scott, James Boswell, Dr Johnson, Robert Burns, Robert Fergusson, Robert Stevenson, Dorothy Dunnett, William Blackwood, *Blackwood's Magazine*.

FURTHER INFORMATION: Open daily and admission is free. Monday to Saturday 9 a.m.–5 p.m. (later in summer); Sunday 1 p.m.–6 p.m. (all year). Guides available (tel: 0131 225 9442).

FURTHER READING: E.J. Cowan, *Montrose: For Covenant and King* (Weidenfeld & Nicolson, 1977); J. Buchan, *Montrose* (House of Stratus, 2001); M. Oliphant and Mrs H. Coghill (ed.), *Autobiography and Letters of Mrs Margaret Oliphant* (1899); J. Ridley, *John Knox* (Oxford Uni. Press, 1968).

(ADVOCATE'S CLOSE)

Site of the first appearance of Bob Skinner, Quintin Jardine's maverick detective

As a city, Edinburgh is a two-faced bitch.
Quintin Jardine, *Skinner's Rules* (1993)

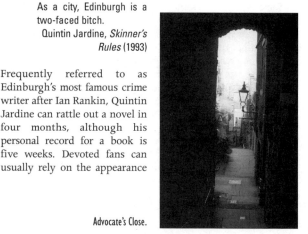

Frequently referred to as Edinburgh's most famous crime writer after Ian Rankin, Quintin Jardine can rattle out a novel in four months, although his personal record for a book is five weeks. Devoted fans can usually rely on the appearance

Advocate's Close.

of two books a year – proof that crime writing may be formulaic, but at least its adherents don't kick their heels for long.

An only child, Jardine was born in Motherwell to parents who were both teachers. Educated at Glasgow High School for Boys, he started his working life as a junior reporter on the *Motherwell Times* and later the *Daily Record*. After a stint as a government press officer, he joined the Scottish Tories as their senior press officer in 1980. In 1985 he set up his own public-relations firm, and in 1997 he defected from the Tories to join the SNP. Jardine began writing in his mid-40s after reading a trashy novel while on holiday. 'I can do better than that,' he thought. Sounds like a cliché, but the result was *Skinner's Rules*, published in 1993, which introduced the unorthodox Edinburgh cop Bob Skinner, a character for whom lovers of the genre seem to have an inexhaustible appetite. Almost equally popular are his books about Oz Blackstone, a private investigator turned Hollywood movie star.

Quintin Jardine. (© Hodder Headline)

Bob Skinner made his first appearance at the mouth of Advocate's Close, opposite St Giles, and has subsequently appeared at many city locations, including: his base at police headquarters in Fettes Avenue; Murrayfield Stadium in the climax of *Stay of Execution*; the Crown Jewel Chamber at Edinburgh Castle in *Festival*; gunplay breaks out in Parliament Hall at the end of *Autographs in the Rain*; Skinner foils a bomb plot at the Edinburgh International Conference Centre in *Thursday Legends*; and the tropical section of the big greenhouse at the Royal Botanic Gardens is where Skinner had a fight almost to the death with Big Lenny Plenderleith.

Today, Quintin Jardine divides his time between his house in Gullane and his retreat in Catalonia, where he does much of his writing. His spin-doctor days are now history, but in a radio interview the inimitable Muriel Gray pitched him the question, 'You were a Tory press officer; what made you want to write fiction?'

FURTHER INFORMATION: In Joan Lingard's children's book *The Sign of the Black Dagger*, the children, both present and past, live in Advocate's Close.

ANCHOR CLOSE

High Street
Site of William Smellie's printing house and Dawney Douglas's Tavern, meeting place of The Crochallan Fencibles

> As I cam by Crochallan,
> I cannily keekit ben:
> Rattlin', roarin' Willie
> Was sitting at yon boord-en'
>> Robert Burns, from 'Rattlin', Roarin' Willie', dedicated
>> to William Dunbar, Colonel of the Crochallan corps

William Smellie printed the works of Robert Fergusson, Adam Smith, Adam Ferguson and later the second edition of Burns's poems, the Edinburgh edition, in 1787. Smellie was not your average, run-of-the-mill printer, but a talented editor and writer who was involved in producing the first edition of the *Encyclopaedia Britannica* (1768–71). He also liked to drink, debate and sing a bawdy song or two, which led to his founding the renowned drinking club The Crochallan Fencibles at Dawney Douglas's Tavern. Dawney liked to sing Gaelic songs and Smellie took the name of one of them, Crodh Challein (Colin's Cattle), for the first half of the club's name, and Fencibles from the city's much-derided volunteer corps of militia. Its members included Adam Smith, Adam Ferguson, Henry Mackenzie and Robert Burns.

Smellie introduced Burns to the club during his first visit to Edinburgh in 1787, and the ploughman poet would have needed no excuse to join in the revelry after a hard day selling himself in the salons of Edinburgh society. It was at Dawney Douglas's Tavern that Burns delivered for the first time his 'Address to a Haggis' – Fair fa' your honest, sonsie face, Great chieftain o' the puddin-race! – now an almost religious rite at every traditional Burns supper. The Crochallan Fencibles also inspired many of the bawdy lyrics of Burns's *The Merry Muses of Caledonia*, verse far removed from the tea parties of the literati:

> There's no a lass in a' the land,
> Can fuck sae weel as I can;
> Louse down your breeks, lug out your wand,
> Hae ye nae a mind to try man
>> From 'Ellibanks'

SEE ALSO: William Smellie, Robert Burns, William Creech, Adam Smith, Henry Mackenzie, Robert Fergusson.

FURTHER INFORMATION: The site of Smellie's printing house, including the room where Burns used to sit and correct his proofs, was at one time occupied by the machine room of the *Scotsman* newspaper. The stools from Smellie's printing house can be seen at The Writers' Museum, Lady Stair's Close.

55 COCKBURN STREET

Fopp

> It cheers me up. Whenever I'm feeling cheesed off or depressed, my wife says, 'Why don't you go to Fopp?' I can always find something there to make me feel better.
>
> Ian Rankin, *The Times*, 8 April 2000

Named after a track by '70s dance band Ohio Players, Fopp was founded in 1981 by Gordon Montgomery, who started his career as a sales assistant with HMV in Coventry before moving to Scotland as a music buyer for Virgin. He opened his first shop in Glasgow in 1985, expanding to a second shop in Edinburgh's Cockburn Street in 1987. Primarily a music store, Fopp also has a keenly priced and eclectic book department. The Velvet

Underground may be blasting out as you walk through its doors, but don't assume its books are all about sex and drugs and rock 'n' roll. Although you may be tempted by the wealth of music biographies (Dylan jostling for space next to the Red Hot

Chili Peppers), it's possible to snatch up children's classics such as *The Little Prince* for a quid, and selected works of the glorious Lemony Snicket for a little over that. However, the attendant bookworm should be warned that hardbacks tend to be arranged in huge stacks and are prone to avalanche suddenly. Fopp stocks titles ranging from the classics to sci-fi, and continues to surprise, sustain low prices and stay cool.

FURTHER INFORMATION: Opening hours: 10 a.m.–6.30 p.m. Monday to Saturday; 11 a.m.–6 p.m. Sunday. Tel: 0131 220 0133. A second, and larger, branch of Fopp is located nearby at 7 Rose Street (tel: 0131 220 0310).

42–4 COCKBURN STREET

Beyond Words Photographic Bookshop

Beyond Words is the only bookshop in Scotland – and one of the very few in the UK – specialising in photographic and photographically illustrated books. The shop and its staff offer a high level of knowledge of photographic books and their availability, a willingness to track down hard-to-get titles, a constantly changing list of remainder titles at about one third of their published price, careful stock handling to ensure their

stock remains in optimum condition and a regular programme of events relating to newly published titles. Their second shop at 45 Broughton Street (0131 556 3377) sells a selection of photographic and other gift books and cards.

FURTHER INFORMATION: Opening hours: 10 a.m.–6 p.m.
Monday to Saturday; 1 p.m.–6 p.m. Sunday. Tel: 0131 226 6636.
Email: info@beyondwords.co.uk.
Website: www.beyondwords.co.uk.

40–1 SOUTH BRIDGE

Forbidden Planet International

Situated minutes from the historic Royal Mile, the Edinburgh

branch of Forbidden Planet stocks a vast variety of science fiction and cult collectable items. The store maintains a range of excellent sci-fi and fantasy novels, from Asimov to Zindell, including local authors such as Iain M. Banks and Charles Stross, along with a huge array of graphic novels, from the popular, such as *Spiderman*, to the work of imported European artists such as Bilal. There is an extensive range of manga titles and, of course, their ever-changing stock of comics and magazines, plus a large selection of merchandise to accompany the literature. Titles are also available via their large webstore and the company blog (web diary) brings personal recommendations from staff, author interviews, news and reviews every week.

FURTHER INFORMATION: Opening hours: 10 a.m.–5.30 p.m. Monday to Saturday; 10 a.m.–6 p.m. Thursdays; 12 p.m.–5 p.m. Sunday. Tel: 0131 558 8226.
Email: fpedinburgh@plus.com.
Website: www.forbiddenplanet.co.uk;
www.fpigraphics.co.uk/blogger.

42 HIGH STREET

Museum of Childhood

> We get lots of telephone enquiries. The other day we got one from someone doing a crossword who wanted to know the colour of Rupert Bear's trousers.
>
> John Hay, Museum Curator

Opened in 1955, this was the first museum in the world to specialise in the history of childhood. One of the best attended

venues in Edinburgh, with around a quarter of a million visitors a year, it has five galleries housing 50,000 items, from Victorian dolls to train sets. Its book collection runs to about 11,000 volumes, but unfortunately the museum doesn't have the space to display them all. A few books are on permanent display, including children's classics, annuals and comics, but the majority of its collection is stored elsewhere. A bibliography is currently being compiled which will enable visitors to select volumes of their choice for perusal. The museum shop also stocks children's books.

FURTHER INFORMATION: Opening hours: 10 a.m.–5 p.m. Monday to Saturday; 12 p.m.–5 p.m. Sunday (July and August only). Admission free. Tel: 0131 529 4142.
Website: www.cac.org.uk.

TWEEDDALE COURT

Former offices of Oliver & Boyd Printers and Publishers

Thomas Oliver founded his printing business in the High Street in 1778, and in 1807 he was joined by bookbinder George Boyd. This was a partnership which would eventually establish them as one of the renowned Victorian publishers. In 1820, they moved to Tweeddale Court. They specialised in publishing Scottish poetry, and worked with many of the literary giants of the day, including Thomas Carlyle and James Hogg. In 1836, theirs became the first business to combine printing, bookbinding and publishing under the same roof.

8 VICTORIA STREET

The Old Town Bookshop

Situated in the heart of the Old Town, close to the Grassmarket, the sign on the street invites you to 'Feed your mind & Feast your eyes' – no overstatement, as this shop is stocked with delights from the ceiling to the floor, including antiquarian and general second-hand books, prints and maps. Art, architecture and photography are strongly represented, a bias stemming from proprietor Ron Wilson's background in art and graphic design. Ron has been described as 'an ageless bohemian', who has painted many of the great cities of the world, and whose staff include the 'glamorously arty' Suzanna and the 'brilliantly erudite' Martin. If you're looking for an introduction to the world of antiquarian books – look no

further. They range from cheap Graham Greenes to Daniell's *Tour of Britain*, which sells for serious shekels.

FURTHER INFORMATION: Opening hours: 10.30 a.m.–5.30 p.m. Monday to Saturday. Tel: 0131 225 9237.

7 COWGATEHEAD

Transreal Fiction

Situated very close to the east end of the Grassmarket, Transreal Fiction sells Scotland's widest range of fantasy and science fiction books. The shop opened in 1997, although the proprietor, Mike Calder, has been selling sci-fi for much longer, having first sold a

science-fiction book to a customer 30 years ago. The latest titles from British and American publishers are carried, together with a comprehensive selection of back-stock. Star Wars, Star Trek, Doctor Who and other genre shows and films are represented, together with sections for novels from Dragonlance, Forgotten Realms, Warhammer, etc. Other specialist sections include fantasy and sci-fi art books, *Lord of the Rings*/Tolkien-related books, and a large selection of faerie books (mainly art – Brian Froud, for instance – but also encyclopedias and other reference books). And calendars, lots of calendars!

FURTHER INFORMATION: Opening hours: 11 a.m.–6 p.m. Monday to Friday; 10 a.m.–6 p.m. Saturday; 12 p.m.–5 p.m. Sunday (August and December only). Tel: 0131 226 2822. Email: enquiries@transreal.co.uk. Website: www.transreal.co.uk.

46–54 CANDLEMAKER ROW

Site of the Harrow Inn, periodic residence of James Hogg, the Ettrick Shepherd (1770–1835)

> Pray, who wishes to know anything about his [Hogg's] life? Who indeed cares a single farthing whether he be at this blessed moment dead or alive? Only picture yourself a stout country lout with a bushel of hair on his shoulders that had not been raked for months, enveloped in a coarse plaid impregnated with tobacco, with a prodigious mouthful of immeasurable tusks, and a dialect that sets all conjecture at defiance . . .
>
> John Wilson (Christopher North)
> 'Noctes Ambrosianae', *Blackwood's Magazine*

James Hogg was a distinct oddity in the Edinburgh literary world of the early nineteenth century. A Border poet with a shepherd's plaid slung across his shoulders, his crudeness and outspokenness sent shockwaves through the salons of the city's literati. Initially, they were charmed and reverential, but eventually they tired of him and often ridiculed him as the novelty of the artistic bumpkin wore thin. A similar reception had greeted the 'ploughman poet' Robert Burns a generation earlier. But Hogg was no transient performing seal for New Town drawing rooms and dining clubs. He evolved into a major writer who was admired by Byron and André Gide, and has influenced Scottish writers from Robert Louis Stevenson to Muriel Spark. In 1824, he wrote one of the masterpieces of Scottish literature: *The Private Memoirs and Confessions of a Justified Sinner*.

Hogg was born the second of four sons in 1770 in the parish of Ettrick in the Scottish Borders. When he was six years old, his father, an impoverished farmer, became bankrupt and he was forced to leave school. Most of his childhood was spent working on farms and, in his mid-teens, he

The guise, poetry and prose of the Ettrick Shepherd are resurrected annually during the first weekend in December by Border poet Walter Elliot (a descendant of Will O'Phaup) at the Scott's Selkirk festival. www.scottsselkirk.com (© Rob Gray/digitalpic)

became a shepherd and taught himself to write and play the fiddle. From his mother, he had learned the oral tradition of ballads and Borders folklore. His mother had inherited these songs and stories from her father, the legendary Will O'Phaup, reputed to have been the last man to converse with the fairies. Soon, Hogg was composing his own songs and verses, publishing his first poem in the *Scots Magazine* in 1793, and in 1801 publishing *Scottish Pastorals*, a small volume of poems. The locals dubbed him 'Jamie the Poeter'.

In the summer of 1802, he first met Walter Scott while working as a shepherd for Scott's friend William Laidlaw when Scott, the newly appointed Sheriff of Selkirk, was scouring the countryside for the disappearing ballads of the Borders. Hogg, with the help of his mother, aided Scott in his search, and the two contemporaries began a lifelong, if sometimes traumatic, friendship.

When Scott's *The Minstrelsy of the Scottish Border* was published in 1802, they came in for severe criticism from Hogg's mother Margaret: 'There was never ane o' my sangs prentit till ye prentit them yoursel', and ye have spoilt them awthegither. They were made for singin' and no' for readin', but ye have broken the charm now, an' they'll never be sung mair.'

In 1810, after his attempts at farming failed, Hogg moved to Edinburgh to try to earn his living as a writer. Scott's assistance to his friend was invaluable, but he eventually achieved fame with the publication of his long poem, *The Queen's Wake*, completed in Deanhaugh Street in 1813, and in 1815 *The Pilgrims of the Sun* was published. He edited the short-lived literary magazine *The Spy*, and many of his stories and poems were published in *Blackwood's Magazine*, in which he first used his now famous sobriquet: the Ettrick Shepherd. He was often caricatured by *Blackwood's* in John Wilson's (Christopher North's) 'Noctes Ambrosianae' as an unsophisticated 'boozing buffoon', a portrayal often accentuated and exploited by Hogg, who played up his celebrity image.

He is best remembered today for his novel *The Private Memoirs and Confessions of a Justified Sinner*. Originally published anonymously, because, Hogg explained, 'it being a story replete with horrors, after I had written it, I durst not venture to put my name to it.' A more likely explanation may be that he didn't want to cause offence to Calvinist Edinburgh.

He lived for five years in Edinburgh at various addresses, including The Harrow Inn, Teviot Row and Ann Street, since demolished to make way for the Waverley Bridge. In 1815, the Duke of Buccleuch granted him a rent-free farm at Altrive (now Edinhope) in Yarrow, where he lived for the rest of his life. In 1820, he married Margaret Phillips, a pious woman from a Nithsdale farming family, with whom he had five children. He died on 21 November 1835, from 'what the country folks call black jaundice' (probably liver failure) and is buried in Ettrick Kirkyard. At his funeral, most of the Edinburgh literati were conspicuous by their absence, except for the towering figure of John Wilson, who wept for his departed friend.

SEE ALSO: Holyrood Park, Sir Walter Scott, John Wilson, *Blackwood's Magazine*.

FURTHER INFORMATION: The James Hogg Society, c/o Dr Robin MacLachlan, 8 Tybenham Road, London SW19 3LA.

FURTHER READING: W. Elliot, *The James Hogg Trail* (Scottish Borders Tourist Board, 2001); Karl Miller, *Electric Shepherd* (Faber, 2003); David Groves, *James Hogg: The Growth of a Writer* (Scottish Academic Press, 1987); Norah Parr, *James Hogg at Home* (D.S. Mack, 1980); Mary Garden (Hogg's daughter), *Memorials of James Hogg, the Ettrick Shepherd* (Paisley, 1885).

1 GREYFRIARS PLACE

Greyfriars Kirkyard

> . . . they finally arrived at the burial-place of the Singleside family. This was a square enclosure in the Greyfriars churchyard, guarded on one side by a veteran angel, without a nose and having only one wing, who had the merit of having maintained his post for a century . . . Here then, amid the deep black fat loam into which her ancestors were now resolved, they deposited the body of Mrs Margaret Bertram; and, like soldiers returning from a military funeral, the nearest relations who might be interested in the settlements of the lady, urged the dogcattle of the hackney coaches to all the speed of which they were capable, in order to put an end to further suspense on that interesting topic.
>
> Sir Walter Scott, *Guy Mannering* (1815)

Greyfriars takes its name from a pre-Reformation Franciscan convent (the grey friars) that stood nearby. In 1562, Mary, Queen of Scots granted the land to the town council for use as a burial ground, and the church, which dates from 1620, became the first church built in Edinburgh after the Reformation. On 28 February 1638, its place in Scottish history was assured when Presbyterians, opposing the Episcopal faith introduced by Charles I, swore to uphold their forms of worship in a National Covenant which was

presented and signed in front of the pulpit (an original copy is displayed in the Visitor's Centre). The Covenanters raised an army in 1639 to defend their religious convictions, but were eventually defeated by the Duke of Monmouth's army at Bothwell Bridge in June 1679. About a thousand Covenanters were imprisoned in Greyfriars Yard for months with no shelter and scant food. Those who signed a bond were freed, but many refused and were transported to slavery in the Colonies. Ironically, near the southern wall stands the mausoleum of the King's Advocate Sir George Mackenzie (1636–91), known as 'Bluidy Mackenzie', the hanging judge, for his vigorous persecution of the Covenanters. From 1650 to 1653, Cromwell used Greyfriars as a barracks during his invasion of Scotland. Little of the original church survives, because in the early eighteenth century the town council stored its gunpowder in a nearby tower which blew up in 1718, taking most of the church with it. Misfortune struck again in 1845 when fire gutted the church. Burial records were not kept until 1658, making the exact location of many graves impossible to determine. In 1979, the Greyfriars congregation united with Highland Tolbooth St John's and a service in Gaelic is now held every Sunday.

Greyfriars Bobby

As a burial place of the great, the good and the bloodcurdlingly infamous, Greyfriars has no equal in the city, but most visitors arrive at this historic churchyard seeking the grave of a man whose life was unremarkable and would have passed unnoticed had he not been the master of a little dog. The story of Greyfriars Bobby, the faithful Skye terrier who kept a vigil for 14 years on his master's grave, is well known. What is not so well known is that Eleanor Atkinson, American author of the bestselling novel *Greyfriars Bobby* (1912), never set foot in Edinburgh, and wrote the novel 3,000 miles away on the other side of the Atlantic. Like many classic animal stories, the book is dripping with sentimentality, but, mixing fact with fiction, Atkinson spins a likeable yarn. Born Eleanor Stackhouse in Indiana in 1863, she worked as a teacher in Indianapolis before joining the *Chicago Tribune* as a reporter, writing under the pseudonym Nora Marks. Her two best-known novels are *Greyfriars Bobby* and *Johnny Appleseed* (1915).

Grave of Auld Jock, master of Greyfriars Bobby.

Bobby was a familiar character on the streets of the Old Town. He was trained to associate Edinburgh Castle's one o'clock gun with his lunchtime, when he would head for John Trail's Temperance Coffee House at 6 Greyfriars Place, a few yards from the gates of the churchyard, near what is now Greyfriars Bobby's bar. Here he was fed daily, returning to his master's grave every evening. The site of Bobby's grave in the churchyard is unmarked, as animals were not permitted to be buried in consecrated ground. He was actually buried in a flowerpot on 14–15 January 1872, in front of the church door beneath a tree. His grave was marked by a stone, which was later removed, no doubt by a conscientious official. The pink granite headstone to which visitors pay tribute at the entrance to the churchyard is a memorial erected by the Dog Aid Society in 1981. John Gray, Bobby's master, who was reputedly a police constable (Atkinson cast him as a shepherd), is buried a few yards up the first path on your right. Bobby's drinking cup, dinner dish, collar and rare photographs of the Trail family with Bobby can be seen at Huntly House Museum in the Canongate.

Edinburgh was twinned with San Diego in 1977. Bob Watt, as chairman of the Edinburgh end of the twinning, decided to present a duplicate of the statue of Greyfriars Bobby to San Diego to mark his retirement from the post. Bob Watt raised around £4,500 and Powderhall Bronze cast the duplicate. British Airways flew the dog to San Diego free of charge.

In San Diego, Bob discovered the city had its own dog from the past: a St Bernard called Bum who was a free-wheeling spirit, had lost a leg and a bit of his tail under a train, become an alcoholic, taken the cure, regularly bitten the dog-catcher and ridden for free when he felt like it on the trains to and from Los Angeles. As he grew older, he mellowed; he ate in different restaurants in San Diego. The restaurateurs posted notices claiming BUM EATS HERE; the city gave him a dog licence and for a time even put his picture on all dog licences. On his death, the children of San Diego chipped in to give him a decent burial in a good cemetery. Interviewed on San Diego television, Bob admitted that if he was ever reincarnated he would rather come back as Bum than Bobby: Bum had led a much more interesting life.

At present, San Diego is creating a historic walk in its oldest area, the Gaslamp District. Bob and Bum sit together at Station 3. The next step is to present a copy of Bum to Edinburgh. The world's first twin dogs will soon be together here and there.

Grave of Duncan Ban MacIntyre (1724–1812)

> My blessing with the foxes dwell,
> For that they hunt the sheep so well.
> Ill fare the sheep, a grey-fac'd nation
> That swept our hills with desolation.
> 'Song to the Foxes'

Although regarded as one of the great Gaelic poets, Donnchadh Ban Mac an t-Saoir never learned to read or write, but with the help of his extensive memory and the pen of his friend, Revd Donald MacNicol, Minister of Lismore, his verses are preserved for posterity. Born in Glen Orchy, he worked there as a forester and gamekeeper, and his love of the countryside inspired his verse. His poems included satires, love songs and drinking songs, but he will be best remembered for his poems about the Argyll–Perthshire border, namely 'Moladh Beinn Dobhrain' ('The Praise of Ben Doran'), which describes his love of deer and deer-hunting, and 'Oran Coire a Cheathaich' ('The Song of Misty Corrie'). He moved to Edinburgh in 1767, where he became a member of the City Guard and served in the Breadalbane Fencibles. MacIntyre and his wife, together with some of his children and grandchildren, are buried in the churchyard.

From the main entrance, follow the path round the right-hand side of the church and take the second (cobbled) path on the right. Near its end, over on the left, stands the large obelisk marking MacIntyre's grave.

Grave of George Buchanan (c.1506–82)
Scholar, poet, dramatist and historian

Best known for his Latin history of Scotland, *Rerum scoticarum historia* (20 volumes, 1582) and *De juri regniapud Scotos* (1579), his decrial of the divine right of monarchs, Buchanan was born near Killearn in Stirlingshire and studied at Paris and St Andrews universities. In 1537, he became tutor to one of the illegitimate sons of James V, but later fled the country after he was charged with heresy on the publication of his poem, 'Franciscanus', in which he satirised the Franciscans. He ended up teaching in Bordeaux, where Montaigne was one of his pupils, and where he wrote his Latin tragedies, *Jeptha* and *Baptistes*. In 1547, he was arrested and imprisoned as a suspected heretic by the Inquisition, but managed to return to Scotland in 1561, now purporting to be a Protestant, where he was appointed Classical tutor to the teenage Mary, Queen of Scots. He later charged her with complicity in the murder of Lord Darnley in the pamphlet 'Ane Detectioun of the Duings of Mary Quene' (1571). His appointments in later life included moderator of the General Assembly of Scotland, keeper of the Privy Seal of Scotland and tutor to the four-year-old King James VI of Scotland (1570–8). He died in an Edinburgh lodging house in 1582 shortly after completing his monumental, but alas unreliable, 20-volume work on the history of Scotland.

George Buchanan's bronze-headed memorial.

From the main entrance, follow the path round the right-hand side of the church. When you reach the end of the building, Buchanan's bronze-headed memorial can be seen in front of you between the trees.

SEE ALSO: Mary, Queen of Scots.

FURTHER READING: I.D. McFarlane, *Buchanan* (Duckworth, 1981).

Where Walter Scott fell in love with Williamina Stuart-Belsches

> Much have I owed thy strains on life's long way,
> Through secret woes the world has never known,
> When on the weary night dawn'd wearier day,
> And bitterer was the grief devour'd alone,
> That I o'erlive such woes, Enchantress! is thine own.
>
> An allusion to Scott's lost love, Williamina Stuart-Belsches, from the envoi of 'The Lady of the Lake' (1810)

One rainy Sunday in 1790 at Greyfriars Churchyard, while Scott was still a teenager, he offered his umbrella to a 14-year-old girl called Williamina and fell instantly in love with her. She was a well-born heiress, the daughter of Sir John Stuart-Belsches, who owned an estate at Fettercairn in Kincardineshire, and Lady Jane, daughter of the Earl of Leven and Melville. They courted and corresponded; Scott felt encouraged, but to support a wife of Williamina's social standing was far beyond his means. In the winter of 1795, Williamina met William Forbes, heir to a banking family, and the following autumn they announced their plans to marry. The jilted Scott was devastated and carried with him the pain of losing Williamina for the rest of his life.

The agony he suffered during this doomed courtship surfaced later in some of his works, namely in the thwarted passions of Wilfred Wycliffe for Matilda in *Rokeby* (1812), the Master of Ravenswood for Lucy Ashton in *The Bride of Lammermoor* (1819) and Darsie Latimer for 'Greenmantle' in *Redgauntlet* (1824).

In September 1797, while touring the Lake District, he was introduced to 27-year-old, French-born Charlotte Carpenter at a ball. Within three weeks of meeting her, Scott proposed, and they were married a few months later on Christmas Eve. Twelve years later, he described his marriage in a letter to Lady Abercorn as 'something short of love in all its forms, which I suspect people feel once in all their lives; folk who have been nearly drowned in bathing rarely venturing a second time out of their depth'. Williamina died at the age of 34 in 1810.

SEE ALSO: Sir Walter Scott.

Grave of Walter Scott (1729–99)
Father of Sir Walter Scott

The grave of Scott's father, a former elder of Greyfriars Kirk, is marked by a bedraggled pink granite slab and, compared to his son's Gothic extravaganza down on Princes Street, the elder Scott's memory seems somewhat neglected. His roots were in the Scottish Borders and on his mother's side he was descended from the Haliburtons of Newmains, who passed on to the Scott family the hereditary right of burial in Dryburgh Abbey, where his famous son now lies. He moved to Edinburgh as a young man to study law, and was studious and successful, becoming senior partner in the firm he was apprenticed to, and later a writer to the Signet. A strict Calvinist with a deep interest in theology, his son described him as 'uncommonly handsome'. In

April 1758, he married Anne Rutherford, with whom he had twelve children, six of whom died in infancy. Scott penned an affectionate portrait of his father, whom he caricatured in *Redgauntlet* (1824) as Saunders Fairford.

From the main entrance, follow the path round the right-hand side of the church until you are standing in front of the archway in the Flodden Wall. Walter Scott's grave is to your left.

SEE ALSO: Grave of Anne Rutherford, Birthplace of Sir Walter Scott, Childhood home of Sir Walter Scott.

Grave of Captain Porteous (d. 1736)
The man responsible for the Porteous Riots, featured in Scott's The Heart of Midlothian

> And thou, great god of Aqua Vitæ!
> Wha sways the empire of this city,
> When fou we're sometimes capernoity,
> Be thou prepar'd
> To hedge us frae that black banditti,
> The City-Guard.
> From 'The Daft Days' by Robert Fergusson (1750–74)

John Porteous, the son of an Edinburgh tailor, served in the army and then joined the City Guard – Fergusson's famous 'black banditti'. History does not record Porteous as a credit to his office, but a man who frequently exceeded the bounds of his commission, dishing out excessive cruelty to his prisoners.

In 1736, two smugglers, Robertson and Wilson, were convicted and sentenced to death. The handcuffed Robertson escaped during a church service, but Wilson was later conducted from the Old Tolbooth Prison (nicknamed The Heart of Midlothian) in the High Street to temporary gallows in the Grassmarket by 50 of the City Guard commanded by Porteous, who was said by a witness to be 'heated by wine'. When the hangman proceeded to cut down Wilson's body, a hail of stones were thrown from the crowd. Porteous ordered the Guard to 'fire and be damned'. Nine of the crowd were left dead and many were wounded. Porteous was subsequently arrested and sentenced to death. Here the tragic story should have ended, but Caroline, the Queen Regent, ordered Porteous's reprieve, and the citizens of Edinburgh were outraged.

On the evening of 7 September 1736, a large mob entered the city, crying out, 'All those who dare avenge innocent blood, let them come here.' The mob stormed the Old Tolbooth, dragged Porteous from his cell and hanged him from a nearby dyer's pole.

This and other such incidents became known as the Porteous Riots and were immortalised by Walter Scott in *The Heart of Midlothian* in 1818:

> 'Away with him – away with him!' was the general cry.
> 'Why do you trifle away time in making a gallows? –
> that dyester's pole is good enough for the homocide.'
> The unhappy man was forced to his fate with
> remorseless rapidity. Butler, separated from him by the

press, escaped the last horrors. Unnoticed by those who had hitherto detained him as a prisoner, he fled from the fatal spot without caring in what direction his course lay. A loud shout proclaimed the stern delight with which the agents of this deed regarded its completion. Butler, then, at the opening into the low street called the Cowgate, cast back a terrified glance, and, by the red and dusky light of the torches, he could discern a figure waving and struggling as it hung suspended above the heads of the multitude, and could even observe men striking it with their Lochaber-axes and partisans. The sight was of a nature to double his horror and to add wings to his flight.

From the main entrance, follow the path round the right-hand side of the church. Take the path to the right just before the archway in the Flodden Wall. Porteous's grave is behind the third tree on your left.

SEE ALSO: The Heart of Midlothian, Holyrood Park, Sir Walter Scott, Robert Fergusson.

FURTHER READING: Alexander Carlyle's *Autobiography* (Thoemmes Press, 1991) relates an eyewitness account of the execution of Wilson.

Grave of William Creech (1745–1815)
Bookseller, publisher and Lord Provost of Edinburgh

[Robert Burns was] coming up Leith Walk brandishing a sapling and with much violence in his face and manner. When asked what was the matter, Burns replied, 'I am going to smash that Shite, Creech.'

Related to John Grierson

William Creech was a bookseller and publisher who had his premises in the Luckenbooths (locked booths), a rabbit-warren of six timber-fronted tenements on six floors, connected to the Old Tolbooth by St Giles. Creech's ground-floor shop, known as 'Creech's Land', was described by Lord Monboddo as 'the natural resort of lawyers, authors and all sorts of literary idlers'. He founded the famous Speculative Society while studying at Edinburgh University, and his house, known as Creech's Levee, in Craig's Close, off Cockburn Street, was the setting for his regular literary salons.

The second edition of Burns's poems, the Edinburgh edition, was published by William Creech in 1787; he had it printed at William Smellie's printing works in Anchor Close, off the High Street. Burns rashly sold the copyright to him for one hundred guineas 'to be payable on demand', but getting money out of Creech was an art in itself, and Burns had to wait over six months to be paid. Creech was also responsible for commissioning Alexander Naysmith (free of charge) to paint his famous portrait of Burns which today adorns thousands of trinkets, tea-towels and shortbread tins. Creech became Lord Provost of Edinburgh in 1811.

From the main entrance, follow the path round the right-hand side of the church. Walk through the archway in the Flodden Wall. Take the last path on your right before the gates. The grave of William Creech is behind the third tree on the left. **SEE ALSO**: Robert Burns, William Smellie.

Grave of William Smellie (1740–1795)
Printer, editor, antiquary, naturalist and founder of The Crochallan Fencibles

> His uncomb'd, hoary locks, wild-staring, thatch'd;
> A head for thought profound and clear, unmatch'd;
> Yet tho' his caustic wit was biting rude,
> His heart was warm, benevolent and good.
> Robert Burns, 'The Poet's Progress'

Described by his friend Robert Burns as 'that old Veteran in Genius, Wit and Bawdry', William Smellie was a man of many talents. The son of a stonemason, he left school aged 12 to become an apprentice printer. In 1763, he married a Miss Robertson, with whom he had 13 children, many of whom died in infancy. In 1765, he set up his own printing house and, with Andrew Bell and Colin MacFarquar, produced the first edition of the *Encyclopaedia Britannica* (1768–71), much of it reputedly written by himself. He also wrote *A Philosophy of Natural History* and was a founder member of the Society of Antiquities in 1780. He printed the second edition

William Smellie.

of Burns's poems, the Edinburgh edition, in 1787 and founded the famous drinking club The Crochallan Fencibles, of which Burns was a member, at Dawney Douglas's Tavern in Anchor Close.

From the main entrance, take the path on your left, following it around the perimeter wall. At the end of the path, two large-gated tombs face you. Smellie's grave is to the right of these tombs.
SEE ALSO: Robert Burns, William Creech, Anchor Close.

Grave of Henry Mackenzie (1745–1831)
Novelist and essayist known as 'the Scottish Addison'

A book I prize next to the Bible.
> Robert Burns praising Mackenzie's
> *The Man of Feeling*

The son of an Edinburgh physician, Henry Mackenzie was educated at the Royal High School and, after studying law at Edinburgh University, earned his living as a lawyer. He is best remembered for his novel *The Man of Feeling*, published anonymously in 1771, which, although criticised for its over-abundant sentimentality, was hugely popular in its day and was one of Burns's 'bosom favourites'. Mackenzie edited two literary periodicals, *The Mirror* and *The Lounger*, and it was in the latter that he gave early recognition to Burns, writing in 1786, 'Though I am far from meaning to compare our rustic bard to Shakespeare, yet whoever will read his lighter and more humorous poems . . . will perceive with what uncommon penetration and sagacity this Heaven-taught ploughman, from his humble and unlettered station, has looked upon men and manners.'

And so the myth of the 'ploughman poet' was born. On the negative side, Mackenzie has been criticised for brokering the deal between Burns and his publisher, William Creech, when he advised Burns to part with his copyright for a hundred guineas. Never a great lover of work written in Scots, Robert Fergusson parodied Mackenzie in his poem 'The Sow of Feeling'. His other novels include *The Man of the World* (1773) and *Julia de Roubigné* (1777). He also wrote a play, *The Prince of Tunis* (1773). Mackenzie died at his house at 6 Heriot Row, but immortality was assured when his friend and fellow romantic, Sir Walter Scott, dedicated *Waverley* to 'Our Scottish Addison, Henry Mackenzie'.

From the main entrance, take the path round the right-hand side of the church. Turn down the second path (cobbled) on your right, then take the second path on your left. Mackenzie's grave is in the middle of the terrace wall.

SEE ALSO: Robert Burns, William Creech.

FURTHER READING: H.W. Thompson, *A Scottish Man of Feeling* (1931).

The Martyrs' Monument

At the northern end of the Kirkyard stands the Martyrs' Monument, erected in 1706 and commemorating some of the 18,000 who died for their faith, with an inscription that begins: 'Halt passenger take heed what thou dost see, This tomb doth shew for what some men did die . . .'

Robert Louis Stevenson was captivated by the Covenanters. His old nurse, Cummy, fed him tales of the martyrs when he was a boy. His mother grew up in Colinton Manse beside the kirkyard where the army of the Covenant bivouacked. As a teenager at Swanston, he was almost within sight of Rullion Green, where 900 bedraggled Covenanters were defeated by

3,000 regular troops of General Sir Thomas Dalyell in 1666, a battle which inspired him to write his pamphlet 'The Pentland Rising', published anonymously in 1866 when he was only 16 years old. The fascination never left him, and long afterwards he wrote from Samoa, 'My style is from the Covenanting writers.'

In *Edinburgh: Picturesque Notes* (1878), RLS devotes a chapter to Greyfriars, where he pours out his feelings for the martyrs:

The Martyrs' Monument.

> . . . down in the corner farthest from Sir George [Mackenzie], there stands a monument dedicated, in uncouth Covenanting verse, to all who lost their lives in that contention. There is no moorsman shot in a snow shower beside Irongray or Co'monell; there is not one of the two hundred who were drowned off the Orkneys; nor so much as a poor, over-driven, Covenanting slave in the American plantations; but can lay claim to a share in that memorial, and, if such things interest just men among the shades, can boast he has a monument on earth as well as Julius Caesar or the Pharaohs. Where they may all lie, I know not. Far-scattered bones, indeed!

On entering through the main entrance, take the first path on your right. The Martyrs' Monument is at the end of the path on the right, beside a hedge.

SEE ALSO: Robert Louis Stevenson, Sir George Mackenzie.

Tomb of Sir George Mackenzie (1636–91)
Also known as 'Bluidy Mackenzie', the hanging judge

> When a man's soul is certainly in hell, his body will scarce lie quiet in a tomb however costly; some time or other the door must open, and the reprobate come forth in the abhorred garments of the grave.
>
> Robert Louis Stevenson

Although a prolific writer of works of fiction, politics, history and law, Mackenzie is best remembered today as a ruthless and brutal persecutor of the Covenanters. Born in Dundee, he was the son of the 2nd Earl of Seaforth. He studied at St Andrews, Aberdeen and Bourges, was called to the Scottish Bar in 1659 and became MP for Ross-shire in 1669. In 1677, he was appointed Lord Advocate and in 1682 he founded the Advocates' Library (now the National Library of Scotland).

His mausoleum has been associated throughout history with hauntings and poltergeist activity, and in *Edinburgh: Picturesque Notes* (1878) Stevenson grimly recalls 'the reprobate' Mackenzie:

> Behind the church is the haunted mausoleum of Sir George Mackenzie: Bloody Mackenzie, Lord Advocate in the Covenanting troubles and author of some pleasing sentiments on toleration. Here, in the last century, an old Heriot's Hospital boy once harboured from the pursuit of the police. The Hospital is next door to Greyfriars – a courtly building among lawns, where, on Founder's Day, you may see a multitude of children playing Kiss-in-the-Ring and Round the Mulberry-bush. Thus, when the fugitive had managed to conceal himself in the tomb, his old schoolmates had a hundred opportunities to bring him food; and there he lay in safety till a ship was found to smuggle him abroad. But his must have been indeed a hard heart of brass, to lie all day and night alone with the dead persecutor; and other lads were far from emulating him in courage. When a man's soul is certainly in hell, his body will scarce lie quiet in a tomb however costly; some time or other the door must open, and the reprobate come forth in the abhorred garments of the grave. It was thought a high piece of prowess to knock at the Lord Advocate's mausoleum and challenge him to appear. 'Bluidy Mackenzie, come oot if ye dar'!' sang the foolhardy urchins. But Sir George had other affairs on hand; and the author of an essay on toleration continues to sleep peacefully among the many whom he so intolerantly helped to slay.

From the main entrance, take the first path on your left around the perimeter wall. Mackenzie's tomb is the large circular structure against the wall.
SEE ALSO: Robert Louis Stevenson.

Memorial to William McGonagall (c.1825–1902) *Scottish writer of doggerel*

> Then, as for Leith Fort, it was erected in 1779, which is really grand,
> And which is now the artillery headquarters in Bonnie Scotland;
> And as for the Docks, they are magnificent to see,
> They comprise five docks, two piers, 1,141 yards long respectively.
> William McGonagall, from 'The Ancient Town of Leith'

Described as the World's Best Bad Poet, William McGonagall's popularity still flourishes and his poetry is still published all over the world, proof that poetry, no matter how execrable, can still find an audience.

The son of an Irish cotton weaver, he was born in Edinburgh

but grew up in Dundee, where his father had moved in search of work. One of five siblings, he worked from the age of eleven as a handloom weaver. He acted in amateur productions at Dundee's Royal Theatre and in 1878 published his first collection of poems, which included his well known 'Railway Bridge of the Silvery Tay'. He gave public readings to derisory applause, ducked missiles thrown at him and was crowned with the ridiculous honour of 'Sir Topaz, Knight of the White Elephant of Burmah'. He sold his broadsheets in the street,

The William McGonagall Memorial.

and once walked all the way to Balmoral, but Queen Victoria denied him an audience. He also tried his luck in London and New York, but returned, as he had arrived, penniless. During his lifetime, he published over 200 poems and his *Poetic Gems* was published in 1890.

He may have died in poverty at South College Street, and is buried in a pauper's grave, but the memory of this naive man, who disregarded everything which makes poetry worth reading, will live forever. His burial records give no clue as to where in Greyfriars Churchyard he was laid to rest. Bob and Pat Watt, founders of the Edinburgh Friends of William McGonagall, raised money for a memorial plaque in the churchyard by running a McGonagall dinner in their home and, with the proceeds, erected a plaque on 6 October 1999. A search of the Edinburgh newspapers of that time gave no clue as to where his remains might be. Having exhausted the resources of this world, Bob decided to search the next world and approached a medium. A vision appeared in the medium's head and he asked Bob if McGonagall had a beard. Bob thought for a minute, then asked the medium if fashions changed in the spirit world; in other words, if you leave your razor in this world, would your beard grow in the next? This was a genuine question, but the medium went a bit huffy and left to investigate some spirits in Egypt.

From the main entrance, follow the path round the right-hand side of the church. Walk straight ahead and through the archway in the Flodden Wall. McGonagall's memorial plaque is in the top-left corner.

SEE ALSO: The Edinburgh Friends of McGonagall, site of William McGonagall's death, Writers' Corner, Tusitala Restaurant.

Grave of Allan Ramsay (1686–1758)
Poet, bookseller and publisher

> Tho' here you're buried, worthy ALLAN,
> We'll ne'er forget you, canty Callan,
> For while your Soul lives in the Sky,
> Your GENTLE SHEPHERD ne'er can die.

Born in the Leadhills and apprenticed to an Edinburgh wig-maker, Allan Ramsay turned to bookselling and published his own poetry. From his bookshop in the Luckenbooths, he launched the first lending library in Britain in 1728. His poetry, written in the vernacular tradition, helped revive interest in Scottish song and poetry, and was a strong influence on Robert Fergusson and Robert Burns.

From the entrance, take the left path around the church, where a memorial stone to Allan Ramsay can be seen high up on the church wall between the last two buttresses.

SEE ALSO: Ramsay Lodge.

25 FORREST ROAD

Sandy Bell's
Favourite watering hole of Hamish Henderson, poet, songwriter and guardian of Scottish folk heritage

> One morning the pub cleaner found a pair o' false teeth sittin' in a yoghurt carton on top o' the bar. A wee while later the phone rings. It's Hamish. 'Did I leave ma teeth there last night?'
>
> Charlie Woolley, landlord, Sandy Bell's

Immortalised as 'Sunday Balls in Fairest Redd' in Sydney Goodsir Smith's *Carotid Cornucopius* (1947), this pub remains very much as it has always been – a no-frills, no-tat, no-nonsense, good old Scottish drinking den. Close to the University, its clientele consists of academics, students, cloth-cap locals, folk enthusiasts and songsters wielding fiddles. Sandy Bell's was also the favourite haunt of the late Hamish Henderson (1919–2002), generally regarded as the father of the Scottish folk revival.

'At the age of seven,' he once recalled, 'I asked my mother about

a song she was singing. We had a book of songs in the house. I asked her where that song was in the book. She said, "Some of the songs we sing are not in books." That started me off as a folklorist and collector.'

Born in Blairgowrie and educated at Cambridge University, where he studied languages, he served as an intelligence officer in North Africa during the Second World War. After the war, he acted as a 'native guide' to the American folklorist Alan Lomax on his visit to Scotland in 1951 and lived for long periods with the travelling people of Scotland, collecting songs, classical ballads and stories passed along 'the carrying stream'.

Hamish Henderson.

'I remember in 1955 in the berry fields of Blairgowrie, picking berries and recording songs,' he said. 'Collecting in the berry fields was a wee bit like holding a tin under the Niagara Falls.'

In the early '50s, he joined the newly founded School of Scottish Studies at Edinburgh University, immersing himself in the Scottish folk tradition and building up a huge archive of songs on tape. His greatest discovery, he always maintained, was the singer Jeannie Robertson, described by A.L. Lloyd as 'a singer, sweet and heroic'. His own works included his collection of verse, *Elegies for the Dead in Cyrenaica* (1948), *Ballads of World War Two* (1947), *Alias MacAlias* (1992), *Armstrong Nose* (1996) and various translations of the modern Italian poets

Charlie Woolley, landlord, Sandy Bell's.

Eugenio Montale, Alfonso Gatto, Salvatore Quasimodo and Giuseppe Ungaretti. Many of his songs have passed into the folk tradition, but the two songs he will be best remembered for are 'The John Maclean March', a tribute to the Red Clydesider John Maclean, and 'Freedom Come All Ye', often referred to as Scotland's unofficial national anthem. A veteran of many Aldermaston and Faslane marches, Henderson was a tireless campaigner for CND and the Anti-Apartheid Movement. He believed he was the target of two assassination attempts by the South African security services, and in 1983 he publicly refused an OBE award in protest at the

Thatcher government's nuclear arms policy – a defiant act for which Radio Scotland listeners voted him 'Scot of the Year'. Hamish Henderson died on 9 March 2002 in an Edinburgh nursing home, aged 82. The friendly atmosphere of 'Sunday Balls in Fairest Redd' is a fitting memorial to this man who dedicated his life to the survival of the Scots folk tradition and believed bursting into song was an essential ingredient of life.
SEE ALSO: Edinburgh Park.

FURTHER INFORMATION: Tel: 0131 225 2751.

FURTHER READING: P. Orr (ed.), *The Poet Speaks* (Routledge, 1966).

CHAMBERS STREET

Museum of Scotland

Housing more than 10,000 artefacts, this museum is dedicated to telling Scotland's story from prehistory to the present day. Opened in 1998 and described by a few over-zealous disciples as the finest Scottish building of the twentieth century, this museum is nothing if not exceptional in its design, with each of its six levels divided into themed areas covering everything from the Jacobite Risings to whisky distilling.

The museum holds various literary artefacts, including a pair of double-barrelled pistols owned by Robert Burns, probably from the period when he was an exciseman. There are letters written by Burns and a cup and saucer which belonged to Nancy McLehose, the inspiration for 'Ae Fond Kiss'. There is also crockery that was used by James Boswell and Samuel Johnson during their epic tour of the Hebrides and a baby basket used by Walter Scott's mother. She gave birth to 12 children, and this basket was probably one of many. A few Samoan artefacts connected to Robert Louis Stevenson include a chief's robe made of leaves and fringed with parrot feathers, and a fly-whisk made of plaited coconut fibre. Augustus Saint-Gaudens' famous bronze plaque of Stevenson, sculpted in New York in 1887, is also on display. Ian Rankin introduced miniature coffins into the plot of *The Falls* (2001) after viewing one of the museum's strangest exhibits: a collection of 17 miniature wooden coffins discovered buried on Arthur's Seat in 1836.

SEE ALSO: Robert Burns, Nancy McLehose, Sir Walter Scott, Robert Louis Stevenson, St Giles Cathedral, Samuel Johnson, James Boswell, Ian Rankin, Holyrood Park.

FURTHER INFORMATION: Opening times: 10 a.m.–5 p.m. Monday to Saturday; 10 a.m.–8 p.m. Tuesday; 12 p.m.–5 p.m. Sunday. Closed Christmas Day. Disabled access throughout. Admission free – although there may be a charge for some special exhibitions.

Tel: 0131 247 4422. Website: www.nms.ac.uk.

GUTHRIE STREET (FORMERLY COLLEGE WYND)

Birthplace of Sir Walter Scott (1771–1832)

Walter Scott (or 'Wattie' as he was known) was born on 15 August 1771, the ninth child of Anne Rutherford, daughter of a former professor of medicine at Edinburgh University, and Walter Scott, a solicitor and writer to the Signet. The house of his birth, along with others, was demolished to make room for the northern frontage of Old College (then known as the new College). It was situated at the top of College Wynd, near Chambers Street, and stood in the corner of a small courtyard. It was a typical dark, overcrowded and airless Old Town tenement; a warren of flats where people lived amid the stink of refuse and bad sanitation; a place where sunlight and fresh air rarely ventured. Six of the Scotts' children had died in infancy behind the walls of this cramped slum, and shortly after Wattie's birth, in 1772, the

College Wynd in 1871, shortly before demolition.

Scotts wisely moved to the clean air and leafy outlook of newly built George Square.

SEE ALSO: Childhood home of W.S., townhouse of W.S., Lasswade Cottage, Parliament Hall, The Heart of Midlothian, Greyfriars Kirkyard, Scott Monument, Holyrood Park, St John's Churchyard, The Writers' Museum, High School, Old College, Sciennes Hill House, Assembly Rooms, J.G. Lockhart, Portobello Sands, Canongate Kirkyard, The Edinburgh Walter Scott Club.

FURTHER INFORMATION: A plaque high up on the eastern wall where Guthrie Street meets Chambers Street commemorates Scott's birthplace. College Wynd was originally named the Wynd of the Blessed Virgin-in-the-Fields as the tall, gabled house at the top was built on the site of Kirk-o'-Field, where Lord Darnley was murdered in 1567 when the house he was staying in was blown to bits.

Irish playwright, novelist and poet Oliver Goldsmith (1730–74) is believed to have lived in College Wynd around 1750 while studying medicine at the University; he left without taking a degree.

34 GRASSMARKET

The White Hart Inn
Scene of the final parting between Robert Burns and Nancy McLehose

> Ae fond kiss, and then we sever,
> Ae fareweel, and then – for ever

Robert Burns lodged at Mr Mackay's White Hart Inn on his last visit to Edinburgh, during the winter of 1791. And it was here that Burns

parted from his beloved Nancy, providing inspiration for the immortal lyric, 'Ae Fond Kiss', one of the greatest poetical farewells ever written. Nancy sailed for Jamaica to join her estranged husband, sailing from Leith in February 1792 on *The Roselle* – the same ship on which Burns had intended to sail from the Clyde in 1786. Her attempt at a reunion with her husband failed, and she returned to Edinburgh in August 1792. Burns never saw her again, although a few letters passed between them.

The White Hart is one of the oldest inns in Edinburgh, dating back to 1516. Only the cellars survive from this time and the present building dates from 1740. William and Dorothy Wordsworth stayed here during their tour of Scotland in 1803.

SEE ALSO: Clarinda, Jean Lorimer, Baxter's Close, Anchor Close, St James Square, Buccleuch Street, Burns Monument, Canongate Kilwinning Lodge, St Giles, William Smellie, William Creech, The Writers' Museum, Sciennes Hill House, Robert Fergusson, Henry Mackenzie, The Blind Poet pub.

FURTHER INFORMATION: Tel: 0131 226 2806.

60 WEST PORT

G.J. Thomson: Foreign Language Books

Opened in 1991 by translator Gordon J. Thomson beside Edinburgh Translations (one of Scotland's oldest independent translation agencies), this mini-bookshop now buys and sells second-hand books in and on all foreign languages. Here you may find anything from Albanian to Ukrainian, but the emphasis is on the major world languages, with French and German language and literature making up a large part of the small but varied stock. Located in Edinburgh's book nook west of the Grassmarket, this is a worthwhile port of call for language enthusiasts and visitors, and a caring home for quality second-hand books in all foreign languages.

FURTHER INFORMATION: Opening hours: 10 a.m.–6 p.m.
Tel: 0131 229 7534. E-mail: edtran@sol.co.uk.
Website: www.edinburghtranslations.co.uk.

62 WEST PORT

Pringle Booksellers

Established in Dundas Street for many years, Pringle Booksellers recently moved to the Old Town and is now trading in the heart of Edinburgh's bookselling community on the West Port. This shop continues to stock a wide range of books with a particular emphasis on Scottish books, literature, art, bibliography, history and antiquarian. The owner is always interested in purchasing good books – from individual items right up to large libraries – and valuations are also conducted. A range of prints and maps is also stocked.

FURTHER INFORMATION: Opening hours: 11 a.m.–5.30 p.m. Monday to Saturday.
Tel: 0131 228 8880.
Website:
www.pringlebooks.co.uk.

68 WEST PORT

Peter Bell Books

Peter has been selling books in Edinburgh for 25 years. His was the third shop to open in the West Port in 1989; now there are five, plus one selling maps and prints. His stock is highly focused, being largely 'scholarly and rare'. The mainly scholarly/academic stock is strong in history, literature, philosophy and Scottish material; the antiquarian stock is an eclectic mixture of the unusual and the rare (in the sense of unlikely to be found elsewhere), mainly books from the nineteenth century. Peter likes obscure little books published on funny subjects in funny places, religious material, Victorian poetry and pamphlets and books published by Edinburgh University Press, of which he has a large backstock.

FURTHER INFORMATION:
Opening hours: 10 a.m.–5p.m.
Tuesday to Saturday.

Tel: 0131 556 2198. Email: books@peterbell.net. Website: www.peterbell.net.

72–4 WEST PORT

Armchair Books

Armchair Books is bursting with a huge quantity of second-hand books on many subjects from Scotland to sci-fi, military to miniature, leather bindings to Ladybirds. Situated in Edinburgh's book corner, just west of the Grassmarket, they specialise in Victorian illustrated books and nice bindings, but they also have a very large, well-organised stock of literature/fiction, poetry and science fiction. Other large sections include: Scottish, military, theology, children's, travel, exploration/mountaineering, social

sciences, cookery, history, modern firsts, art and architecture and others. If you're a student, a book dealer or just plain poor, then you qualify for a ten per cent discount. **FURTHER INFORMATION**: Opening hours: 10 a.m.–6 p.m., seven days a week. Tel: 0131 229 5927. Email: armchairbooks@hotmail.com. Website: www.armchairbooks.co.uk.

145–7 WEST PORT

West Port Books

Established in 1977, West Port Books is a vast warren of loosely connected rooms crammed with art, academia, upmarket remainders and music. Described by its owner, Bert Barrott, as 'decidedly not twee or overly sophisticated, this shop is a serendipitist's garden of delights and an organised man's vision of hell'. Specialisms include fine arts, Indian history and classical

music. They also publish reprints of Edinburgh classics, both in print and as audiobooks. Bert also likes to emphasise the shop's other function as 'a drop-in day centre for various n e ' e r - d o - w e l l intellectuals and layabouts who consume my tea in vast quantities'.

FURTHER INFORMATION: Opening hours:

    10.30 a.m.–5.30 p.m. Monday, Tuesday and Friday;

    12 p.m.–6 p.m. Wednesday, Thursday and Saturday.

    Tel: 0131 229 4431.

    Email: west@portbooks.freeserve.co.uk.

(8 LAURISTON STREET)

Main Point Books

The name says it all. Books are the main point. The proprietor is Richard Browne, whose favourite writers are Flann O'Brien, Brautigan, Sebald, Vonnegut, Kerouac and Rumi and his style is appreciated by those who enjoy an offbeat sense of humour. He specialises in 'reliable rereads': mountaineering, walking, maps, transport, military, fishing, fiction, film, theatre, photography, biography and a great deal of poetry. There is a lively esoteric section spanning everything from aromatherapy to Zoroastrianism. Main Point Books is also the home of *Scottish Book Collector* magazine, which has now become *textualities*, an annual publication, while at www.textualities.net you'll find a great selection of features on writing and book collecting, as well as books for sale.

FURTHER INFORMATION: Opening hours: 11 a.m.–5.30 p.m. Tuesday to Saturday.

    Tel: 0131 228 4837.

    Email: rich@textualities.net.

Canongate

Site of Boyd's Inn, at which Dr Johnson arrived in Edinburgh in 1773

> Oats. A grain, which in England is generally given to horses, but in Scotland supports the people.
>
> Dr Johnson, *A Dictionary of the English Language* (1755)

On Saturday, 14 August 1773, James Boswell received a note at his house at 501 James Court, off the Lawnmarket, that Dr Samuel Johnson had arrived at Boyd's Inn (now demolished), at the head of the Canongate. Johnson had come to Edinburgh to begin his tour of Scotland and the Hebrides with his friend James Boswell, a journey which would eventually produce two classic works of travel literature: Johnson's *A Journey to the Western Islands of Scotland* (1775) and Boswell's *Journal of a Tour to the Hebrides* (1785). 'Late that evening . . . I went to him directly,' Boswell wrote.

> He embraced me cordially; and I exulted in the thought, that I now had him actually in Caledonia . . . the Doctor had unluckily had a bad specimen of Scottish cleanliness. He then drank no fermented liquor. He asked to have his lemonade made sweeter; upon which the waiter, with his greasy fingers, lifted a lump of sugar, and put it into it. The Doctor, in indignation, threw it out of the window . . . He was to do me the honour to lodge under my roof . . . Mr Johnson and I walked arm-in-arm up the High Street, to my house in James Court: it was a dusky night: I could not prevent his being assailed by the evening effluvia of Edinburgh. I heard a late baronet, of some distinction in the political world, observe, that 'walking the streets of Edinburgh at night was pretty perilous, and a good deal odoriferous'. The peril is much abated, by the care which the magistrates have taken to enforce the city laws against throwing foul water from the windows; but, from the structure of the houses in the Old Town, which consist of many stories, in each of which a different family lives, and there being no covered sewers, the odour still

continues. A zealous Scotsman would have wished Mr Johnson to be without one of his five senses upon this occasion. As we marched slowly along, he grumbled in my ear, 'I smell you in the dark!' But he acknowledged that the breadth of the street, and the loftiness of the buildings on each side, made a noble appearance.

SEE ALSO: James Boswell, David Hume, St Giles.

FURTHER INFORMATION: A plaque can be seen commemorating Dr Johnson's visit at the junction of Boyd's Entry and St Mary's Street.

OLD PLAYHOUSE CLOSE

Site of the Playhouse Theatre (1747–69)

Whaur's yer Wullie Shakespeare noo?
Shouted from the audience on
the first night of *Douglas*

The powerful tragedy called *Douglas* was first performed at the Playhouse Theatre on 14 December 1756 and was a brilliant success. It was written by John Home (1722–1808), a Church of Scotland minister at Athel- staneford in East Lothian, but Home ended up paying a heavy price for its triumph as the play gave such offence to the Edinburgh Presbytery that he was forced to resign from the ministry. Home's play, although rarely performed today, was influential in its day because it was instrumental in breaking down the belief of the Church that all drama was immoral, which eventually led to the licensing of Edinburgh's Theatre Royal in 1767 in Shakespeare Square at the east end of Princes Street.

John Home.

John Home was born in a house in Quality Street (now Maritime Street), Leith, and educated at Edinburgh University. He fought on the government side in the 1745 Jacobite Rebellion and was captured after the Battle of Falkirk and imprisoned in Doune Castle, from where he escaped using the age-old trick of tying his blankets together to form a rope. He became a minister in 1747, and after his enforced resignation in 1757, he became tutor to the Prince of Wales (later George III).

After the success of *Douglas* in Edinburgh, David Garrick decided to produce it on the London stage. Garrick also produced Home's next play, *The Siege of Aquileia* in 1760. Other works of Home's include *The Fatal Discovery* (1769), *Alonzo* (1773), *Alfred* (1778) and *A History of the Rebellion of 1745* (1802). John Home is buried in the graveyard of South Leith Parish Church, Henderson Street, Leith.

FURTHER INFORMATION: Old Playhouse Close is situated opposite New Street. A plaque marks the site of John Home's birthplace at 28 Maritime Street, Leith.

FURTHER READING: H. Mackenzie, *An Account of the Life and Writings of John Home* (1822).

22 ST JOHN STREET

Lodgings of Tobias Smollett (1721–71)
Historian and writer of picaresque comic novels

> The city [of Edinburgh] stands upon two hills . . . which with all its defects, may very well pass for the capital of a moderate kingdom.
>
> Tobias Smollett, *The Expedition of Humphry Clinker* (1771)

Although born on a farm in Dumbartonshire, and educated at Glasgow University, Smollett was never really considered 'Scotland's own', partly because he lived most of his life in

Tobias Smollett.

London and later moved abroad for his health. Where Robert Louis Stevenson turned exile into legend, Smollett was probably too anglicised, too caustic, too prejudiced and too out of touch with his roots for many Scottish people to really identify with him.

He was a surgeon's mate in the Royal Navy and later practised in London, but his main calling and career was as a man of letters. It was his picaresque novels which brought him fame, namely *Roderick Random* (1748), *Peregrine Pickle* (1751) and *The Expedition of Humphry Clinker* (1771). In 1753, he edited the *Critical Review*, but his criticism was so savage it led to his imprisonment for libel in 1760. He was a noted historian, writing his *History of England* (three volumes, 1757–8), and another major achievement was his translation of Cervantes' *Don Quixote* into English in 1755.

During the summer of 1766, he stayed with his sister, Mrs Telfer, who occupied the second flat of 182 Canongate (now renumbered 22 St John Street) above the pend (vaulted entrance), and it was here he wrote part of his last and most popular novel, *The Expedition of Humphry Clinker*. Written during the last two years of his life, the story is told by its characters through a series of letters on a journey encompassing Wales, London and Scotland, where Edinburgh disgusts them by its filth.

For health reasons, his last years were spent abroad, and he died in Livorno, Italy. Shortly before his death he visited his mother at St John Street, confiding to her that he was ill and not long for this world. To

The pend, St John Street.

this, she replied, 'We'll no' be very long pairted onie way. If you gang first, I'll be close on your heels. If I lead the way, you'll no' be far ahint me.'

SEE ALSO: Holyrood Palace.

FURTHER READING: L.M. Knapp, *Doctor of Men and Manners* (1940); G.M. Kahrl, *Tobias Smollett: Traveller-Novelist* (1945).

ST JOHN STREET

Hall of the Canongate Kilwinning Lodge of Freemasons Visited by Robert Burns in 1787

> There's many a badge that's unco braw
> Wi' ribbon, tape and lace on;
> Let kings and princes wear them a'
> Gie me the Master's Apron.
> > Robert Burns, 'The Master's Apron'

Burns became a Freemason when he was 23, in 1781, when he was initiated into the Lodge St David at Tarbolton in Ayrshire. Five years later, he visited Edinburgh for the first time in an attempt to secure enough patronage to publish a second edition of his poems. He carried with him letters of introduction from his Masonic contacts in Ayrshire, which opened many doors for him and were instrumental in assuring his success.

On 1 February 1787, he made his only recorded visit to the Canongate Kilwinning Lodge. He was later reputedly made their Poet Laureate, an office which was held by James Hogg, the Ettrick Shepherd, in 1835.

SEE ALSO: Anchor Close, St James Square, Buccleuch Street, Burns Monument, White Hart Inn, St Giles, William Smellie,

William Creech, The Writers' Museum, Sciennes Hill House, Robert Fergusson, Clarinda, Jean Lorimer, Henry Mackenzie, The Blind Poet pub.

FURTHER INFORMATION: The Lodge site is on the west side of St John Street, near the vennel. At no. 10 lived the printer of the Waverley novels, James Ballantyne, friend and misfortune of Sir Walter Scott.

175 CANONGATE

The Old Children's Bookshelf

Specialising in children's literature of yesteryear, the shelves of this tiny shop are filled with books from the 1920s to the 1950s, a time when kids eagerly buried their noses in books about holiday adventures, schools and ponies, Girl Guides and the

exploits of Fatty and the Five Find-outers. This golden age gave birth to some of the great classics of children's literature from the pens of Arthur Ransome, E. Nesbit, C.S. Lewis and others. Further nostalgia can be found in the shop's collection of annuals, comics and storypapers, including editions of *Eagle*, *Girl*, *Dandy*, *Bunty*, *Lion* and *Meccano Magazine*. Books are bought and a catalogue is issued quarterly (ask to be added to the mailing list).

FURTHER INFORMATION: Opening hours: 10.30 a.m.–5 p.m. Monday to Friday; 10 a.m.–5 p.m. Saturday. Tel: 0131 558 3411. Email: shirleyocb@aol.com.

152 CANONGATE

Canongate Kirkyard

The original Canongate Kirk was located at the now ruined Abbey of the Holy Rood, adjacent to the Palace of Holyroodhouse. King James VII (James II of England) appropriated the Abbey church for use as a Chapel of the Order of the Thistles and built the present church for parishioners as a replacement in 1690.

Grave of Adam Smith (1723–90)
Scottish philosopher and economist

> With the greater part of rich people, the chief
> enjoyment of riches consists in the parade of riches,
> which in their eyes is never so complete as when they
> appear to possess those decisive marks of opulence
> which nobody can possess but themselves.
>
> Adam Smith, *The Wealth of Nations* (1776)

Best known for his influential book *The Wealth of Nations*, Smith was one of the great eighteenth-century moral philosophers whose ideas led to modern-day theories. He is also regarded as the world's first political economist. Born in Kirkcaldy, Fife, he was sent to Oxford at the age of 17. On his return home, he joined 'the brilliant circle in Edinburgh which included David Hume, John Home, Hugh Blair, Lord Hailes and Principal Robertson'. In 1751, aged 28, he became professor of logic at Glasgow University. In 1752, he took the chair of moral philosophy, and his *Theory of Moral Sentiments* was published in 1759.

Grave of Adam Smith.

A shy, clumsy and absent-minded man, he lived a quiet bachelor's life with his mother, who lived to be 90. Loved by his students, he had the gift of oratory and a considerable reputation as a lecturer. He was a good friend of David Hume, and discussed his ideas with the great thinkers of his day, including Samuel Johnson and Benjamin Franklin. In 1760, he travelled to France, where he met Voltaire and began writing *An Inquiry into the Nature and Causes of the Wealth of Nations*, a book which transformed the economic theories of the day by analysing the results of economic freedom, and recognising the division of labour, rather than land or money, as the main ingredient of economic growth. Smith moved to London in 1776 and the book was published that year. In 1778, he returned to Edinburgh as commissioner of Customs. He died on 17 July 1790, after an illness. From the main entrance, his grave is over on the far left against the rear wall of the Old Tolbooth building.

SEE ALSO: David Hume, John Home.

FURTHER READING: I.S. Ross, *The Life of Adam Smith* (Clarendon, 1995).

Grave of Robert Fergusson (1750–74)
Scottish poet who was a major influence on Robert Burns

> Mr Fergusson died in the cells.
>
> Entry in the superintendent's log,
> Edinburgh's Bedlam, 16 October 1774

'O thou, my elder brother in Misfortune/By far my elder brother in the Muse,' wrote Robert Burns in epitaph on Robert Fergusson. Fergusson's poetry had a deep influence on Burns; his 'The Farmer's Ingle' clearly inspired 'The Cotter's Saturday Night'.

David Annand's bronze figure of Robert Fergusson.

Robert Fergusson was born in Edinburgh on 5 September 1750 in the Cap and Feather Close, near Niddry's Wynd (now Niddry Street). The Close was demolished with the construction of North Bridge, which provided easier access to the seaport of Leith and the land on which the New Town now stands.

Robert was a second son born into a lower-middle-class family. His father, a clerk, came from Aberdeen farming stock. Educated privately at the Royal High School in Edinburgh for four years, Robert was awarded a bursary from the Donald Fergusson fund, enabling him to attend the Dundee High School and then St Andrews University.

He enjoyed university life. He was a good singer – with a voice encouraged by a glass or several – and was popular amongst his fellow students. The University was less enamoured with the young man and on at least one occasion he stood on the doorstep of expulsion. The 'rabbit grace' best illustrates his relationship

Robert Fergusson's headstone – erected by Robert Burns.

with the staff and students. At that time it was the practice in the University for lecturers and students to eat dinner together. Each day, the students had to take it in turn to say grace over the food. Robert recited a quatrain that he had quilled:

> For rabbits young and for rabbits old
> For rabbits hot and rabbits cold
> For rabbits tender and for rabbits tough
> Our thanks we render for we've had enough.

The staff frowned, the students cheered, and it was reported that there were fewer rabbits purchased after that event.

In May 1768, following the death of his father, Robert abandoned his studies without graduating and returned to Edinburgh to support his mother and family. In September 1778, he was working as a clerk copyist in the Commissary Records Office, quilling page after page of copperplate script at a penny a page. When the Tron Kirk bell chimed eight o'clock, the town stopped work. Robert enjoyed life; he danced, he sang, he drank, he became a member of the Cape Club. Each member of this club was dubbed with a 'knighthood'. Robert became Sir Precenter.

His first poems were published in *Ruddiman's Weekly Magazine* in 1771 and were written in imitation of the English style. 'Daft Days' was his first Scots poem, published in 1772, and a slim volume of his works appeared in 1773, inspiring Burns to emulate his artistic vigour.

Tragically, however, Fergusson suffered from manic depression and, following a fall which exacerbated this condition, he was committed to the public asylum. He died shortly afterwards in Darien House, which, originally built in 1698 as the offices and stores of the Darien Company, had degenerated in the following century into a pauper lunatic asylum. The Bedlam Asylum stood behind the building which is now the Bedlam Theatre in Forrest Road. Fergusson's body was interred in a pauper's grave two days after his death. A young doctor, Andrew Duncan, had attended him in the last few weeks of his life. Appalled by the conditions and treatment of the inmates in Bedlam, Andrew Duncan went on to pioneer methods for improving the treatment of the insane.

Robert Fergusson wrote 33 poems in Scots and 50 poems in English, and will chiefly be remembered for 'Auld Reekie' (1773), which traces a day in the life of the city. Other well known poems include 'Elegy on the Death of Scots Music', 'Hallow Fair', 'To the Tron Kirk Bell', 'Leith Races' and 'The Rising of the Session'.

Burns was saddened to discover that Fergusson had been buried in an unmarked grave and, in February 1787, he sought permission to erect a headstone. After it was in place, Burns took five years to settle his account with the Edinburgh architect who designed the stone, commenting in a letter that 'He was two years in erecting it, after I commissioned him for it; and I have been two years paying him, after he sent me his account; so he and I are quits . . . He had the hardiesse to ask me interest on the sum; but considering that the money was due by one Poet, for putting a tomb-stone over another, he may, with grateful surprise, thank Heaven that ever he saw a farthing of it.'

Erected and commissioned by the Friends of Robert Fergusson, a bronze figure sculpted by David Annand commemorates the poet outside the gates of the kirkyard. The statue was the brainchild of George Philp and Bob Watt, and was unveiled on 17 October 2004. Stewart Conn, the Edinburgh Makar, composed and delivered a poem to mark the occasion. 'Robert Burns' (Chris Tait) emerged from a crowd of about 2,000 to say how pleased he was.

Robert Fergusson (1750–74)
On the unveiling of his statue in the Canongate, Sunday,
17 Oct 2004
By Stewart Conn

> The image uppermost in my mind
> was of him crouching in his cell in squalor,
> his head adorned with a crown of straw
> he had neatly plaited with his own hand.
> Now we see this trig figure
> caught in mid-stride among the thrang,
> a reminder that guid gear can gang
> intil sma' buik – not just in literature.
> Though too late to revivify a spirit broken
> in his lifetime it rekindles recognition
> of his artistry, humanity and vision
> and the plain braid Scots he spoke in.
> Besides cocking a snook at the literati
> of his day, his presence will regenerate
> the native vigour of the Canongate
> (no need to muster the black banditti).
> Long may those sturdy 'wee rosiers'
> spring from his grave; his affinity
> with common folk, his ribaldry and pity,
> move us to laughter and to tears.
> So let us – in fancied ritual – celebrate
> his genius by washing down our oysters
> with reaming noggins . . . raised in roisterous
> praise of Auld Reikie's peerless laureate.

SEE ALSO: Robert Burns.

FURTHER INFORMATION: Fergusson's grave is situated close to the western wall of the church, bordered by a low chain fence. The statue and the grave are the primary memorials for Robert Fergusson, but there are a number of other tributes in the city, as follows: a plaque in St Giles; a plaque in the new Royal High School; the male and female wards in the Royal Edinburgh Hospital, which are named after him; a lock of his hair in Edinburgh University Library; and his portrait hangs in the Scottish National Portrait Gallery. The Cape Club is still in existence today. Tel: 0131 553 1052.

FURTHER READING: A. Law, *Robert Fergusson and the Edinburgh of his Time* (Edinburgh City Libraries, 1974); D. Irving, *The Life of Robert Fergusson* (1799); T. Sommers, *The Life of Robert Fergusson, the Scottish Poet* (1803).

Fergusson destroyed his papers just before he died. There

are inscribed copies of his 1773 *Poems* and some scraps among the Cape Records, MSS 2041–4, in the National Library of Scotland, and a few manuscripts in the Laing Collection at the Edinburgh University Library. The Edinburgh Room of the Edinburgh Central Public Library maintains a folder of newspaper clippings.

Grave of Mary Brunton (1778–1818)
Scottish novelist

Born on the island of Burra in Orkney, Mary Brunton (née Balfour) is best remembered for her novel *Self-Control*, published anonymously in 1812. Anonymity was often not a choice but a necessity for women writers in the early nineteenth century, who could not be seen to step over the boundaries of the home and their household duties. Not only were they denied the credit for their art, but, as in Brunton's preface in *Self-Control*, they were often made to feel apologetic for it: '[it] was begun at first merely for my own amusement, and to reconcile my conscience to

Mary Brunton.

the time which it has employed, by making it in some degree useful'. She married the Revd Alexander Brunton in 1798 and lived in Bolton, near Haddington, East Lothian, before moving to Edinburgh in 1803 when her husband took on the chaplaincy at Greyfriars. Their first home was at 3 St John Street, opposite the Masonic lodge. Her other works included *Discipline* (1814) and *Emmeline* (1819).

FURTHER INFORMATION: The tablet marking Mary Brunton's grave is fixed to the western wall, near the top-left corner of the kirkyard.

Grave of Dugald Stewart (1753–1828)
Scottish philosopher and biographer

> Wealth, honours, and all that is extraneous of the man, have no more influence with him than they will have at the Last Day.
>
> Robert Burns

Dugald Stewart held the chair of moral philosophy at Edinburgh University for 25 years and became a celebrated philosopher and masterful teacher, whose persuasive arguments influenced many of his students, including Walter Scott and philosopher James Mill. Stewart was a disciple of Thomas Reid's 'common sense' philosophy and taught the first course on economics given in Britain. He is best remembered for his *Elements of the*

Philosophy of the Human Mind (three volumes, 1792, 1814, 1827). A circular Corinthian monument was erected to his memory on Calton Hill in 1831. His nondescript tomb is situated in the north-west corner of the kirkyard, first on the left as you enter the area dominated by the tall monument erected to the memory of the soldiers who died in Edinburgh Castle.
SEE ALSO: Monument to Dugald Stewart.

Grave of James Ballantyne (1772–1833)
Childhood friend, printer, publisher and secret partner of Sir Walter Scott

> In prospect of absolute ruin, I wonder if they would let me leave the Court of Session. I would like, methinks, to go abroad, 'And lay my bones far from the Tweed.'
> Sir Walter Scott, *Journal* (1826)

James Ballantyne's friendship with Scott began during their boyhood at Kelso Grammar School, where they shared a bench together. Ballantyne went on to study law, but in 1797 he set up as a printer and launched the *Tory Kelso Mail*, and in 1802 printed the first two volumes of Scott's *Border Minstrelsy*. Scott encouraged him to move to Edinburgh and, with money loaned from Scott, he moved to a small shop at Abbeyhill, near Holyroodhouse, where the third volume of *The Minstrelsy* was printed. He later moved to larger premises in the Canongate and in 1805 Scott bought a quarter share in Ballantyne's printing business, setting up James and his younger brother John in a publishing business four years later in Hanover Street. Scott's involvement in these ventures, which eventually led to his financial downfall, were kept intensely secret.

John Buchan, in his biography of Scott, describes James Ballantyne as 'enthusiastic, excitable, a muddler in finance, incapable of presenting at any time an accurate statement of his assets and liabilities', and Lockhart's judgement on his father-in-law's partnership in his *Life* is an accurate assessment of a madcap enterprise:

> It is an old saying, that wherever there is a secret there must be something wrong; and dearly did he pay the penalty for the mystery in which he had chosen to involve this transaction . . . Hence, by degrees, was woven a web of entanglement from which neither Ballantyne nor his adviser had any means of escape.

Although the printing business was successful, the publishing side was a disaster. Its complex credit structure, coupled with its tangled involvement with Archibald Constable, who was ruined in 1826, inevitably led to Ballantyne's downfall the same year, with debts amounting to around £130,000. Scott subsequently wrote his way out of debt, a task which took him six years.

Buchan recalls that in 1829, 'James Ballantyne was no longer the jolly companion he had been, for he had lost his wife, retired to the country, and taken to Whiggism and piety.'

He died four years later and is buried beside his brother John (see below).

SEE ALSO: John Ballantyne, Sir Walter Scott, J.G. Lockhart, R.M. Ballantyne.

FURTHER INFORMATION: In 1870, the Ballantynes moved to Clare House in Newington, following the expansion of Waverley Station. In 1878, a London branch was opened and in 1916 the Edinburgh printing works finally closed. James Ballantyne's nephew was the novelist R.M. Ballantyne, author of *Coral Island* (1858).

Grave of John Ballantyne (1774–1821)
Printer, publisher and secret partner of Sir Walter Scott

> I believe Scott would as soon have ordered his dog to be hanged, as harboured, in his darkest hour of perplexity, the least thought of discarding 'jocund Johnny'.
>
> J.G. Lockhart, *The Life of Sir Walter Scott* (1837–8)

John Ballantyne, the younger brother of James, Walter Scott's school friend, was born in Kelso and was described by Lockhart as 'a quick, active, intrepid little fellow . . . so very lively and amusing . . . liked his bottle and his bowl, as well as, like Johnny Armstrong, "a hawk, a hound, and a fair woman"'. His father sent him to London where he worked in a banking house and he later trained as a tailor. Success, however, eluded him in life. In 1805, his goods were sold off to cover his debts, and his brother James offered him a post as clerk in his printing business. Both brothers became inextricably linked with Scott when he secretly bought a share of their printing business and later created a publishing house to be run by John, a move which would end in insolvency for Scott and the Ballantynes.

Lockhart recalls a touching scene beside John Ballantyne's grave in his *Life*:

> As we stood together a few days afterwards, while they were smoothing the turf over John's remains in the Canongate churchyard, the heavens, which had been dark and slaty, cleared up suddenly, and the midsummer sun shone forth in his strength. Scott, ever awake to the 'skiey influences', cast his eye along the overhanging line of the Calton Hill, with its gleaming walls and towers, and then turning to the grave again, 'I feel,' he whispered in my ear, 'I feel as if there would be less sunshine for me from this day forth.'

He died as he had lived: ignorant of the situation of his affairs, and deep in debt.

SEE ALSO: James Ballantyne, Sir Walter Scott, J.G. Lockhart.

FURTHER INFORMATION: John and James Ballantyne are buried in unmarked graves in front of the tomb of Sir William Fettes. From the main entrance, take the path leading round the right-hand side of the church. Follow the path downhill. On your right is the enormous tomb of Fettes, where a plaque at the bottom left marks the spot.

Grave of Clarinda (Agnes McLehose 1759–1841)
Inspiration for Robert Burns's 'Ae Fond Kiss'

> I'll ne'er blame my partial fancy,
> Naething could resist my Nancy:
> But to see her was to love her;
> Love but her, and love for ever.
> > Robert Burns, from 'Ae Fond Kiss'

Robert Burns first met Mrs Agnes (Nancy) McLehose after she engineered an invitation for him to a tea party given by Miss Erskine Nimmo at her brother's flat in Alison Square (now demolished), off Nicolson Street, on 4 December 1787. They seem to have been well and truly smitten with each other, and that night she hurriedly sent him a letter inviting him to tea at her house in

Clarinda's headstone.

Potterrow. He never kept the appointment as he dislocated his knee shortly afterwards when his coach reputedly overturned on his way home following an evening of revelry. And so the circumstances fell into place for the start of an impassioned correspondence between the two from December until mid-March, during which time around 80 letters were written between them, and a relationship blossomed which would eventually inspire Burns to write one of his greatest love songs.

It is doubtful whether today's postal system could have coped with their copious correspondence – sometimes six letters each a day – but since 1773 the Edinburgh penny post had been in operation, offering deliveries of letters and small parcels every hour throughout the day. Burns, who was then lodging at 2 St James Square (now demolished), used the penny post, but Nancy, careful of her reputation, often used her maid, Jennie Clow, to convey her letters.

On 8 December, Burns wrote to Nancy, stating:

> I cannot bear the idea of leaving Edinburgh without seeing you – I know not how to account for it – I am strangely taken with some people; nor am I often mistaken. You are a stranger to me; but I am an odd being: some yet unnamed feelings; things not

> principles, but better than whims, carry me farther than boasted reason ever did a philosopher.

Nancy replied:

> These 'nameless feelings' I perfectly comprehend, tho' the pen of Locke could not define them . . . If I was your sister, I would call on you; but tis a censorious world this; and in this sense 'you and I are not of this world'. Adieu. Keep up your heart, you will soon get well, and we shall meet. Farewell. God bless you.

Nancy has been described by an acquaintance as 'short in stature, her form graceful, her hands and feet small and delicate. Her features were regular and pleasing, her eyes lustrous, her complexion fair, her cheeks ruddy, and a well-formed mouth displayed teeth beautifully white.' Another said she was 'of a somewhat voluptuous style of beauty, of lively and easy manners, of a poetical cast of mind, with some wit, and not too high a degree of refinement or delicacy'. She was also married to, but estranged from, James McLehose, a Glasgow lawyer whom she had married when she was 18 and whom she had borne four children (two dying in infancy) by the time she was 23. McLehose ended up in a debtors' prison and afterwards sailed to a new life in Jamaica, leaving Nancy struggling to make ends meet as a single parent in a flat at General's Entry (now demolished) off Potterrow on Edinburgh's Southside. Although separated, Nancy was still in the eyes of the law a married woman and therefore had to be careful in her letters to Burns that she was not in any way compromised. Soon, therefore, they adopted for discretion's sake the Arcadian noms de plume

Clarinda's Tea Room – a short walk away at 69 Canongate.

Sylvander and Clarinda. Burns's injury made it difficult for him to have any opportunity to consummate the relationship and some of his letters – through frustration – got a little overheated, one stating 'had I been so blest as to have met with you in time, it might have led me – God of love only knows where'. To which Nancy replied, 'When I meet you, I must chide you for writing in your romantic style. Do you remember that she whom you address is a married woman?'

They did meet after Burns recovered, but there is no evidence that their relationship ever became sexual. Burns eventually left Edinburgh in February 1788, later marrying his former lover Jean Armour. They did, however, meet once more before Nancy's departure to join her husband in Jamaica in a failed attempt to rebuild her marriage. Her diary entry at the time reveals she was still in love with Burns 'till the shadow fell . . . This day I can never forget. Parted with Robert Burns in the year 1791 never more to meet in this world. Oh may we meet in heaven.' Before her departure, Burns sent her a card with a lyric scrawled on it from Sanquhar Post Office in Dumfriesshire, which began 'Ae fond kiss, and then we sever, Ae fareweel, and then – for ever . . .'

Nancy outlived Burns by 45 years, dying aged 82 in 1841 at her flat beneath Calton Hill. Her grave is situated against the eastern wall of Canongate Kirkyard. The site of the house where she corresponded with Burns is marked by a plaque at the corner of Potterrow and Marshall Street. In November 1788, Nancy's maid, Jennie Clow, gave birth to Burns's illegitimate son, conceived while acting as courier for Sylvander and Clarinda.

SEE ALSO: Robert Burns.

FURTHER INFORMATION: It was the Clarinda Burns Club that proposed that a plaque should be erected on the site of Clarinda's house at General's Entry in Potterrow on the wall of Bristo School in 1937. Edinburgh Corporation Education Committee thought 'the idea was totally unacceptable. It is beneath the dignity of our city to sanction such a tablet in view of Clarinda's character.' Questions were raised in the House of Commons. However, the Clarinda Burns Club stood firm, and a plaque was finally erected on 22 January 1937.

Clarinda's Tea Room is at 69 Canongate (0131 557 1888), near the entrance to Canongate Kirkyard.

VIEWCRAIG GARDENS

The Hutton Garden
A place to read

If you want a place to read in Edinburgh, there are few better than the Hutton Garden. Good views of East Lothian, Arthur's Seat, the old Royal High School and the new Parliament: a mix of history unique to the town.

The Garden is on the site of James Hutton's house. As you sit there, feel the gaists (ghosts) of Adam Smith, David Hume and Joseph Black – Edinburgh's Enlightenment stars – around you. Look at the Crags behind you: the view helped James Hutton – the man who gave us his theory of the Earth – become the father of modern geology. As you sit there, feel the past as James did, read Walter Scott's *Guy Mannering* as James did and, in winter, wear thick underwear as James did. The Hutton Garden is accessed by steps up from Viewcraig Gardens, off Holyrood Road.

Holyrood

The Palace of Holyroodhouse and Holyrood Abbey

> The Palace of Holyrood-house is an elegant piece of architecture, but sunk in an obscure, and, as I take it, unwholesome bottom, where one would imagine it had been placed on purpose to be concealed. The apartments are lofty, but unfurnished; and as for the pictures of the Scottish kings, from Fergus I to King William, they are paltry daubings, mostly by the same hand, painted either from the imagination, or porters hired to sit for the purpose.
>
> Tobias Smollett, *The Expedition of Humphry Clinker* (1771)

The twelfth-century Abbey of the Holy Rood is a roofless ruin today, but the Palace still stands in its high-born glory after 500 years of turbulent history. Construction was started by James IV (1473–1513) and finished off by his son James V (1513–42) after his father fell at Flodden Field in 1513.

William Dunbar (*c*.1460–*c*.1520) was one of many poets in history who depended on Court patronage for their survival, and during the reign of James IV he was frequently outspoken and candid, often criticising the powers that be with the clout of his piercing verse. Little is known of his life, but he is said to have been born in East Lothian, attended St Andrews University and then entered the priesthood. He later became secretary to some of James IV's embassies to foreign courts. In 1500, he was

given a Royal pension and in 1503 he wrote the political allegory *The Thrissill and the Rois*, the thistle being James IV, and the rose his wife, Margaret Tudor. Other poems included *Tua Mariit Wemen and the Wedo* and *The Dance of the Sevin Deidly Synnis*. His name disappears from all records after the Battle of Flodden, indicating he probably died in battle. Hugh MacDiarmid rated Dunbar a greater poet than Burns.

Poet and playwright David Lyndsay (*c.*1490–1555) also sought patronage from the court of James IV. His hilarious and irreverent political satire *The Thrie Estaites* was first performed in Cupar, Fife, in June 1552 and is the earliest Scottish play to have survived.

The Palace is best known for being the home of Mary, Queen of Scots (1542–87), who was twice married in the Abbey and who witnessed the murder of her secretary, David Rizzio, by her jealous husband, Lord Darnley, in her antechamber, where the bloodstains can still be seen. Mary was the daughter of James V, King of Scots, by his second wife, Mary of Guise, and she arrived at Holyrood from France in 1561, a Catholic queen in a Protestant country. All her literary output was in French, which was widely spoken by the Scottish nobility. Her library held more than 300 books, which included the largest collection of French and Italian poetry in Scotland. She wrote sacred poems and love sonnets, but little of her work was published during her lifetime. This was rectified in 1873 when the *Poems of Mary, Queen of Scots* were edited and published by Julian Sharman. Mary was beheaded in 1587 when she was implicated in a plot against her cousin, Elizabeth I. An extract from a sonnet written during her incarceration at Fotheringay reveals her despair:

> Que suis-je hélas? Et de quoi sert ma vie?
> Je ne suis fors qu'un corps privé de coeur,
> Une ombre vaine, un objet de malheur
> Qui n'a plus rien que de mourir en vie.
> (Alas what am I? What use has my life?
> I am but a body whose heart's torn away,
> A vain shadow, an object of misery
> Who has nothing left but death-in-life.)

The other turbulent event that took place at Holyrood Palace was during the 1745 Jacobite uprising, when the Palace served briefly as the headquarters of Bonnie Prince Charlie, recreated by Sir Walter Scott in *Waverley* (1814):

> By this time they reached the Palace of Holyrood, and were announced respectively as they entered the apartments ... It is not, therefore, to be wondered that Edward, who had spent the greater part of his life in the solemn seclusion of Waverley-Honour, should have been dazzled at the liveliness and elegance of the scene now exhibited in the long-deserted halls of the Scottish Palace. The accompaniments, indeed, fell short of splendour, being such as the confusion and hurry of the time admitted; still, however, the general

John Buchan, in his role as Lord High Commissioner to the General Assembly of the Church of Scotland, leaving Holyrood Palace in 1933.

effect was striking, and the rank of the company considered, might well be called brilliant.

Sir Arthur Conan Doyle's father, Charles Doyle (1832–93), a talented artist and designer, was a clerk of works at the Office of Works in the Palace in the mid-nineteenth century, and is credited with designing its fountain. His son, Arthur, recounts Rizzio's murder in his story 'The Silver Mirror'. In the spring of 1933, John Buchan was made Lord High Commissioner to the General Assembly of the Church of Scotland and his headquarters were at the Palace, which he recalled in his autobiography *Memory Hold-the-Door* (1940) as a place 'where he entertains the Church and the World according to his means and his inclination'.

David I founded the Abbey of Holy Rood in 1128 on the spot where a stag which was about to gore him vanished into thin air, leaving him holding the holy rood (cross). The Abbey was run by the Augustinian Order and has seen a succession of Scottish monarchs married, crowned and buried there. Much of it was destroyed during the Reformation, and it was pillaged by the Earl of Hertford on his march through Scotland in 1544. In 1688, it was again plundered, by a mob celebrating the accession of William of Orange, when royal coffins were smashed and the head of Darnley was stolen. A new roof was erected in 1758, but was such a botched job it collapsed ten years later, and was never replaced, resulting in the ruin we see today.

The Holyrood Abbey Sanctuary was a safe haven for over 700 years for debtors trying to avoid imprisonment. Whether aristocrat or commoner, all were given refuge. In literary history, it is famous for giving shelter to the poverty-stricken Thomas De Quincey (1785–1859), who was imprisoned for debt on numerous occasions and was forced to take refuge there for a time, and in Joan Lingard's children's book *The Sign of the Black Dagger*, The Comte D'Artois arrives from France seeking shelter at the sanctuary.

The sanctuary was established in the twelfth century under a charter granted by King David I. On entering the sanctuary, a debtor had to submit an application to the Bailie of Holyrood for the 'benefit and privilege' of sanctuary. If the Bailie ruled in the debtor's favour, he was issued with 'letters of protection' and

allowed to reside within the sanctuary grounds out of reach of the law. Holyrood Park was within its boundary and most of its accommodation was provided by lodging houses and inns at the foot of the Canongate, some of which are still standing in Abbey Strand, at the bottom of the Canongate, between the roundabout and the gates of the Palace. On Sundays, the Abbey lairds (debtors) were free to step outside the sanctuary's boundary as legal proceedings could not be implemented on Sunday under Scots law. Part of its boundary is marked today by a row of three S-shaped brass studs sunk into the top of Abbey Strand where the cobbles meet the tarmac. Although imprisonment for debt was abolished in 1880, Holyrood's ancient right of sanctuary has never been revoked.

SEE ALSO: Thomas De Quincey, Sir Arthur Conan Doyle, Sir Walter Scott, John Buchan, Robert Louis Stevenson, Tobias Smollett, Holyrood Park, St Stephen Street.

FURTHER INFORMATION: Opening times: 9.30 a.m.–4.30 p.m. November to March; 9.30 a.m.–6 p.m. April to October. Tel: 0131 556 5100. Website: www.royal.gov.uk.

FURTHER READING: J. Lingard, *The Sign of the Black Dagger* (Puffin, 2005); S. Mapstone, *William Dunbar, 'The Nobill Poyet'* (Tuckwell Press, 2001); R. Bell (ed.), *Bittersweet Within My Heart: The Love Poems of Mary, Queen of Scots* (Chronicle Books, 1993); R. Sabatini, *The Historical Nights' Entertainment* Vol. 1 (House of Stratus, 2001); Mr Chrystal Croftangry relates tales of the sanctuary in Sir Walter Scott's *Chronicles of the Canongate* (Penguin, 2003).

HOLYROOD PARK

> We set out upon our walk, and went through many streets to Holyrood House, and thence to the hill called Arthur's Seat, a high hill, very rocky at the top, and below covered with smooth turf, on which sheep were feeding. We climbed up till we came to St Anthony's Well and Chapel . . .
>
> Dorothy Wordsworth, *Recollections of a Tour Made in Scotland*, AD 1803

There are not many cities in the world that can boast a 650-acre geological spectacle within walking distance of the city centre, encompassing ancient volcanoes, fossilised beaches, crags and lochs. Sometimes known as the Queen's Park (or the King's Park, depending on the sex of the ruling monarch), wordsmiths have often utilised and been stimulated by its primeval beauty.

At St Anthony's Well, Robert Wringham 'was subject to sinful doubtings' and had a heavenly vision while contemplating murdering his brother in James Hogg's *The Private Memoirs and Confessions of a Justified Sinner* (1824). The discovery in 1836 of 17 miniature coffins of wood, each containing a wooden image of a human figure dressed for burial, in a recess of the rock on the north-east side of Arthur's Seat inspired Ian Rankin to weave miniature coffins into the plot of *The Falls* (2001).

Rankin also used the top of Salisbury Crags as the setting for the suicide of Jim Margolies in the prologue of *Dead Souls* (1999):

> 'Salisbury Crag' has become rhyming slang in the city. It means skag, heroin. 'Morningside Speed' is cocaine. A snort of coke just now would do him the world of good, but wouldn't be enough. Arthur's Seat could be made of the stuff: in the scheme of things, it wouldn't matter a damn.

In the 1830s, Thomas De Quincey relished the immunity his strolls in the park gave him from his creditors, falling, as it did, within the boundary of the Holyrood Abbey Sanctuary for debtors. If he'd still been around a few decades later, he would have spotted a young Robert Louis Stevenson, who, when not skating on Duddingston Loch, was filching kestrels' eggs from the high rocks of Arthur's Seat, which he described as 'a hill for magnitude, a mountain by reason of its bold design'. The Crags are said to have inspired young Edinburgh medical student Arthur Conan Doyle to create the towering plateau in *The Lost World* (1912). Sir Walter Scott used the mustering of the Jacobite army in the Park to great effect in *Waverley* (1814) and gives us a striking description of Salisbury Crags in *The Heart of Midlothian* (1818), depicting them as 'a close-built, high-piled

Salisbury Crags.

city, stretching itself out beneath in a form, which, to a romantic imagination, may be supposed to represent that of a dragon'. Beneath the Crags runs the Radical Road, built in 1820 at Scott's suggestion by a group of unemployed weavers who were believed to hold radical political views following the end of the Napoleonic wars. J.G. Lockhart, Scott's biographer and son-in-law, proposed on Scott's death in 1832 the erection of 'a huge Homeric Cairn on Arthur's Seat – a land and sea mark'. It was the Scott Monument on Princes Street which finally became Scott's memorial, though had it been erected on the top of Arthur's Seat, it would have stood out like a beacon for miles. James Hogg, the Ettrick Shepherd, while paddling in the sea at Portobello, exclaimed upon spying the peak of Arthur's Seat, 'Isna Embro a glorious city? Sae clear the air, yonner you see a man and a woman stannin on the tap o' Arthur's Seat!'

SEE ALSO: Sir Walter Scott, Thomas De Quincey, Robert Louis Stevenson, Ian Rankin, Sir Arthur Conan Doyle, James Hogg, J.G. Lockhart, National Museum of Scotland.

FURTHER INFORMATION: No explanation has ever been found for the burial of the 17 miniature coffins discovered on Arthur's Seat. Some of the surviving coffins are on display at the National Museum of Scotland, Chambers Street.

Calton

Old Calton Burial Ground

Grave of David Hume (1711–76)
Scottish philosopher, historian and political thinker

> In all ages of the world, priests have been enemies of liberty.
>
> David Hume, *Essays Moral, Political and Literary* (1741–2)

Empiricist and sceptic, David Hume's powerful arguments exposed serious defects in accepted accounts of rationality, causation and morality, concluding that the domain of reason in human affairs was more narrow than had been supposed and tradition and custom were the principal sources of accepted morality. He is best remembered for *A Treatise of Human Nature* (1739), *Political Discourses* (1752) and his *History of England* (five volumes, 1754–62).

Fearful that the rumour that he had entered into a conspiracy with the Devil was taken seriously, his friends, in order to prevent any violation of his grave, mounted guard over his tomb for eight nights after his funeral with pistols and lanterns. No physical or metaphysical intrusion was recorded.

SEE ALSO: Former home of David Hume.

FURTHER INFORMATION: As you climb the steps from street level, David Hume's imposing tomb can be seen in the top-right corner.

Tomb of David Hume.

Grave of 'Indian Peter', Peter Williamson (1730–99)
Possible inspiration for David Balfour in Stevenson's Kidnapped

Robert Louis Stevenson based many of his characters on real people. W.E. Henley inspired Long John Silver, and a John Silver is buried in Old Calton Cemetery. A John Pew, immortalised as 'Blind Pew' in *Treasure Island*, is buried in

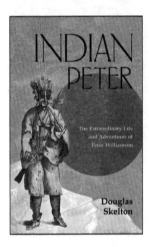

South Leith Churchyard. The name and description of Alan Breck appears in the custom records of Leith. Stevenson would, without a doubt, have read Peter Williamson's colourful accounts of his kidnapping and adventures in the Americas. It cannot be proved, but it is certainly probable, that Peter Williamson was a stimulus in the creation of David Balfour and *Kidnapped* (1886).

Williamson was born at Hinley Farm, near the village of Aboyne in Aberdeenshire. When he was a boy, visiting his aunt in Aberdeen, he was kidnapped from the quayside, shipped off to America and sold into slavery. After seven years of servitude, he married and began life as a farmer, but in 1754 his farm was attacked by Indians during the French and Indian War (1754–63) and he was forced to travel with them as a slave. He later escaped and joined the British Army to fight the French and their Indian allies. Captured by the French after his regiment surrendered, he was eventually freed after a POW exchange and made his way back to Scotland. He settled in Edinburgh where he established a coffee room in Parliament House in Old Parliament Close. In 1770, he organised the city's first penny post and in 1773 he produced the first Edinburgh street directory.

SEE ALSO: Robert Louis Stevenson, W.E. Henley, The Hawes Inn.

FURTHER INFORMATION: Peter Williamson was interred in an unmarked grave 15 paces north-east of the political martyrs' monument. The Williamson family memorial (an 8-ft-square pillar) marks the spot. Peter Williamson is often wrongly assumed to have been the inspiration for the novel and film *A Man Called Horse*.

FURTHER READING: Douglas Skelton, *Indian Peter* (Mainstream, 2004); Peter Williamson, *The Travels of Peter Williamson* (R. Fleming, 1768); Peter Williamson, *French and Indian Cruelty* (Bryce and Paterson, 1758); Peter Williamson, *Life and Curious Adventures* (John Orphoot, 1812).

Grave of William Blackwood (1776–1834)
Bookseller and publisher of Blackwood's Magazine

It is ironic that William Blackwood is buried just a few yards from his great publishing rival, Archibald Constable. Blackwood was a Tory and Constable was a Whig, but, political differences aside, both men contributed enormously to Edinburgh's literary heritage.

Born in Edinburgh, Blackwood was apprenticed at 14 to the bookseller Bell and Bradfute at their shop in Parliament Square. After a period in London and Glasgow, he established himself as a bookseller and publisher in 1804, when he set up his own business at 64 South Bridge. In 1816, he took the extremely radical step of relocating his business to the New Town at 17 Princes Street; this was an unprecedented move, as traditionally the bookselling and publishing trade was located in the Old Town. Contrary to

William Blackwood.

popular opinion, Blackwood wasn't ruined – his business prospered – and his new premises were described by J.G. Lockhart in *Peter's Letters to his Kinsfolk* as 'the only great lounging book-shop in the New Town of Edinburgh'. He became the Scottish agent of Byron's publisher, John Murray, and spotted the talent of John Galt and Susan Ferrier. In 1817, as a rival to Constable's *Edinburgh Review*, he founded *Blackwood's Magazine*, which evolved into a highly influential magazine that launched many writers' careers during its 180 years until its closure in 1980. William Blackwood died on 16 September 1834 and was succeeded by his two sons, Alexander and Robert.

SEE ALSO: *Blackwood's Magazine*, John Wilson, J.G. Lockhart, James Hogg, Archibald Constable, the *Edinburgh Review*.

FURTHER INFORMATION: When entering the graveyard from Waterloo Place, walk straight up the path and follow it round to the right. Keep walking until you can go no further. The black gates of Blackwood's tomb, which backs on to Waterloo Place, are directly in front of you. The Blackwood archives can be consulted at the National Library of Scotland, George IV Bridge.

FURTHER READING: F.D. Tredrey, *The House of Blackwood, 1804–1954* (W. Blackwood & Sons, 1954); M. Oliphant, *Annals of a Publishing House* (W. Blackwood & Sons, 1897).

Grave of Archibald Constable (1774–1827)
Regarded as the first modern publisher

Archibald Constable was born in Carnbee, Fife, where his father was land steward to the Earl of Kellie. In 1788, aged 14, he was apprenticed to Peter Hill, an Edinburgh bookseller, and in 1795 he went into business for himself as a dealer in rare and curious books on the Royal Mile. His business soon flourished, and he bought the *Scots Magazine* in 1801 and launched the *Edinburgh Review* in 1802, which became notorious for its savage literary articles. Apart from his natural flair for publishing and his regard for editorial independence, one of the reasons for his success was that he actually paid writers fees which matched their talents, something unheard of in early-nineteenth-century publishing. Lord Henry Cockburn (1779–1854) described Constable in *Memorials of his Times* (1856) as a man who 'confounded not merely his rivals in trade, but his very authors, by his unheard-of prices. Ten, even twenty, guineas for a sheet of review, £2,000 or £3,000 for a single poem . . . [he] drew authors from dens where they would otherwise have starved.' In 1805, jointly with

Archibald Constable.

Longman & Co., Constable published Walter Scott's *Lay of the Last Minstrel*, followed by *Marmion* in 1808. In 1812, he purchased the rights to the *Encyclopaedia Britannica*. He suffered insolvency in 1826 due to the collapse of his London agents, but surfaced again in 1827 when he published *Constable's Miscellany*, an early form of mass-market literature, reproducing works on art, literature and science in cheap editions. He died on 21 July 1827 and can rightly be called the first modern publisher.

SEE ALSO: The *Edinburgh Review*, Francis Jeffrey, Thomas Carlyle, Walter Scott, *Blackwood's Magazine*, William Blackwood.

FURTHER INFORMATION: When entering the graveyard from Waterloo Place, walk straight up the path and follow it round to the right. Keep walking until you can go no further. Constable's grave is on your right in the corner and possibly obscured by ivy. Some of Constable's correspondence and business papers are held by the National Library of Scotland, George IV Bridge.

CALTON HILL

Monument to Dugald Stewart (1753–1828)
Scottish philosopher and biographer

An exalted judge of the human heart.

Robert Burns

The rhetoric and elegant prose of Dugald Stewart has excited and inspired many, including the young Walter Scott, who remembered his 'striking and impressive eloquence'. Another student wrote, 'To me his lectures were like the opening of the heavens. I felt I had a soul.'

Born and educated in Edinburgh, Dugald Stewart was the son

of the professor of mathematics at Edinburgh University, a post that father and son held jointly from 1775. He was professor of moral philosophy from 1785 to 1810 and became one of the most distinguished philosophers in Britain. He was greatly influenced by Thomas Reid's 'common sense' philosophy and his lectures on political economy were attended by all four founding members of the *Edinburgh Review*. He was in France during the French Revolution, where he met Benjamin Franklin and Thomas Jefferson, and while on holiday

in Ayrshire he met Robert Burns. He returned with a copy of Burns's Kilmarnock edition of poems, which he showed to Henry Mackenzie, who subsequently wrote his famous influential review in *The Lounger*. This review contributed significantly to Burns's success. It was Stewart who first compared Edinburgh to Athens, christening his native city 'the Athens of the North' for posterity.

Dugald Stewart.

He was a prolific writer and is best known for *Elements of the Philosophy of the Human Mind* (three volumes, 1792, 1814, 1827). His other work includes *Outlines of Moral Philosophy* (1793), *Philosophical Essays* (1810) and *Biographical Memoirs* (1810) which chronicles the lives of Adam Smith, William Robertson and Thomas Reid. The monument to him on Calton Hill, built in 1831, was designed by William Playfair, and is modelled on one erected by Lysicrates in Athens in the fourth century.

Stewart lived for many years in Horse Wynd, Canongate (now the site of the Scottish Parliament) and from 1806 to 1812 at Whitefoord House in the Canongate, afterwards moving to 7 Moray Place, where he died in 1828. He is buried near the south-west corner of Canongate Kirkyard.

SEE ALSO: Canongate Kirkyard.

REGENT ROAD

The Burns Monument

Situated on the south side of Calton Hill, this monument crowns a rock ten feet higher than the level of the street and was erected in 1830, after a design by Thomas Hamilton. It is a circular

Corinthian cyclo-style of twelve columns, raised on a quadrangular base, surmounted by a cupola in imitation of the monument of Lysicrates at Athens (as is the monument to Dugald Stewart), and contains a bust of Burns by W. Brodie and, reputedly, a number of relics connected to the poet. A marble statue of Burns – sculptor John Flaxman's last work – which stood formerly in the monument is now in the National Portrait Gallery.

SEE ALSO: Anchor Close, St James Square, Buccleuch Street, Burns Monument, Canongate Kilwinning Lodge, White Hart Inn, St Giles, William Smellie, William Creech, The Writers' Museum, Sciennes Hill House, Robert Fergusson, Clarinda, Jean Lorimer, Henry Mackenzie, The Blind Poet pub.

New Calton Burial Ground
Site of the Stevenson family tomb

> 10 May 1887
> Sir, The favour of your Company to attend the Funeral of my father, from his house here, to the place Interment in the New Calton Burial Ground, on Friday the 13th curt at 1/2 past 2 o'clock, will much oblige, Sir your obedient servant
>
> Robert Louis Stevenson

The walled tomb of the Stevensons is the last resting place of this dynasty of engineers and their families, notably RLS's parents, Thomas (1818–87) and Margaret (1828–97), and his grandparents, Robert (1772–1850) and Jean (1799–1846). Other family members interred here include Jean's father, Thomas Smith (1752–1815), Robert's son, Alan (1807–1865), and Alan's son, Bob Stevenson (1847–1900).

Thomas Stevenson died in the early hours of Sunday, 9 May 1887, at 17 Heriot Row. His funeral 'would have pleased him', wrote Louis. 'It was the largest private funeral in man's memory here.' Louis, sadly, was too ill to attend. His mother's diary entry for 13 May, the day of the funeral, reads, 'My darling was "gathered to his fathers" today in the new Calton burying ground. Lou had cold and could not be present. Bob was chief mourner.'

The Stevenson tomb.

SEE ALSO: Howard Place, Inverleith Terrace, Heriot Row, Pilrig House, Colinton Manse, Swanston Cottage, Baxter's Place, Glencorse Kirk, Rutherford's Howff, Old Calton Burial Ground, St Giles, Hawes Inn, Rullion Green, W.E. Henley, Alison Cunningham, Henderson's School, Deacon Brodie, The Writer's Museum, *Kidnapped* Statue, RLS Club, Museum of Scotland, George Mackenzie, Martyrs' Monument, Edinburgh Castle, Old College, Parliament Hall, Holyrood Park, Royal College of Surgeons' Museum, R.M. Ballantyne, RLS Memorial, Writers' Corner.

FURTHER INFORMATION: The entrance to the New Calton Burial Ground is situated beside the large circular monument to Robert Burns on Regent Road. On entering, walk straight ahead down the path in front of you, following it round to the right. The Stevenson tomb is against the eastern wall, about halfway along on your left.

35 ROYAL TERRACE

Birthplace of Helen Bannerman (1862–1946)
Author and illustrator of *The Story of Little Black Sambo*

The publication in 1899 of *The Story of Little Black Sambo* established Helen Bannerman's reputation as an innovator in children's picture books. With its short, sharp, repetitive and rhythmic narrative, vividly colourful illustrations and unique size for tiny hands, it became an instant bestseller. With success also came worldwide condemnation for its stereotypical depiction of black people – fuzzy hair, thick lips, rolling eyes, bony knees and the demeaning names of the characters, Sambo and his parents Mumbo and Jumbo; but despite over 100 years of criticisms and bannings, *The Story of Little Black Sambo* still remains in print today. Bannerman, who was born Brodie Cowan Watson at 35 Royal Terrace, the daughter of an Army chaplain, spent many of her formative years in distant outposts of the British Empire. She was educated by her father until she was ten, when she was sent to school in Scotland. She later studied French and German, obtaining a degree through correspondence courses from London's St Andrew's University.

In 1889, she married William Burney Bannerman, a surgeon in the Indian Medical Service. The Bannermans spent 30 years in India, mostly based in Madras, where tropical diseases were rife. For much of the year, their two daughters lived up-country with their nanny in the healthier hill country of Kodaikanal, a two-day train journey away. It was on one of these tortuous train journeys, according to her daughter Day, that she created *The Story of Little Black Sambo* to amuse her children.

A friend of the family, Alice Bond, thought the illustrated story would interest a publisher, and persuaded Bannerman to let her take the manuscript with her to London. Bannerman, who had not written the book with a view to publication, agreed, insisting only that she retain copyright. Unfortunately for Bannerman, Alice Bond's role as acting literary agent proved not to be her forte in life. In London, she presented the book to publisher Grant Richards, who offered to publish it, but only on the condition that they could buy the copyright for five pounds, to which Bond agreed. It is easy with hindsight to condemn Bond for accepting this paltry offer, but one would like to think she had probably been doing the rounds unsuccessfully for days with publishers and that, just as she was about to call it a day, Grant Richards showed a little interest. Faced with the choice of publication for a fiver or consigning the book to a mildewed trunk back in Kodaikanal, Bond took the fiver.

35 Royal Terrace.

As the book gained popularity, and neither Grant Richards nor Bannerman retained any copyright control, rogue versions of the book started to appear in other countries, especially in the USA, where some illustrators were responsible for editions which contained some of the worst instances of racial caricaturing. David Pilgrim, curator of the Jim Crow Museum of Racist Memorabilia at Ferris State University in Big Rapids, Michigan, comments on the word sambo's history: 'If you say "sambo"', he states, 'it's not as bad as "nigga", but it's certainly as bad as "darky" or, to some extent, "pickaninny" . . . How can you write a book whose central character has a name that you would not call a black person?'

Attempts have been made in recent years to clean up the book's image. A title change – *The Story of Little Babaji* – from Harper Collins in 1996 and an edition with socially acceptable illustrations in 2003 from Handprint Books in New York have made an appearance. The book will always have its champions as well as its opponents, but whether you regard it as racist literature, a product of a bygone era or just a favourite story read to you on your father's knee, *The Story of Little Black*

Sambo – love it or loathe it – has established itself as a classic in the world of children's literature and refuses to return to where it rightly belongs – amid the setting suns of the British Raj.

FURTHER INFORMATION: Helen Bannerman died on 13 October 1946. She was cremated and her ashes were placed on her husband's grave at Grange Road Cemetery, Edinburgh.

FURTHER READING: Elizabeth Hay, *Sambo Sahib: The Story of* Little Black Sambo *and Helen Bannerman* (P. Harris, 1981).

The Southside

The Royal High School of Edinburgh
Former school of Sir Walter Scott

> I was never a dunce, nor thought to be so, but an incorrigibly idle imp, who was always longing to do something else than what was enjoined him.
> J.G. Lockhart, *The Life of Sir Walter Scott* (1837–8)

Facing you at the foot of Infirmary Street is the former building of the old High School, now occupied by a department of Edinburgh University. In October 1779, at the age of eight, young Wattie entered the second class, taught by Mr Luke Fraser, 'a good Latin scholar'. Younger than most of his classmates, Wattie's Latin was rusty, and he made little headway, until three years later when he entered the class of the headmaster, Dr Adam. Through Adam's inspirational teaching, Wattie began to learn the value of knowledge, and what before had been a burdensome task evolved into a lifelong love affair with Latin poetry and prose.

In J.G. Lockhart's *The Life of Sir Walter Scott* (seven volumes, 1837–8) he fondly recalled his schooldays:

> Among my companions, my good nature and a flow of ready imagination rendered me very popular. Boys are uncommonly just in their feelings, and at least equally generous. My lameness, and the efforts which I made to supply that disadvantage, by making up in address what I wanted in activity, engaged the latter principle in my favour; and in the winter play-hours, when hard exercise was impossible, my tales used to assemble an admiring audience round Lucky Brown's fireside, and happy was he that could sit next to the inexhaustible narrator. I was also, though often negligent of my own task, always ready to assist my friends; and hence I had a little party of staunch partisans and adherents, stout of hand and heart though somewhat dull of head – the very tools for raising a hero to eminence. So on the whole, I made a

91

brighter figure in the yards than in the class.

The old Royal High School.

Scott's father also employed a private tutor for him during these years, but in the spring of 1783 he left the High School to spend the summer with his Aunt Janet in Kelso, prior to entering university in the autumn.

SEE ALSO: Birthplace of W.S., childhood home of W.S., townhouse of W.S., Lasswade Cottage, Parliament Hall, Greyfriars Kirkyard, St John's Churchyard, The Heart of Midlothian, Holyrood Park, The Writers' Museum, Old College, Sciennes Hill House, Scott Monument, Assembly Rooms, J.G. Lockhart, Portobello Sands, Canongate Kirkyard, The Edinburgh Walter Scott Club.

FURTHER INFORMATION: The Royal High School of Edinburgh, known today as the old High School, was built in 1777 by Alexander Laing at a cost of £4,000. In 1829, a new Royal High School was opened on the side of Calton Hill to be closer to the expanding New Town and the old school closed. In 1832, the building reopened as a surgical hospital and in 1906 the building was acquired by Edinburgh University. Legend has it that Walter Scott carved his initials into the stone on the exterior of the left-hand side of the main doorway, which can still be seen today.

Site of the Old Royal Infirmary
Where W.E. Henley, inspiration for Long John Silver, was hospitalised from 1873 to 1875

> It was the sight of your maimed strength and masterfulness that begot John Silver in *Treasure Island*.
>
> Robert Louis Stevenson acknowledging Henley as his inspiration in 1883.

The son of a Gloucester bookseller, William Ernest Henley (1849–1903) came to Edinburgh in 1873 to be treated by Professor Joseph Lister for tubercular arthritis, which, seven years previously, had resulted in the amputation of his left leg below the knee. Lister's skills saved his other leg and probably his life, but the treatment was painful and he was hospitalised in Edinburgh for almost two years. Henley is chiefly remembered today as a poet, notably for his 'Invictus' (1875) – 'I am the master of my fate, I am the captain of my soul' – but Henley was an imperialist and a Tory, and much of his poetry was a platform for his jingoistic patriotism. His 'Hospital Sketches', first published in the *Cornhill Magazine* in 1875,

The old Royal Infirmary.

grimly recall his distressing time at the Infirmary. He was also a critic and an editor, and first met Robert Louis Stevenson through their mutual friend and colleague Leslie Stephen, editor of the *Cornhill Magazine* and father of Virginia Woolf.

Stevenson described the meeting to Frances Sitwell in a letter dated 13 February 1875:

> Yesterday, Leslie Stephen, who was down here to lecture, called on me and took me up to see a poor fellow, a bit of a poet, who writes for him, and who has been eighteen months in our infirmary and may be, for all I know, eighteen months more . . . Stephen and I sat on a couple of chairs and the poor fellow sat up in his bed, with his hair and beard all tangled, and talked as cheerfully as if he had been in a King's Palace, or the great King's Palace of the blue air. He has taught himself two languages since he has been lying there. I shall try to be of use to him.

Stevenson became a close friend of Henley, taking him out for carriage rides and even carrying an easy chair on his head all the way from Heriot Row to the Infirmary for Henley's use. They collaborated on a number of plays together between 1880 and 1885, none of which was successful. Henley held a series of editorships including *Pen* (1880) and *Magazine of Art* (1881–6), and in 1889 he returned to Edinburgh to edit the *Scots Observer*. A stinging critic and a fearless editor, Henley published the works of Hardy, Barrie, Kipling, H.G. Wells, Stevenson, Yeats and Henry James. He also published the struggling Joseph Conrad's *The Nigger of the Narcissus* in *The New Review*. 'Now that I have conquered Henley,' wrote Conrad, 'I ain't afraid of the divvle himself.'

His friendship with Stevenson was all but destroyed after their play-writing escapades, but when Henley accused Stevenson's wife of being a plagiarist over a story she'd had published, the slander was too much for Stevenson, who wrote to a friend saying, 'I fear that I have come to the end with Henley.' The incident terminated their friendship, and they never communicated again. He was, of course, immortalised as Long John Silver in *Treasure Island*, and Jim Hawkins's last words on Silver could well be Stevenson's lament for Henley:

> Of Silver, we have heard no more. That formidable seafaring man with one leg has at last gone clean out of my life; but I dare say he met his old negress, and perhaps still lives in comfort with her and Captain Flint. It is to be hoped so, I suppose, for his chances of comfort in another world are very small.

W.E. Henley.

SEE ALSO: Robert Louis Stevenson, John Gray, Deacon Brodie.

FURTHER INFORMATION: According to J.H. Millar, author of *A Literary History of Scotland*, W.E. Henley invented the phrase 'the Kailyard School', derived from the popular American novel *Mrs Wiggs of the Cabbage Patch*. The Kailyard (cabbage patch) School comprised a group of Scottish writers, namely J.M. Barrie, Ian Maclaren and S.R. Crockett, who created a false, cosy, sentimental and romantic image of Scottish life written in local patois, lasting from around 1888 to 1896.

Henley used to address J.M. Barrie as 'friend', and reputedly Henley's only daughter, Margaret, mispronounced it as 'fwend' and 'fwendy-wendy'. This was Barrie's inspiration for the name of his Wendy character in *Peter Pan*. Margaret died aged four in 1894. Henley is buried beside her in the churchyard of St John the Baptist, Cockayne Hatley.

The old Royal Infirmary was built between 1738 and 1748 and was on the south side of Infirmary Street on the site now occupied by the buildings of the former Infirmary Street school and swimming baths. It was eventually superseded by the Royal Infirmary at Lauriston Place in 1879. The gateway of the old Infirmary can still be seen at the entrance of what was the 'New Surgical Hospital' (now part of Edinburgh University) built in 1853 on nearby Drummond Street.

Terrorist Timothy McVeigh chose Henley's 'Invictus' as his final statement prior to his execution for bombing the Federal Building in Oklahoma City.

FURTHER READING: J.M. Flora, *W.E. Henley* (Irvington, 1970); Bill Yule, *Matrons, Medics and Maladies: Edinburgh Royal Infirmary in the 1840s* (Tuckwell Press, 1999).

53–62 SOUTH BRIDGE

Site of James Thin's Bookshop
Formerly the largest bookselling establishment in the city

> Alf Jamieson, who used to run our antiquarian and
> second-hand books department, could be quite sharp
> with customers. One day, two eminent Free Church
> Professors were questioning him on the price of a book
> they were interested in, and hinting that they hoped for
> a slight reduction. Alf impatiently barked, 'What do you
> think this is, a bloody bazaar?', turned on his heel and
> left them to it.
> *James Thin, 150 Years of Bookselling 1848–1998* (1998)

In 1836 James Thin (1823–1915) was apprenticed to the bookseller
James McIntosh at 5 North College Street. His starting wage was
two shillings and sixpence a week, out of which he had to provide
himself with pen and pencil. His working hours were from 9 a.m.
to 9 p.m. and meals were eaten in the shop. After 12 years of
training, he set himself up in business in 1848, when he bought
the stock of a failed bookseller and leased a shop at 14 Infirmary
Street. His first day's sales totalled five shillings and sevenpence.
Concentrating mainly on academic books and working closely
with the University, his business prospered and expanded. He was
also a keen hymnologist and had a personal collection of 2,500
hymnbooks. Three generations later, his family were still
controlling the business.

In 1891, aged 67, James Thin was interviewed by *The
Publisher's Circular*, who drew from him a delightful insight
into Edinburgh's literati and their tastes:

> Mr Thin has met most of the famous men who have visited
> Edinburgh, or been associated with its history during the
> past half-century. He remembers Macaulay well, and
> speaks with enthusiasm of the historian's oratorical
> power. He also knew Christopher North, 'the lion-headed'.
> 'A man of great power,' said Mr Thin, 'who never did
> himself justice, and who seems to be entirely forgotten by
> the younger generation.' De Quincey used to visit Mr
> Thin's shop in search of scarce books. The author of *The*

James Thin around 1904
in his office in the South
Bridge bookshop.

Confessions of an Opium Eater was described by Mr Thin as a meagre, nervous, shrivelled little man, who went skulking about after nightfall as if he could not stand the garish light of day ... But of all the great men whom he has known, Mr Thin speaks with the greatest cordiality of Carlyle – indeed, he talks of the sage of Chelsea with a deep and open reverence . . . Mr Thin remembers the sudden rise of 'Pickwick' and the slower ascent of Thackeray. In those days, it was all Dickens. Now the better class of readers are forsaking him for his once neglected rival – a circumstance that strikes Mr Thin rather favourably . . . Lord Tennyson is, of course, immensely popular; and since their death Arnold and Newman have both been much in demand, especially the former. It does not appear that academic Edinburgh cares much for Mr Ruskin.

SEE ALSO: Blackwell's.

FURTHER INFORMATION: The Blackwell family took over James Thin on South Bridge in 2002 and a further eight branches were acquired by Ottakar's.

FURTHER READING: *James Thin, 150 Years of Bookselling 1848–1998* (Mercat, 1998).

53–9 SOUTH BRIDGE

Blackwell's

In 1995, www.blackwell.co.uk became the first transactional online bookstore in the UK, giving people across the world access to over 150,000 titles – a far cry from the 12-ft-square bookshop opened by Benjamin Henry Blackwell on Broad Street in Oxford on New Year's day in 1879. Benjamin, a God-fearing teetotaller, prospered and created a publishing and bookselling empire, lining the walls of academic institutions and homes throughout the British Empire and America. Blackwell's took over James Thin on South Bridge in 2002 and embarked upon a process of extensive modernisation. The shop today is a vibrant and exciting place, with  products ranging from stationery to sheet music to medical instruments, and is the largest retail bookselling establishment in Edinburgh, with access to over three million titles.

FURTHER INFORMATION: Opening hours: 9 a.m.–8 p.m. Monday to Saturday (except Tuesdays: 9.30 a.m.–8 p.m.); 12 p.m.–6 p.m. Sunday. Tel: 0131 622 8222.

Email: edinburgh@blackwell.co.uk.

SEE ALSO: James Thin.

SOUTH BRIDGE

The University of Edinburgh: Old College

> Men bred in the universities of Scotland cannot be expected to be often decorated with the splendours of ornamental erudition, but they obtain a mediocrity of knowledge, between learning and ignorance, not inadequate to the purposes of common life ...
>
> Samuel Johnson, *A Journey to the Western Islands of Scotland* (1775)

The literal translation from Latin of alma mater is 'bounteous mother', and Old College – and the Tounis College which stood on the same site before it – can certainly lay claim to a staggering roll-call of literary offspring. The 13-year-old Walter Scott attended Old College intermittently from 1783 to 1786, where he studied for a general Arts degree, and recalled the moral philosophy class of Mr Dugald Stewart, 'whose striking and impressive eloquence riveted the attention even of the most volatile students'. He left Old College in 1786 and became

apprenticed to his father's legal firm. Divinity student Thomas Carlyle enrolled in 1809 and left ten years later without taking his degree, bemoaning the fact that 'within its learned walls, I have not one single friend, not even an acquaintance that I value; which, after 15 years' residence, says but little for my moral qualities.' Robert Louis Stevenson attended Old College from the late 1860s until 1875, first studying engineering, before transferring to law. A bohemian at heart, the world of academia didn't hold much attraction for RLS, who frequently rushed out in the middle of lectures for 'pencils';

Rowand Anderson's Old College dome, erected in 1887, on top of which stands John Hutchison's 'Golden Boy', added in 1888, and modelled on Edinburgh athlete Anthony Hall.

in reality, this was an excuse for sinking a pint at Rutherford's, across the road in Drummond Street. Stevenson was also a member of the Speculative Society, the University's literary and debating society, founded in 1764, and whose members have included Sir Walter Scott, Francis Jeffrey and Hugh MacDiarmid. Arthur Conan Doyle began studying medicine at Edinburgh in 1876, and would regularly walk between Old College and the Surgical Hospital where the University held its anatomy classes at the foot of Infirmary Street (formerly the old High School). As a student, he was taught by Dr Joseph Bell (his inspiration for Sherlock Holmes) and the father of antiseptic surgery, Joseph Lister. Although Doyle was born and studied in Edinburgh, he never had any great love for the city or its university, commenting, 'Edinburgh University may call herself, with grim jocoseness, the "alma mater" of her students, but if she is to be mother at all, she is one of a very stoic and Spartan cast, who conceals her maternal affection with remarkable success. The only signs of interest she ever deigns to evince towards her alumni

James Matthew Barrie, MA (Edin.), 1882.

are upon those not infrequent occasions when guineas are to be demanded from them.'

In 1878, J.M. Barrie entered Old College, where he struggled with mathematics but was inspired by the lectures of the great scholar Professor Masson. Barrie never experienced any great financial hardships at university, but did recall 'three undergraduates who lodged together in a dreary house at the top of a dreary street; two of them used to study until two in the morning, while the third slept. When they shut up their books, they woke number three, who rose, dressed and studied until breakfast time.' S.R. Crockett, another exponent of the Kailyard School, existed for three years on nine shillings a week while attending university, living on meals of porridge and penny rolls washed down with milk.

Other literary alumni include Henry Mackenzie, David Hume, Oliver Goldsmith, Charles Darwin, John Brown, Norman MacCaig, Robert Garioch and Peter Mark Roget. Former Lord Chancellors of the University include J.M. Barrie and John Buchan; in 1866, Thomas Carlyle became Lord Rector.

The original College of the University of Edinburgh was founded in 1583 by the Town Council of Edinburgh and for many years it was known as the Tounis College of Edinburgh. It was built in the grounds of the Collegiate Church of St Mary's in the Fields, known locally as Kirk o' Field, and it was here that Mary, Queen of Scots's second husband, Lord Darnley, was murdered in 1567. The new building, now known as Old College, was started in 1789 and took 40 years to complete. The original plan of the building was by Robert Adam, who died in 1792, before it was completed. Work was then interrupted by the Napoleonic Wars, but in 1816 William Playfair was appointed to complete the building, which he finally accomplished in the late 1820s. Much of Adam's design survived in the building, including the huge vaulted entrance on South Bridge. Playfair was responsible for the vast quadrangle (Adam's design proposed a cross building splitting it in two), the surrounding terrace and the 190-ft-long Playfair Library hall. At the rear of the building is the Talbot Rice Gallery, containing a small permanent exhibition of Dutch and Italian old masters.

SEE ALSO: Sir Walter Scott, Robert Louis Stevenson, J.M. Barrie, Sir Arthur Conan Doyle, Thomas Carlyle, S.R. Crockett, Henry Mackenzie, David Hume, Norman MacCaig, Robert Garioch, John Buchan, Rutherford's Howff.

FURTHER INFORMATION: The interior of Old College is not open to the public, but visitors are welcome to stroll around the quadrangle. Appointments can be made in advance to view the Playfair Library hall. Tel: 0131 650 1000/2093.

FURTHER READING: R. Footman and B. Young, *Edinburgh University, An Illustrated Memoir* (1983).

8 DRUMMOND STREET

Rutherford's Howff
Favourite drinking den of Robert Louis Stevenson (1850–94)

> Last night as I lay under my blanket in the cockpit . . . There was nothing visible but the southern stars, and the steersman there out by the binnacle lamp . . . the night was as warm as milk; and all of a sudden, I had a vision of – Drummond Street. It came to me like a flash of lightning; I simply returned thither, and into the past. And when I remembered all that I hoped and feared as I pickled about Rutherford's in the rain and the east wind: how I feared I should make a mere shipwreck, and yet timidly hoped not; how I feared I should never have a friend, far less a wife, and yet passionately hoped I might; how I hoped (if I did not take to drink) I should possibly write one little book, etc. etc. And then, now – what a change! I feel somehow as if I should like the incident set upon a brass plate at the corner of that dreary thoroughfare, for all students to read, poor devils, when their hearts are down.
>
> RLS writing to his friend Charles Baxter aboard the yacht *Casco* in the South Pacific on 6 September 1888

Untouched by the Brigadoon mimicry of much of city-centre Edinburgh, Rutherford's still retains the sparse decor and friendly atmosphere of the traditional Scottish howff (tavern). It first opened its doors in 1834 and became a popular watering hole for the students of Edinburgh University just around the corner in South Bridge. Electric lighting has been installed and the price of a pint has increased dramatically, but one gets the feeling that Rutherford's hasn't changed very much since the late 1860s when the young velvet-jacketed engineering student Robert Louis Stevenson sauntered through its doors to down his first pint of the day after

tedious hours of note taking on the stress factors of lighthouses.

Stevenson was no model student, regularly playing truant, dozing and doodling in class. Despite coming from a family of engineers, he eventually gave up engineering to study law, passing his Bar exams in 1875. He never, however, actually practised law. No stranger to the howffs of the Old Town and its squalid underbelly, drink, revelry and the haunches of a whore were a delight to him. 'I was the companion,' he said, 'of seamen, chimney-sweeps and thieves; my circle was being continually changed by the action of the police magistrate.'

Of all his haunts, Rutherford's seemed to hold a special place in his heart, which he never forgot. A few RLS portraits and memorabilia now hang on the walls. However, the pub's homage doesn't go off the deep end into sacred-shrine territory. Among the many other thirsty undergraduates and word-smiths to have regularly entered Rutherford's portals were a young medical student named Arthur Conan Doyle and the poet Hugh MacDiarmid.

San Francisco RLS fans toast the great Tusitala.

J.M. Barrie, who was ten years younger than Stevenson, also studied at Edinburgh University. The two admired each other greatly and corresponded in later life, but never met, much to Barrie's sincere regret. Long after Stevenson's death, Barrie wrote about a fictional encounter with him in the 1925 edition of Rosaline Masson's anthology of memoirs entitled *I Can Remember Robert Louis Stevenson*: 'he led me away from the Humanities to something that he assured me was more humane, a howff called Rutherford's where we sat and talked by the solid hour.'

SEE ALSO: Howard Place, Inverleith Terrace, Heriot Row, Pilrig House, Colinton Manse, Swanston Cottage, Baxter's Place, Glencorse Kirk, New Calton Cemetery, Old Calton Burial Ground, St Giles, Hawes Inn, Rullion Green, W.E. Henley, Alison Cunningham, Henderson's School, Deacon Brodie, *Kidnapped* Statue, RLS Club, Museum of Scotland, George Mackenzie, Martyrs' Monument, Edinburgh Castle, Old College, Parliament Hall, Holyrood Park, Royal College of Surgeons Museum, R.M. Ballantyne, RLS Memorial, Writers' Corner.

CORNER OF DRUMMOND STREET AND SOUTH BRIDGE

Edinburgh's Writers' Corner

On the corner of Drummond Street and the Bridges is the first signpost of the creation of Edinburgh's Writers' Corner: a plaque dedicated to Robert Louis Stevenson. As City of Literature, the city should have such a corner. Robert Louis Stevenson passed this corner daily, strolling from Old College to Rutherford's Bar. The plaque's initiator, Bob Watt, has a saying, 'If no one is complaining, it can't be Edinburgh, it must be somewhere else.' This was never more true than at the unveiling of the RLS plaque. After all the effort in fundraising and placing the plaque just where Stevenson had hypothesised in his letter to Charles Baxter, a voice said off-stage, as it was being unveiled, 'It's bronze. Stevenson would have liked brass.' Tetchy Bob replied, 'Had you been willing to polish it weekly for the next 200 years, it would have been brass. You did not volunteer, so it's bronze.'

Diagonally across the road from the Stevenson plaque in South College Street is a plaque to William McGonagall. On the opposite corner of Drummond Street, a plaque is in the pipeline to mark the spot where J.K. Rowling wrote much of the first *Harry Potter* book. The fourth corner is up for grabs. Send ideas to Bob Watt or Allan Foster, care of Mainstream.

SEE ALSO: Robert Louis Stevenson, William McGonagall, J.K. Rowling.

(5 SOUTH COLLEGE STREET)

Site of William McGonagall's death

> How dare they try to steal our McGonagall, perhaps the greatest genius to come from the east coast of Scotland, and Dundee in particular?
>
> Dundee Councillor, John Corrigan, objecting to Edinburgh Councillor Eric Milligan's civic card, which carries a picture of the South College Street plaque.
> *Edinburgh Evening News*, 4 January 2003

> If you were a poet, would you sooner live in Edinburgh or Dundee?
>
> Bob Watt, The Edinburgh Friends of William McGonagall

'Poetry in the Garden', a fundraising event organised by The Edinburgh Friends of William McGonagall, raised the money for the plaque erected at 5 South College Street, where William McGonagall (1825–1902) died. Robin Harper MSP unveiled the plaque in his capacity as Rector of Edinburgh University on 27 October 2002.

Many people deride McGonagall's work, especially other poets. One cannot help thinking that there may be a touch of jealousy there. Here was a man of poor education and low economic status who did not start to write until he was 54, and yet his work has never been out of print since.

McGonagall always carried an umbrella. This was not for rain showers, but to defend himself against the peas blown at him or the rotten fruit fired at his head. On one occasion in the Captain's Bar, next to the plaque in South College Street, Eric Milligan, the then Lord Provost, regretted not carrying an umbrella. It had been suggested by Bob Watt, founder of The Edinburgh Friends of William McGonagall, that the Captain's Bar might be renamed McGonagall's Bar, and the story subsequently appeared in *The Scotsman*. By coincidence, Eric Milligan paid a visit to the Captain's Bar on the evening of the publication. On entering, he was greeted with a barrage of crisps, peanuts and expletive-filled slogans, the most printable of which was, 'Leave our pub alane, ye bastard'. McGonagall's umbrella would have been a welcome defence. Needless to say, the Captain's Bar remains the Captain's Bar.

SEE ALSO: Greyfriars Churchyard, The Edinburgh Friends of William McGonagall, Tusitala Restaurant.

6A NICOLSON STREET

Buffet King Restaurant (Formerly Nicolson's)
Where J.K. Rowling wrote parts of *Harry Potter and the Philosopher's Stone*

> We won't be selling any *Harry Potter* books . . . It teaches people how to cast spells on people. Ordinary people can't cast spells, but you can by the power of Satan. It's not a laughing matter; it's quite serious. If you educate children to witchcraft, you don't know where it's going to end. It could even end with children dying.
> Theodore Danson-Smith, Edinburgh bookseller,
> *The Scotsman*, 10 June 2003

J.K. Rowling first appeared at the Edinburgh International Book Festival in 1997, an unknown writer promoting her first book about a boy wizard. Her audience totalled just 20 people. At the same festival in 2004, the event was closed off to everyone but herself and her fans. She was given her own purpose-built signing tent and her queue of devotees stretched into the street. Signed copies of first editions of the *Harry Potter* books now sell for colossal prices at auction and her books are sold in every corner of the planet. When *Harry Potter and the Order of the Phoenix* went on sale in China in 2003, a huge balloon in the shape of a Chinese lantern was suspended in Beijing above the Avenue of Eternal Peace. 'Harry Potter is here,' it said. 'Are you?'

Eddie Ng, manager of Buffet King.

Born and bred in the West Country, Rowling attended Exeter University, where she studied French. After various secretarial jobs, she went to Portugal when she was 26 to teach English as a foreign language, and it was while she was there that she began writing stories about Harry Potter. She met and married a Portuguese television journalist, and in 1993 their daughter Jessica was born. Four months later, however, their marriage collapsed, and Rowling decamped with her daughter to Edinburgh, where her younger sister lived. By this time, she was living on benefits and experiencing the plight of many single mothers: poverty, loneliness, poor housing and inadequate or expensive childcare. She lived in Leith, in a flat at South Lorne Place, for a few years (cashing her benefits from Leith Walk Post Office), before moving to Hazelbank Terrace in Shandon, off Slateford Road, in 1997.

The flats at South Lorne Place.

She enjoyed writing in cafés, particularly Nicolson's on the Southside:

> I would go to Nicolson's café, because the staff were so nice and so patient there and allowed me to order one espresso and sit there for hours, writing until Jessica woke up. You can get a hell of a lot of writing done in two hours if you know that's the only chance you are going to get.

She trained as a teacher at Moray House Teacher Training College in Holyrood Road, studying by day and writing at night, and it was while working as a French teacher that her

J.K. Rowling. (© Richard Young)

first book, *Harry Potter and the Philosopher's Stone*, was accepted for publication. A few months later, the American rights were sold, and she was able to give up teaching and write full-time. She still lives in Edinburgh and has a country retreat in Perthshire, but is rarely seen in cafés these days.

After her first book was published, she visited some pupils at Leith Academy, where she used to teach. 'They avoided the issue for half of the class,' she said, 'then someone said, "Miss! You're rich now, eh?"'

SEE ALSO: Edinburgh Book Lovers' Tour.

FURTHER INFORMATION: Buffet King is an excellent Chinese restaurant, but unfortunately you can't order a cup of espresso and sit in a corner writing your latest novel any more, as the restaurant is now geared to buffet meals. The staff, however, welcome visitors who just want to pop in and see the corner where J.K. Rowling penned much of Harry Potter. Buffet King will also deduct ten per cent from the bill for anyone who can produce a ticket for the Edinburgh Book Lovers' Tour.

Buffet King, 1st Floor, 6a Nicolson Street, Edinburgh
(opposite Festival Theatre).
Open seven days, 12 p.m.–11p.m.
Tel: 0131 557 4567.
Website: www.buffetkingedinburgh.com.

(18 NICOLSON STREET)

The Royal College of Surgeons Museum
Location of the death mask of serial killer William Burke, who, together with accomplice William Hare, provided the inspiration for Robert Louis Stevenson's 'The Body Snatcher'

Stevenson's spine-chilling short story 'The Body Snatcher' was
written in June 1881 at Kinnaird Cottage, Pitlochry, and was
originally destined to be one of a series of horror stories, or
'crawlers' as he described them, in a book entitled *The Black Man
and Other Tales*. From this collection of tales, 'Thrawn Janet' and
'The Merry Men' appeared in the *Cornhill Magazine*, but 'The
Body Snatcher' was 'laid aside [by Stevenson] in a justifiable
disgust, the tale being horrid'. By 1884, however, he obviously
thought the readers of *The Pall Mall* were ready to cope with it,
as he submitted it for their Christmas edition, describing it to the
editor as 'blood-curdling enough – and ugly enough – to chill the
blood of a grenadier'. *The Pall Mall* responded by sending its
publicity campaign for the story into overdrive, but when the
campaign hit the streets, it was deemed so repulsive by the
authorities that the police were ordered to suppress it.

Stevenson's inspiration for 'The Body Snatcher' was
Edinburgh's most famous murdering duo, Burke and Hare, who,
between 1827 and 1828, delivered at least 16 of their victims to
the dissecting rooms of Dr Knox in Surgeons' Square for seven
pounds and ten shillings a cadaver. Contrary to popular legend,
no evidence has ever been uncovered confirming that Burke and
Hare were grave-robbers. Rather, all their victims were
murdered by suffocation – guaranteed undamaged and fresh on
delivery.

William Burke and William Hare both left their native
Ireland to work as labourers on the new Union Canal, but they
did not become acquainted with each other until Burke and his
partner, Helen McDougal, moved into Logs Lodging house in

Surgeons' Square,
1829.

105

Surgeons' Square today.

Tanners Close (now demolished) in the West Port, where Hare had settled with the widowed proprietress. One day, a male lodger died owing Hare four pounds in rent. To recoup his loss, Hare decided, with Burke's help, to sell the corpse to Dr Knox's Anatomy School at Surgeons' Square. At the funeral of the deceased lodger, unbeknown to the mourners, the coffin was weighted with a sack of bark. After this incident, Burke and Hare got the taste for easy money, and their first murder victim was a sickly, bedridden miller who was boarding at their lodgings. After getting him drunk, they suffocated him and carted his corpse off to Dr Knox. From then on, their victims tended to be selected from the weak, the poor and the intoxicated lowlife of Edinburgh's squalid backstreets: people

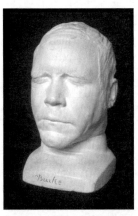

Death mask of William Burke. Note the mark of the hangman's noose on his neck. (© The Royal College of Surgeons of Edinburgh)

no one would miss. In the end, they got careless and lazy, and when their last victim was discovered under a bed at their lodgings, the game was up.

The trial began on Christmas Eve 1828. Hare turned King's evidence and was released in February 1829, as were both their partners, much to the public's anger, but Burke was found guilty and sentenced to hang. Between 30 and 40,000 people witnessed his execution at the Lawnmarket on Wednesday, 28 January 1829. Burke's corpse went the way of his victims and ended up on a slab in an anatomy class, where it was put on public display. His skeleton and an anatomy text-book covered with his skin are on display at the Surgeons' Hall Museum.

The authorities investigated Knox's role in the affair and decided that, though neither he nor his staff had been aware the cadavers were murdered, he had acted incautiously and should have made enquiries. This judgement, however, did not stop the public rioting outside Knox's house and burning his effigy. As a consequence of the Burke and Hare case, the Anatomy Act was passed in 1832 for regulating the supply of bodies to anatomy departments, sanctioning the bodies of the poor to be taken from hospitals and workhouses to be used in teaching. Today's Anatomy Act permits only bequests that have been written into the will or verbally agreed with relatives of the deceased before death.

SEE ALSO: Old Glencorse Kirk.

FURTHER INFORMATION: William Burke's death mask and a few other related artefacts, including the anatomy text book covered with his skin, can be viewed at Surgeons' Hall Museum of the History of Surgery, 9 Hill Square, to the rear of the Playfair building on Nicolson Street. Opening hours: 12 p.m.–4 p.m. Monday to Friday. Tel: 0131 527 1649. Admission free.

Surgeons' Square, where Dr Knox's Anatomy School was located, still exists and is behind the Old High School at the foot of Infirmary Street, accessed through the vennel to the right of the building. Dr Knox's house and anatomy school were situated in the south-west corner of the square, to the right of the steps leading up to Drummond Street.

FURTHER READING: W. Roughead (ed.), *Burke and Hare* (W. Hodge, 1948); O.D. Edwards, *Burke and Hare* (Polygon, 1984); I. Rae, *Knox the Anatomist* (Oliver & Boyd, 1964).

116 NICOLSON STREET

Oxfam Book and Music Shop

Benefiting from its location near the University, this shop has built a reputation for securing a consistently high standard of stock with a rapid turnover. Staffed by enthusiastic, knowledgeable and friendly volunteers, the goodwill generated by the Oxfam name means donations frequently include first editions and rare books. Top local authors such as Christopher

Jo Christison of Oxfam Books and Music.

Brookmyre, Ian Rankin and Alexander McCall Smith have called in to sign donated books. Throughout August, the window displays are changed daily, reflecting the programme of the Book Festival and showcasing the authors and themes of the world's premier literary event. The extensive Scottish section is very popular with overseas visitors, who add to the animated atmosphere of the store. The shop also has a small team of volunteers who actively sell through the Internet, so the shop's customer base can extend in any one day from Nicolson Street to South Korea. There is no doubt that customers benefit from the excellent value and choice the shop offers, but, along with those who donate books, they also contribute enormously to Oxfam's humanitarian work around the world.

FURTHER INFORMATION: Opening hours: 9.30 a.m.–5.30 p.m. Monday to Saturday; 1p.m.–5p.m. Sunday.
Tel: 0131 667 9150.

45 CLERK STREET

Barnardo's Bookshop

A charity bookshop with a good general second-hand and academic stock. Sections include: fiction, classics, poetry, biography, history, reference, general non-fiction and children's books. They have a competitively priced 'old and interesting' section with a good selection of unusual and antiquarian stock including many Scottish titles. New review copies are donated by local publications, booksellers and publishers at much reduced prices. All proceeds from the bookshop help with the important work undertaken by  Barnardo's with children and young people.

FURTHER INFORMATION: Opening hours: 10 a.m.–5 p.m. Monday to Saturday; 12 p.m.–4 p.m. Sunday. Tel: 0131 668 3142.

43 WEST NICOLSON STREET

Word Power

> When I meet people from Scotland, I ask them if they know Word Power. I ask them as if it were an old friend of mine, someone who I love, someone who inspires me.
> Benjamin Zephaniah

Word Power bookshop was opened by Booker Prize-winner James Kelman on 1 December 1994 and is committed to promoting radical literature, making it more accessible and thereby supporting small presses and new writers. 'The world of books,' they say, 'is a precious resource: books are not just commodities to be marketed on the shelves alongside baked beans. The range of books we offer gives you fast-track entrance to a world of publishing outwith the mainstream, a world where independent publishers, small presses, new writers with no prior sales history, individuals producing their own 'zines all have an equal voice.'

Although essentially a radical bookshop, Word Power can obtain any book in print, and fast. In 2003, they launched an online book service and their website offers a staggering information resource. They are also the organisers of the Edinburgh Independent Radical Book Fair.

FURTHER INFORMATION: Opening hours: 10 a.m.–6 p.m. Monday to Friday; 10.30 a.m.–6 p.m. Saturdays. Tel: 0131 662 9112. Email: books@word-power.co.uk. Website: www.word-power.co.uk.

32 WEST NICOLSON STREET

The Blind Poet pub

> . . . a very elegant genius, of a modest backward temper, accompanied with that delicate pride which so naturally attends virtue in distress.
> David Hume describing Dr Blacklock

This pub commemorates the life of the Scottish poet Dr Thomas Blacklock (1721–91). Born in Annan, the son of a bricklayer, he lost his sight after contracting smallpox as a child. He studied divinity at Edinburgh University and was ordained minister of Kirkcudbright in 1762, but blindness limited the duties he

could perform and he retired on a small annuity in 1762. He survived by writing, tutoring and running a student lodging house. In the 1770s, Dr Blacklock and his wife lived in the upper floors of West Nicolson House (now the Pear Tree pub, a few yards west of The Blind Poet). He produced his first book of poems in 1746 and continued writing verse for the next 40 years, but he is probably best remembered for his association with Robert Burns.

Blacklock recognised the genius of Burns's poems, commenting that they had 'a pathos and a delicacy'. In September 1786, he wrote a letter to Burns encouraging him to come to Edinburgh, where he might try for a second edition of his by then out-of-print Kilmarnock edition. Burns's life at this juncture was in turmoil. The Kilmarnock printer wanted money up-front for a second edition, which Burns didn't have. Jean Armour was pregnant with twins and her parents were threatening legal action, and

Burns was involved in a new relationship with Mary Campbell, a local nursery-maid. He was seriously planning to emigrate to the West Indies with Mary and had even booked a passage with a shipping agent. 'I had taken the last farewell of my friends,' he said in an autobiographical letter to Dr Moore, 'my chest was on the road to Greenock; I had composed my last song I should ever measure in Caledonia . . . when a letter from Dr Blacklock to a friend of mine overthrew all my schemes by rousing my poetic ambition. The Doctor belonged to a set of Critics for whose applause I had not even dared to hope. His idea that I would meet with every encouragement for a second edition fired me so much that away I posted to Edinburgh without a single acquaintance in town.'

Burns really had nothing to lose by going to Edinburgh. If all failed, his ship to the West Indies was departing from Leith anyway. He needn't have worried, as his debut in Edinburgh was a great success and not only resulted in a second edition but also brought him fame and celebrity. And had Dr Blacklock not written inviting Burns to Edinburgh, he may well have boarded the *Roselle* bound for Jamaica and never have been heard of again.

SEE ALSO: Robert Burns.

FURTHER INFORMATION: Dr Blacklock and his wife are buried in the graveyard of Buccleuch Church, on the west side of Chapel Street. Two indecipherable white stones on the west wall mark their graves.

(BUCCLEUCH PEND)

Lodgings of Robert Burns during his visit to Edinburgh of 1786–7

> O Willie brew'd a peck o' maut,
> And Rob and Allan cam to see;
> Three blyther hearts, that lee-lang night,
> Ye wid na found in christendie.
> We are na fou, we're nae that fou,
> But jist a drappie in our e'e;
> The cock may craw, the day may daw,
> And ay we'll taste the barley bree.
>
> Robert Burns, from 'Willie Brew'd a Peck O' Maut'

'Willie Brew'd a Peck O' Maut' was written for Burns's schoolmaster friend William Nicol after an evening of revelry in Moffat. Nicol taught Latin at the Royal High School in Infirmary Street and lived in Buccleuch Street, over the pend leading into St Patrick's Square, opposite Buccleuch Place. Burns moved into Nicol's attic on 7 August 1787 from his lodgings in Baxter's Close, off the Lawnmarket. Up until the late nineteenth century, there existed an underground tavern beneath the pend, a favourite watering hole of Burns and Nicol, run by Lucky Pringle. On 25 August 1787, the two of them set off on a tour of the Highlands by coach, covering 600 miles in 22 days. Burns described the experience of travelling with Nicol as like 'travelling with a loaded

Buccleuch Pend.

blunderbuss at full cock'. Despite Nicol's volatile character, their friendship was still intact after their Highland tour, and Burns continued to stay with Nicol until he moved to lodgings at St James Square in October 1787.

SEE ALSO: Baxter's Close, Anchor Close, St James Square, Burns Monument, White Hart Inn, St Giles, Canongate Kilwinning Lodge, William Smellie, William Creech, The Writers' Museum, Sciennes Hill House, Robert Fergusson, Clarinda, Jean Lorimer, Henry Mackenzie, The Blind Poet pub.

FURTHER INFORMATION: Burns's lodgings at Buccleuch Pend were demolished in 1949, and a new pend was rebuilt on the site between 15 and 27 Buccleuch Street.

30 BUCCLEUCH STREET

Pickering's Books

Pickering's Books (formerly McFeely's Bookstore) is a small-to medium-sized general shop near the University, selling a range of selected second-hand books with an emphasis on academic subjects in the humanities. The shop also stocks literary fiction and crime novels, some US and UK remainders (largely academic), and some antiquarian or older books. The owner, Stephanie

Pickering, took over the premises from Gerry McFeely in the early summer of 2004. More years ago than she cares to remember, she started West Port Books (still extant under the benevolent rule of the excellent Bert Barrott and now one of Edinburgh's oldest bookstores). She moved abroad and spent the intervening years raising a family and working as a freelance editor. The stated aim of this new venture is a simple one – 'to sell interesting books to people who like to read'.

FURTHER INFORMATION: Opening hours: 10 a.m.–5.30 p.m. Monday to Saturday. Tel: 0131 662 8570.
Email: stephaniepickering@blueyonder.co.uk.

18 BUCCLEUCH PLACE

Former residence of Francis Jeffrey (1773–1850) and birthplace of the *Edinburgh Review* (1802–1929)

> This will never do!
> Francis Jeffrey on Wordsworth's 'The Excursion'
> (1814) in the *Edinburgh Review*, November 1814

One of the greatest achievements of the publisher Archibald Constable was the launching of the *Edinburgh Review*, a magazine which, although not wholly literary, expressed its opinions on literature in an unreserved and often remorseless manner. Thomas Carlyle described it as 'a kind of Delphic oracle'. Byron was less romantic and penned his lengthy satirical poem, 'English Bards and Scotch Reviewers', as a retort to its acerbic reviews. The reading public, however, couldn't get enough of it, and its circulation rose rapidly, reaching a peak of 14,000 monthly copies in 1818.

18 Buccleuch Place.

It was founded by the Reverend Sydney Smith and advocates Henry Brougham, Francis Horner and Francis Jeffrey at Jeffrey's third-floor flat at 18 Buccleuch Place in the spring of 1802. The idea for a Whig review was Smith's, who at that time was a private tutor. Jeffrey, who was initially sceptical of the idea, became its first editor. Henry Brougham wrote:

> There was himself [Smith] ready to write any number of articles, and to edit the whole; there was Jeffrey, *facile princeps* in all kinds of literature; there was myself, full of mathematics and everything relating to the colonies; there was Horner for political economy, and Murray for political subjects. Besides, might we not, from our great and never-to-be doubted success, fairly hope to receive help from such leviathans as Playfair, Dugald Stewart, Thos. Brown, Thomson and others? All this was irresistible.

The first issue contained no fewer than 29 articles and 252 pages. Early contributors included William Hazlitt, Thomas Carlyle, John Allen, George Ellis and Henry Hallam. Walter Scott was also a frequent contributor until Jeffrey published a savage 35-page review of *Marmion* in April 1808:

> To write a modern romance of chivalry, seems to be such a phantasy as to build a modern abbey or an

> English pagoda. For once, however, it may be excused
> as a pretty caprice of genius, but second production of
> the same sort is entitled to less indulgence, and
> imposes a sort of duty to drive the author from so idle a
> task, by a fair exposition of the faults which are, in a
> manner, inseparable from its execution.

Jeffrey effectively shot himself in the foot with this review, as Scott, along with his 'pretty caprice of genius', transferred his allegiance shortly afterwards to the new London-based magazine, the *Tory Quarterly Review*.

Jeffrey was enthusiastic about Keats and Byron, but was never

Francis Jeffrey.

passionate about the Lake school of poetry and often responded with scathing reviews. The Irish poet Thomas Moore became so incensed at Jeffrey's articles that he challenged him to a duel in 1806, which was fortunately halted by the police.

In 1829, Jeffrey gave up his editorship and was elected dean of the Faculty of Advocates. He continued to write articles and, in 1830, he obtained a seat in the House of Commons after becoming lord advocate of Scotland. The *Edinburgh Review* continued publication for another 100 years, publishing most of the major writers and critics of the nineteenth and early twentieth centuries, until its demise in 1929.

SEE ALSO: Dean Cemetery, Archibald Constable, *Blackwood's Magazine*, Thomas Carlyle, Sir Walter Scott.

FURTHER INFORMATION: Francis Jeffrey was born at 7 Charles Street. He also lived at 62 Queen Street, 92 George Street, 24 Moray Place and Craigcrook Castle off Craigcrook Road, the former home of Archibald Constable. Jeffrey is buried in Dean Cemetery.

5 GEORGE SQUARE

Former location of George Watson's Ladies College
School of novelist and journalist Rebecca West (1892–1983)

> Rebecca West could handle a pen as brilliantly as ever
> I could and much more savagely.
>
> George Bernard Shaw

Once a household name, Rebecca West's popularity has waned in recent years, probably due mainly to the difficulty in categorising her work. She wrote in every literary genre, including biography, essays, novels, history and investigative

George Watson's Ladies College, 1905 (Cicily Fairfield, back row, fifth from the left).

journalism. Her association with H.G. Wells, which forever labelled her as a famous novelist's mistress, didn't help either.

She was born Cicily Isabel Fairfield in London's Paddington in 1892 and was the youngest of three sisters. Her father, Charles Fairfield, was a journalist who deserted his family in 1901 and sailed to Africa, where he died penniless five years later. Her mother, Isabella Mackenzie, was a former governess, who, following the collapse of her marriage, returned with her family to her native city of Edinburgh in 1902. Their first home was at 2 Hope Park Square, and they later moved to Buccleuch Place.

West was enrolled at George Watson's Ladies College on 13 January 1903 and won the school's junior essay prize in 1907. Notebooks were discovered in 1996 at the Rebecca West archive in Tulsa University which were the draft of a novel entitled *The Sentinel*. The start of the manuscript was dated 1909 and written when West was still a schoolgirl. Watson's later became John Thompson's Ladies College in her 1922 novel, *The Judge*. On leaving school, she attended RADA and briefly pursued an unsuccessful acting career.

She began her writing career as a columnist on the suffragist weekly *The Freewoman* in 1911, and it was here she first used the pen name Rebecca West, taken from the strong-willed heroine of Henrik Ibsen's drama *Rosmersholm*. She contributed to various newspapers and socialist magazines, and her first book, *Henry James*, was published in 1916.

She first met H.G. Wells after writing an unfavourable review of his novel *Marriage* in 1912. 'Mr Wells is the Old Maid among novelists,' she wrote. 'Even the sex obsession that lay clotted on Ann Veronica like cold white sauce was merely old maid's mania,

The former George Watson's Ladies College.

114

the reaction towards the flesh of a mind too long absorbed in airships and colloids.' Shortly afterwards, aged nineteen, she began an affair with her 'old maid' which lasted ten years. Their son and her only child, Anthony West, was born in 1914.

She was a staunch supporter of the suffragist movement, participating in marches, protests and riots, but she was never imprisoned. Her essay *A Reed of Steel* (1933), about Emmeline Pankhurst, is one of her best works.

Her first novel, *The Return of the Soldier* (1918), about a shell-shocked soldier, was followed by *The Judge* (1922), *The Strange Necessity* (1928) and *Harriet Hume* (1929). Her autobiographical novel, *The Fountain Overflows*, was published in 1956.

In 1930, she married the banker Henry Maxwell Andrews and settled in Ibstone, in Buckinghamshire. The pair were widely travelled, and a journey they made to Yugoslavia inspired *Black Lamb and Grey Falcon* (1941). Their marriage lasted 38 years and was mostly celibate – a preference of Henry's. After his death, she wrote, 'I get the impression that I married an odd but very nice man who, to all intents and purposes, died about seven years after we were married and I have been living with a zombie ever since.' After her husband's death in 1968, she lived in London. She was present at the Nuremberg trials, and her writings were published as *A Train of Powder* (1955). Curiously, she defended McCarthyism and the crusade against Communism in the 1950s. The novel *Sunflower* (1986), published after her death, explores her relationships with H.G. Wells and Lord Beaverbrook.

FURTHER INFORMATION: The draft of West's teenage novel discovered in notebooks at Tulsa University is now published by the European Humanities Research Centre at Oxford University, introduced and annotated by Kathryn Laing, the doctoral student who discovered them. The former George Watson's Ladies College at 5 George Square is now part of Edinburgh University.

FURTHER READING: C.E. Rollyson, *Rebecca West: A Saga of the Century* (Sceptre, 1996); Anthony West, *H.G. Wells: Aspects of a Life* (Hutchinson, 1984).

25 GEORGE SQUARE

Childhood Home of Sir Walter Scott

> Born for nae better than a gangrel scrape-gut . . .
> The teenage Walter Scott described by his father

George Square was designed by the architect James Brown and pre-dates the New Town by 20 years. It wasn't named after royalty or a worthy man of letters, but James's brother George. It was a fashionable place to live, but more importantly it was a healthy place to live, especially if you'd just arrived in 1772, like the Scotts had, from a tenement ghetto in the Old Town, where six of their children had died in infancy.

Young Wattie, however, did not spend his early childhood at

George Square. In 1773, when he was about 18 months old, he contracted poliomyelitis and lost the use of his right leg, which left him with a limp for the rest of his life. Doctors could do nothing for him, and on the advice of his grandfather, Dr Rutherford, he was sent to live with his paternal grandfather at Sandyknowe Farm in the Scottish Borders, where it was hoped fresh air and exercise would improve his health.

Thus began Wattie's lifelong love affair with the Border country. Amongst his earliest memories were being wrapped in the newly flayed skin of a sheep to attempt a cure, being carried by the ewe-milkers to the crags above the house, and winter evenings round the fireside listening to his grandmother's tales. Border life didn't mend his leg, but his general health improved, and when he was four years old, the family decided to try another remedy.

In the summer of 1775, he left the Borders with his Aunt Janet for the waters of Bath. The visit didn't cure his lameness, but he did pick up an English accent and learn the rudiments of reading at a local dame-school. They returned to Sandyknowe the following summer, and two years later, between the ages of seven and eight, he returned to George Square. 'I felt the change,' he

25 George Square.

wrote, 'from being a single indulged brat, to becoming a member of a large family, very severely.'

His mother, Anne, was a small, plain woman, who was sagacious, friendly and lived to the ripe old age of 87. She had a head full of ballads and stories which she passed on to Wattie, and was the first person to introduce him to the world of poetry. Her husband, Walter, was a solicitor and a staunch Calvinist. Almost teetotal, he possessed no hobbies, but had an intense interest in theology, doling out long sermons from the family Bible on the Sabbath. Anne and Walter's marriage was a happy one, apart from the day he threw out of the window a cup in which his wife had thoughtlessly given tea to the traitor Murray of Broughton, who betrayed his fellow Jacobites after Culloden. History does not record if any passers-by or any of the Scotts' illustrious neighbours were injured. These neighbours included the Lord Advocate Lord Melville, writer Henry Mackenzie and the 'hanging judge' Lord Braxfield, the inspiration for Robert Louis Stevenson's *Weir of Hermiston*.

Scott's siblings consisted of four brothers and one sister. Robert, the eldest, joined the Navy and later the East India Company, and died of malaria aged 41. John became a soldier and died aged 47. Thomas (his favourite brother), a couple of years younger than Wattie, died a regimental paymaster in

Canada, aged 50. Daniel, the youngest, ended up being employed on a plantation in Jamaica, where he was accused of cowardice during a slave uprising, indelibly staining the family name. Wattie shunned him on his return and did not attend his funeral or wear mourning for him. His only sister, Anne, a year younger than him, was a highly strung and sickly girl who was terribly accident-prone. Her perilous escapades included crushing her hand in an iron door, almost drowning in a pond and seriously burning her head after her cap caught fire. She died in her late 20s.

In 1779, when he was eight, Wattie attended the High School in Infirmary Street, and in 1783, aged thirteen, he entered Edinburgh University. His studies were frequently interrupted by ill health and in 1784–5 he was forced to convalesce once again in the Borders at his Aunt Janet's house in Kelso. By this time, he was a voracious reader, reading 10 times the average quota for a boy his age. He had mastered French and by the time he was 15 he was proficient enough in Italian to read Dante and Ariosto in the original.

In 1786, he signed up for a five-year apprenticeship in his father's legal firm, where the laborious task of copying legal documents (he once wrote 10,000 words without rest or food) was invaluable training for his future career as a novelist, and in 1792 he qualified as an advocate.

As a teenager, his lameness didn't seem to be any great impediment. Long walks and horse-riding did not daunt him. He could lift a blacksmith's anvil by the horn, and James Hogg once described him as the strongest man of his acquaintance. He became involved in the city's social life and was accustomed to the hard drinking and revelry of gentlemen's clubs, often not returning home until the early hours, prompting his father to complain once that he was 'born for nae better than a gangrel scrape-gut'. One of these clubs was the famous Speculative Society, a hub of literary and legal talent.

As an advocate, he walked the floor of Parliament Hall waiting to be hired. He defended destitute prisoners for no fee, and on his Border circuits his clients included sheep stealers, poachers and drunkards. It was his exploration of the Borders which drew him deeper into its ancient traditions and inspired him to collect its ballads and tales before they vanished forever. A Tory who valued tradition and the monarchy, Scott was prompted by the country's fear of rising republicanism and the threat of a French invasion to join the newly formed Royal Edinburgh Volunteer Light Dragoons in 1797. In July of the same year, he met French émigrée Charlotte Carpenter while holidaying in the Lake District, and after a whirlwind romance they were married on Christmas Eve in St Mary's Church, Carlisle. Shortly afterwards, the couple moved into rented accommodation on the second floor of 108 George Street, then to 10 South Castle Street and finally to 39 North Castle Street, his townhouse for the next 28 years.

SEE ALSO: Birthplace of W.S., townhouse of W.S., Lasswade Cottage, Heart of Midlothian, Greyfriars Kirkyard, Scott Monument, Holyrood Park, St John's Churchyard, The

Writers' Museum, High School, Old College, Sciennes Hill House, Assembly Rooms, Parliament Hall, J.G. Lockhart, Portobello Sands, Canongate Kirkyard, The Edinburgh Walter Scott Club.

FURTHER INFORMATION: Sandyknowe Farm is situated two miles south-west of the village of Smailholm, in the shadow of Smailholm Tower, Roxburghshire, about 40 miles south of Edinburgh, approximately halfway between Kelso and Earlston. It is not open to the public. His Aunt Janet's house at Kelso can be seen opposite The Knowes car park. A bust of Scott is fixed to the wall facing the street. It is not open to the public. The school he attended is now the Abbey Row Community Centre, next to Kelso Abbey.

FURTHER READING: For a full account of Scott's Border haunts see W. Elliot's *Sir Walter Scott Trail* (2001); J. Buchan, *Sir Walter Scott* (House of Stratus, 2001); A.M. Clark, *Sir Walter Scott: The Formative Years* (W. Blackwood, 1969); J.G. Lockhart, *The Life of Sir Walter Scott* (Uni. Press of the Pacific, 2002).

(1 HOPE PARK CRESCENT)

Till's Bookshop

This late-opening bookshop has been running for 20 years. It holds a general stock of second-hand books covering many subjects and includes one of the largest sections of fiction in Edinburgh (literature, sci-fi, fantasy, mystery, thriller). Other sections include children's books, show business, rock/popular music, Scottish, a large self help/new age section, foreign languages, poetry/drama, politics, philosophy, psychology/sociology, travel, history, popular science, the arts, comics, LPs, CDs and Rick's old original cinema posters. To quote a recent review, 'Everything that you want is here. There's always a stream of new books coming in, too, a really friendly shop, and very helpful. If all second-hand bookshops were like Till's, the world would be a better place.' Go in and see for yourself.

Rick Till.

FURTHER INFORMATION: Opening hours: 12 p.m.–7.30 p.m. Monday to Friday; 11 a.m.–6 p.m. Saturday; 12 p.m.–5.30 p.m. Sunday. Tel: 0131 667 0895. Shopping website opening soon. Email and they'll send you a message when they're up and running: tillsbookshop@btconnect.co.uk.

NEWINGTON

East Preston Street Burial Ground

Grave of Jean Lorimer (1775–1831)

> Lassie wi' the lint-white locks,
> Bonie lassie, artless lassie,
> Wilt thou wi' me tent the flocks?
> Wilt thou be my dearie O?
>
> Robert Burns, chorus of
> 'Lassie wi' the Lint-White Locks'

Robert Burns wrote more verse to this 'lassie wi' the lint-white locks' than any other of his many romantic attachments, including 'Whistle and I'll Come To Ye My Lad', 'It Was the Charming Month of May' and 'Come Let Me Take Thee To My Breast'. Jean Lorimer was a great beauty and had clearly infatuated Burns, who described her as 'one of the finest women in Scotland . . . and is in a manner to me what Sterne's Eliza was to him; a Mistress or Friend, or what you will, in the guise of Platonic Love'.

Jean was born at Craigieburn, near Moffat, the daughter of William Lorimer, a merchant and farmer. She had no shortage of admirers and eloped while still in her teens with a squanderer called Whelpdale who deserted her after three weeks of marriage and ended up in a debtors' prison. She returned to her father's farm and in later life became a governess. She died at Newington.

SEE ALSO: Anchor Close, St James Square, Buccleuch Street, Burns Monument, Canongate Kilwinning Lodge, White Hart Inn, St Giles, William Smellie, William Creech, The Writers' Museum, Sciennes Hill House, Robert Fergusson, Clarinda, Henry Mackenzie, The Blind Poet pub.

FURTHER INFORMATION: Jean Lorimer's grave is marked by a large cruciform near the main entrance. Regrettably, the gates of this old burial ground are often locked.

Mayfield

Abden House
Former lodgings of John Buchan (1875–1940)

John Buchan, father of the modern espionage novel and best remembered as the author of *The Thirty-Nine Steps*, was a frequent visitor to Edinburgh. In 1907, he became a partner in the Edinburgh publishing house of Thomas Nelson & Sons, through his old Oxford friend Tommy Nelson. Although mainly based at their London office, he was, together with his wife Susan, very familiar with the city. Nelson's Parkside works were situated opposite the Commonwealth Pool, between Holyrood Park Road and Parkside Terrace, on the site now occupied by an insurance company. Buchan became editor of Nelson's new magazine, the *Scottish Review*, and his intentions were 'to make it the centre of a Scottish school of letters such as Edinburgh had [in the *Edinburgh Review* and *Blackwood's Magazine*] a hundred years ago'. The magazine's readership, however, had other intentions, and it folded after two years. He next edited the famous Nelson Sixpenny Classics.

During their first visit to Edinburgh, the newly-wed Buchans stayed at Abden House, a Gothic villa which is now in the grounds of Edinburgh University's Pollock Halls of Residence off Dalkeith Road. 'It was enormous,' recalled Buchan's wife Susan, 'even judged by the standards of yesterday, but we existed happily in a corner of it with two excellent Scots servants. The garden had sweeping green lawns and a view of Arthur's Seat which redeemed the gloom of the heavy carved woodwork and the sombre curtains which almost stood up by themselves.'

Buchan resigned from Nelson's in 1929.

SEE ALSO: Thomas Nelson, Holyrood Palace, Old College, John Buchan Society.

FURTHER INFORMATION: Abden House today is a conference and events venue (0131 651 2169). The Buchans also frequently stayed with their friends the Maitlands at 6 Heriot Row.

All those who are interested in John Buchan, whether they are fans of long standing or are meeting him for the first time, should visit the John Buchan Centre, situated at the south end of Broughton village on the A701, 29 miles south of Edinburgh. Located in a former church where Buchan and his family worshipped, it houses many items relating to his diplomatic, military and literary careers. The Centre also features work by his sister Anna, who wrote under the pen-name O. Douglas. The Centre is open on Easter weekend and from May to mid-October, 2 p.m.–5 p.m. daily. There is a small admission charge.

FURTHER READING: J.A. Smith, *John Buchan* (Hart-Davis, 1965); A. Lownie, *John Buchan, The Presbyterian Cavalier* (Pimlico, 2002).

(210 DALKEITH ROAD)

The Bookworm

Peter Ritchie, proprietor of The Bookworm.

According to Eddie Fenwick's *Second-hand and Antiquarian Bookshops in Scotland*, The Bookworm has 'the best stock of military history in Scotland'. It also stocks military history DVDs and war-game figures of 15 mm and 25 mm, and can arrange for blank figures to be painted. All general subjects are covered, with a large stock of crime fiction. The shop has two levels, with the front selling paperbacks and the upper level mostly hardbacks. Eighteen years in the business, its customer base is widespread, covering the Borders, Fife, the Highlands and overseas.

FURTHER INFORMATION: Opening hours: 9.30 a.m.–5.30 p.m. Monday to Friday; 9.30 a.m.–5.15 p.m. Saturday. Tel: 0131 662 4357 (Peter Ritchie).

Sciennes

SCIENNES HOUSE PLACE

Sciennes Hill House
First and only meeting of Walter Scott and Robert Burns

Scott met Burns only once in his life: when he was a lad of 15 in
1786–7, at Sciennes Hill House, the residence of philosopher
and historian Adam Ferguson. He graphically recalled this
meeting in Lockhart's *Life*:

> I saw him one day at the late venerable Professor
> Ferguson's, where there were several gentleman of
> literary reputation, among whom I remember the
> celebrated Mr Dugald Stewart. Of course we
> youngsters sate silent, looked and listened. The only
> thing which I remember which was remarkable in
> Burns's manner, was the effect produced upon him by
> a print of Bunbury's, representing a soldier lying dead
> on the snow, his dog sitting in misery on the one side,
> on the other his widow, with a child in her arms . . . He
> actually shed tears. He asked whose the lines [written
> beneath] were, and it chanced that nobody but myself
> remembered that they occur in a half-forgotten poem of
> Langhorne's called by the unpromising title of 'The
> Justice of the Peace'. I whispered my information to a
> friend present, who mentioned it to Burns, who
> rewarded me with a look and a word, which, though of
> mere civility, I then received, and still recollect, with
> very great pleasure.
>
> His person was strong and robust; his manners rustic,
> not clownish; a sort of dignified plainness and
> simplicity . . . the eye alone, I think, indicated the
> poetical character and temperament. It was large and
> of a dark cast, and glowed (I say literally glowed) when
> he spoke with feeling or interest. I never saw such an
> eye in a human head, though I have seen most
> distinguished men of my time. His conversation
> expressed perfect self-confidence, without the
> slightest presumption. Among the men who were the
> most learned of their time and country, he expressed
> himself with perfect firmness, but without the least
> intrusive forwardness; and when he differed in opinion
> he did not hesitate to express it firmly, yet at the same

time with modesty. I do not remember any of his
conversation distinctly enough to be quoted, nor did I
ever see him again, except in the street, where he did
not recognise me, as I could not expect he should.

SEE ALSO: Sir Walter Scott, Robert Burns, Old College.

FURTHER INFORMATION: A plaque on the restored remains of the
mid-eighteenth-century Sciennes Hill House (aka Sciennes
Hall) commemorates the only meeting of Scott and Burns.
Partly demolished in 1868, it is the back of the original house
that faces the street today, and the modified front faces the
rear. Originally, it was the home of Robert Biggar, who lost
his fortune after investing in the Darien Scheme. An old
Jewish burial ground lies opposite. Sciennes is a corruption
of Sienna, and the name is derived from St Catherine of
Sienna, to whom was dedicated a convent erected here about
1514.

Marchmont

(ARDEN STREET)

Former home of Ian Rankin (1960–) and home of the fictitious Inspector Rebus

> Once I caught a train to Cardenden by mistake . . .
> When we reached Cardenden, we got off and waited
> for the next train back to Edinburgh. I was very tired
> and if Cardenden had looked more promising, I think I
> would have simply stayed there. And if you've ever
> been to Cardenden you'll know how bad things must
> have been.
> Kate Atkinson, *Behind the Scenes at the Museum* (1995)

Described by the crime fiction writer James Ellroy as the 'king of tartan noir', Ian Rankin was born in 1960 in the village of Cardenden in Fife. He now lives and works in Edinburgh, where most of his novels are set, graphically contrasting the picturesque 'Athens of the North' with its concrete housing schemes and criminal underclass.

Rankin writes in his introduction to *Rebus: The Early Years* (1999):

Ian Rankin. (© Rankin)

> I was living in a room in a ground-floor flat in Arden
> Street, so my hero, John Rebus, had to live across the
> road. When the book was published, I found to my
> astonishment that everyone was saying I'd written a
> whodunit, a crime novel. I think I'm still the only crime
> writer I know who hadn't a clue about the genre before
> setting out . . .

'Before setting out', Rankin had a variety of jobs: chicken-factory worker, alcohol researcher, swineherd, grape-picker, punk musician, tax collector, assistant at the National Folktale Centre in London and journalist with the monthly magazine *Hi-Fi Review*. Writing prose, poetry and pop lyrics for as long as he can remember, his influences ranged from *The Beano* to Muriel Spark. 'My dad saw himself in most of my characters,' he

124

Arden Street.

remarked in *Rebus: The Early Years*, 'even if that character was a nun. "Yes," he'd say, "but she speaks just like me."'

Rankin attended Edinburgh University, where he won several literary prizes. One of his short stories evolved into a novel called *The Flood*, but in the mid-'80s he started writing a book which updated Dr Jekyll and Mr Hyde to present-day Edinburgh. *Knots and Crosses* was published in 1987 and appropriately introduced Detective Sergeant John Rebus with 'water seeping into his shoes' standing before the grave of his father. Rebus was intended as a one-off, but the public's appetite for this sardonic, obstinate, world-weary cop has ensured his immortality with each successive bestseller. In 1988, Rankin was elected a Hawthornden Fellow and in 1991–2 he won the Chandler-Fulbright Award, one of the world's most prestigious detective-fiction prizes.

Rebus is now on a par with the legends of the detective genre, from Marlowe to Morse, but one of the great allures of Rebus is the way Rankin weaves real places and events into his stories: Arthur's Seat in *The Falls*, the new Scottish Parliament building in *Set in Darkness*, the Mull of Kintyre helicopter crash in *A Question of Blood*, and Rebus's and Rankin's local pub, the Oxford Bar.

In an interview on 17 November 2000, Ian Rankin explained the origins of Rebus's unusual name:

> I was a student of English Literature when I wrote the first Rebus book, *Knots and Crosses*, and I was studying deconstruction, semiotics, etc. A rebus is a picture puzzle, and it seemed to click. After all, we already had Inspector Morse (a type of code), and in the first book, Rebus was being sent picture puzzles to solve . . . so I made him Rebus, thinking it was only for one book (I never intended turning him into a series) so it didn't matter if I gave him a strange name. Recently, I bumped into a guy called Rebus in my local pub. He lives in Rankin Drive in Edinburgh. Truth is always stranger than fiction . . .

SEE ALSO: Rebus Tours, Oxford Bar, Holyrood Park, Fopp.

FURTHER INFORMATION: Ian Rankin lived in a ground-floor flat at 24 Arden Street in the mid-'80s, before moving to Dalkeith Road.

The Grange

GRANGE ROAD

Grange Cemetery

Grave of Thomas Nelson and Sons
Prolific Edinburgh publishers and inventors of the rotary printing press

> On the eve of the [First World] war we must have been one of the largest businesses of the kind in the world, issuing cheap editions of every kind of literature not only in English, but in French, German, Magyar, and Spanish.
>
> John Buchan

Thomas Nelson was born into a pious family on a small farm in Throsk, Stirlingshire, in 1780, and by the age of 16, he had become a teacher. After various jobs, he headed for London, where he became employed as a publisher's apprentice. When he was 18, he returned to Edinburgh and opened a second-hand bookshop in the Grassmarket. Within a few years, he began publishing affordable Christian works and classic literature for the 'common folk'.

Thomas Nelson, senior.

His distribution and sales methods, which included selling books at fairs and auctions, low prices and sending out sales reps, were extremely innovative. The book trade was initially sceptical of this pious upstart, but his company soon began to flourish.

His two teenage sons, William and Thomas, joined the company in the 1830s and in 1839 took over its management. In 1844, a London office was opened and by 1853 Nelson had become the largest printing and publishing house in Scotland, specialising in religious works, school texts, and stories of travel and adventure for children.

Thomas Nelson Jr invented the rotary printing press in 1850

and revolutionised the industry. Using a continuous web sheet, the rotary press was faster than others and printed on both sides simultaneously. He exhibited his invention at the Great Exhibition of 1851 but, oddly, he never patented it, and it was copied throughout the world.

In the 1840s, the company moved into premises at Hope Park on Edinburgh's Southside, where employees were well cared for – this included the provision of meals, often accompanied by a sermon from the clergy. The Hope Park premises were completely destroyed by fire in 1878 and new premises were built in Parkside on the edge of Holyrood Park. Nearby, Thomas Jr built himself a castellated Gothic mansion named St Leonards, now part of Edinburgh University's Pollock Halls on Dalkeith Road.

In the early 1900s, John Buchan became involved in the company's management through his friendship with Thomas Jr's son Tommy, to whom he dedicated *The Thirty-Nine Steps*. Buchan edited the Nelson Sixpenny Classics and in 1907 launched the short-lived magazine the *Scottish Review*. He also wrote a history of the First World War and the life of Montrose for Nelson.

Thomas Nelson, the company's founder, died in 1861. When informed that his death was approaching, he calmly replied, 'I thought so; my days are wholly in God's hands. He doeth all things well. His will be done!' He then lifted his Bible from his bedside table and said, 'Now I must finish my chapter.'

SEE ALSO: John Buchan.

FURTHER INFORMATION: In 1960, Nelson merged with The Thomson Organisation and in 1969 it was bought by Sam Moore, an American Bible and Christian text publisher based in Nashville.

Bruntsfield

160 BRUNTSFIELD PLACE

Birthplace of Muriel Spark (1918–)
Scottish novelist, short-story writer, biographer and poet

> But Edinburgh, said the man, was a beautiful city, more
> beautiful then than it is now. Of course the slums have
> been cleared. The Old Town was always my favourite.
> We used to love to explore the Grassmarket and so on.
> Architecturally speaking, there is no finer sight in
> Europe.
>
> Muriel Spark, *The Prime of Miss Jean Brodie* (1961)

Although Muriel Spark has written over 20 novels, it is her
sixth novel, *The Prime of Miss Jean Brodie*, published in 1961
and adapted for stage and screen, which is her best known and
most discussed work. In fact, she could probably write another
20 novels, but all roads would still lead back to this one, which,
although easy to read and written in a relaxed style, is more
complex in its theme and composition than it at first appears.
And this is the reason why readers and critics keep returning to
this novel, which can be read on many different levels. *The
Prime of Miss Jean Brodie*, like all great classics, refuses to fade
into obscurity.

Muriel Spark was born in 1918 to Sarah and Bernard
Camberg, an engineer. She was enrolled at James Gillespie's
School in 1922, where she became known as the school's 'poet
and dreamer'. Her work regularly appeared in the school
magazine, and in 1932 she was crowned 'Queen of Poetry'.

The former James
Gillespie's School on
Bruntsfield Links, now
part of Edinburgh
University.

Muriel Spark in 1947.

When she was eleven, the young Muriel encountered Miss Kay, whose eccentric teaching and idealism formed the basis for the fictional character in her 1961 novel, *The Prime of Miss Jean Brodie*. After leaving school, she attended Heriot Watt College in Chambers Street, and at 18 took a job in the office of Small's department store at 106 Princes Street. In 1937, aged 19, she married Sydney Spark in Salisbury, Southern Rhodesia, and their son Robin was born in Bulawayo a year later. Her husband became increasingly mentally unstable, and, following her return to Britain in 1944, the couple were divorced. She joined the political department of the Foreign Office secret intelligence service, MI6, during the Second World War. After the war, she remained in London, where she became general secretary of the Poetry Society and editor of the *Poetry Review* (1947–9). She started writing seriously after the war and in 1951 she won *The Observer*'s short-story competition with 'Seraph and the Zambesi'. Her first collection of poems, 'The Fanfario and Other Verse', was published in 1952, and in 1954 she was converted to Roman Catholicism, an event which influenced her later writing. Her first novel, *The Comforters* (1957), was praised by Evelyn Waugh as 'brilliantly original and fascinating', and during the next four years she penned a further five novels: *Robinson* (1958), *Memento Mori* (1959), *The Bachelors* (1960), *The Ballad of Peckham Rye* (1960) and *The Prime of Miss Jean Brodie* (1961).

The Prime of Miss Jean Brodie was first published in *The New Yorker* magazine to great acclaim, prompting her move to New York in the early '60s, where she worked for the magazine with fellow contributors J.D. Salinger, John Updike and Vladimir Nabokov. During this period, she wrote two further novels, *The Girls of Slender Means* (1963) and the prize-winning *The Mandelbaum Gate* (1965). In the late '60s, she moved to Rome and in 1979 settled in Tuscany, where she lives and writes today. Her later works include *The Abbess of Crewe* (1974), *Loitering with Intent* (1981) and *A Far Cry from Kensington* (1988). The first volume of her autobiography, *Curriculum Vitae*, was published in 1992.

SEE ALSO: Christina Kay, The Muriel Spark Society.

FURTHER INFORMATION: The building which was James Gillespie's School (the model for the Marcia Blaine School in the novel *The Prime of Miss Jean Brodie*) is on nearby Bruntsfield Links and is now Edinburgh University student accommodation. Today, James Gillespie's School is situated in Lauderdale Street, Bruntsfield.

FURTHER READING: A. Bold, *Muriel Spark* (Routledge, 1986).

28 BRUNTSFIELD PLACE

The Book-Swop

The Book-Swop was set up in 1995 to recycle new and used books. All books bought here can be returned and Book-Swop will reimburse one-third of the selling price towards the purchase of your next book. New titles are also available. Books are wanted as part exchange, in good condition, and recently published.

Browsers are welcome.

FURTHER INFORMATION: Opening hours: 10 a.m.–5 p.m. Monday to Saturday. Tel: 0131 229 9451.

7 LEAMINGTON TERRACE

Former home of Norman MacCaig (1910–96)
Scottish poet

> Hugh MacDiarmid: After I am gone, my poetry will be remembered and read for hundreds of years, but after you have gone, your poetry will soon be forgotten.
> Norman MacCaig: Ah, but I am not planning to go!

Norman MacCaig was one of the great Scottish poets, who wrote not in Scots or Gaelic, but in English in a simple way, observing nature, people and especially his friends. From rhyme to free verse, MacCaig produced unique poetry which, despite MacDiarmid's tongue-in-cheek prediction, will not be forgotten.

He was born on 14 November 1910 to Robert McCaig and Joan MacLeod. His father, who came from Haugh of Urr in

Dumfriesshire, was a chemist who had a shop at 9 Dundas Street, and the family lived in a tenement flat at 11 Dundas Street. His mother, who had never been taught to read or write, was from Scalpay, off Harris. Norman was the youngest of four children; he was educated at the Royal High School and studied classics at Edinburgh University. He became a primary-school teacher and remained in teaching until 1967, when he was appointed as fellow in creative writing at Edinburgh

University. In 1970, he joined the Department of English Studies at the University of Stirling and became a reader in poetry, retiring in 1978.

His first volumes of poetry, *Far Cry* (1943) and *The Inward Eye* (1946), earmarked him as a devotee of the 'anti-cerebral' New Apocalypse, a group of writers who, for a brief time in the 1940s, reacted against the 'classicism' of Auden with savage and disorderly verse. Other collections included *Riding Lights* (1955), *Measures* (1965), *Rings on a Tree* (1968), *A Man in my Position* (1969) and *Collected Poems* (1985).

He first met the poets of the Scottish Renaissance (including Hugh MacDiarmid, Sydney Goodsir Smith and Sorley Maclean) in the Southern Bar in South Clerk Street in 1946. In a radio interview with Roderick Watson, he recalled his early meetings with them: 'For a while, they despised and rejected me, of course, because I write in English: "Lickspittle of the English ascendancy; stabber in the back of the Scottish movement; cultural Quisling." But, of course, when they got to know me and found that I was tall, handsome, rich and could sing in tune, they decided I wasn't so bad after all and Douglas Young invented a phrase, he said, "It's a pity Norman doesn't write in Scots but he's got a Scots accent of the mind." Whatever that means.'

After the pubs had closed, the sessions of debate and flyting often continued at MacCaig's flat in Leamington Terrace, where he lived from 1943 to 1996. 'In his own house, he was a generous host,' recalled George Mackay Brown. 'In this, he had a good partner in Isabel, his wife. By 10 p.m., closing time in those days, the burn of lyricism and laughter was only beginning to gather head. Often a group of merry figures was to be seen at a bus stop, burdened with "cerry-oots".'

MacCaig never wrote long, continuous screeds of verse, and critics have sometimes claimed his poetry is lightweight and without political clout. Once, when asked how long it takes him to write a poem, he replied, 'Two fags. Sometimes, it's only one.' He died in the Astley Ainslie Hospital on 23 January 1996, aged 85.

SEE ALSO: Hugh MacDiarmid, Sydney Goodsir Smith.

Morningside

CLINTON ROAD

East Morningside House
Former home of Susan Ferrier (1782–1854), 'Scotland's Jane Austen'

> One thing let me entreat you: if we engage in this undertaking, let it be kept a profound secret from every human being. If I was suspected of being accessory to such foul deeds, my brothers and sisters would murder me and my father bury me alive.
>
> Susan Ferrier writing to her friend Charlotte Clavering, revealing her yearning to write a novel

Like many women writers throughout history who dared to defy convention and go beyond their expected duties of looking after the family and the home, Susan Ferrier, in order to avert scandal, wrote her first two novels anonymously. But unlike her contemporary Jane Austen, to whom she is often compared, Susan Ferrier has drifted into obscurity.

She was born in a flat in Lady Stair's Close, off the Lawnmarket, on 7 September 1782, the tenth child of Helen Coutts and James Ferrier, a successful lawyer who became principal clerk of session. When she was two years old, her family moved to 25 George Street and later acquired the first villa to be built in Morningside – East Morningside House – as a summer residence. In 1797, when Susan was 14 years old, her mother died. All of her siblings eventually married, while Susan took over the role of looking after her father, remaining a spinster all her life.

She wrote only three novels. The first two, *Marriage* (1818) and *The Inheritance* (1824), were published anonymously by Blackwood

The gateway to East Morningside House.

132

and were immensely popular. Her novels were intended to instruct, but were also filled with humour and astute observation. Published the same year as Jane Austen's *Northanger Abbey* and Mary Shelley's *Frankenstein*, her novel *Marriage*, she explained, would 'warn all young ladies against runaway matches'. In the moralising attitudes and manners of her day, she remarked, 'I expect it will be the first book every wise matron will put into the hand of her daughter, and even the reviewers will relax of their severity in favour of the morality of this little work.' Most of *Marriage* was written in the oak-panelled study at East Morningside House.

She was good friends with Sir Walter Scott, who described her as 'simple, full of humour, and exceedingly ready at repartee, and all this without the least affectation of the blue-stocking'. Scott offered to negotiate with publishers Blackwood over her third novel, *Destiny*, which was published in 1831 and is dedicated to him. Scott was also a friend and colleague of Ferrier's father and was a regular visitor to East Morningside House.

Ill health, failing eyesight and conversion to the Free Church led to her abandoning writing in later life. She died aged 70 in her townhouse at 38 Albany Street in 1854 and is buried in the family grave in St Cuthbert's Churchyard in Lothian Road.

SEE ALSO: St Cuthbert's Churchyard, *Blackwood's Magazine*, John Wilson, Sir Walter Scott.

FURTHER INFORMATION: Legend has it that a white rose bush still grows in the garden from which Bonnie Prince Charlie and the Jacobite army plucked blooms for their bonnets as they passed along Cant's Loan (now Newbattle Terrace) en route to Holyrood Palace. An old willow tree which grows against the Clinton Road wall is said to have been grown from a cutting taken from Napoleon's garden on St Helena. East Morningside House is not open to the public.

FURTHER READING: M. Cullinan, *Susan Ferrier* (Twayne, 1985); N. Paxton, *Subversive Feminism: A Reassessment of Susan Ferrier's* Marriage, *Women and Literature* (1976).

77 FALCON AVENUE

St Peter's Church
Church of Father John Gray (1866–1934), the original Dorian Gray in Oscar Wilde's *The Picture of Dorian Gray*

> It is false art and false to human nature. Mr Wilde has brains, art, and style; but if he can write for none but outlawed noblemen and perverted telegraph boys, the sooner he takes to tailoring (or some other decent trade) the better for his own reputation and morals.
> Critic W.E. Henley's response to
> *The Picture of Dorian Gray*

The only novel of Oscar Wilde (1854–1900), *The Picture of Dorian Gray*, was condemned when it was first published in

1890 as an affront on polite society and contributed to his downfall, which ended in his imprisonment for homosexuality in 1895. It tells the story of young, handsome and hedonistic Dorian Gray who, after having his portrait painted, dreams of remaining young forever while his painted visage grows old and corrupt. Offering up a prayer, he volunteers his soul in exchange for perpetual youth.

There is no single person who can be defined as the original inspiration for Dorian Gray – Wilde knew many

St Peter's Church.

fascinating and beautiful young men – but his friendship with John Gray, with whom he had an intimate relationship and from whom he received letters signed 'Dorian', leads us to believe that if Wilde was not modelling Dorian on John Gray, he was certainly out to beguile him. Wilde at this time was besotted with Gray, who recalled 'having received from someone' a letter stating, 'The world is changed because you are made of ivory and gold. The curves of your lips rewrite history.'

A poet, critic and playwright, John Gray's origins were very different from the London literati he courted in 1890s Victorian

Drawing by A.W. Spare of John Gray in 1910.

London. He was born in London, the son of a wheelwright and carpenter. On leaving school, he became a metal turner at Woolwich Arsenal. Self-educated, he passed his civil service examinations and took up the position of clerk in the Foreign Office library.

He first met Wilde in the summer of 1889 at a supper party in a Soho restaurant and has been described by George Bernard Shaw as 'one of the more abject of Wilde's disciples'. In 1893, Gray's *Silverpoints*, a book of 29 poems, was published by the Bodley Head, with Wilde agreeing to underwrite the costs. This was a contract from which Wilde later withdrew. By this time, Gray's relationship with Wilde was sidelined by the ascendancy of Wilde's latest lover, Lord Alfred Douglas; the jilted Gray told friends he was seriously contemplating suicide.

He was rescued from the depths of despair by an extremely wealthy Russian emigré Jew named André Raffalovich, who began publishing critical articles, poems and fiction and meeting many prominent men of letters in his 'at homes'. Raffalovich, now a Roman Catholic convert, fell in love with Gray. During these years, Gray and Raffalovich collaborated on several unsuccessful plays. Drawn towards Catholicism himself, Gray entered the Scots College in Rome in 1898 and was subsequently ordained as a priest. He served as curate initially

at St Patrick's Church in the slum parish of Edinburgh's Cowgate.

Raffalovich was probably of the opinion that Gray deserved a lot better in life and made the archdioceses of St Andrews and Edinburgh an offer they couldn't refuse – a gift of the site and construction costs for a new church to be built in prospering middle-class Morningside, at a cost of around £5,500. There were no strings attached, except that he 'proposed' Gray as its new priest. No objections were raised.

André Raffalovich in 1886 by A.D. May.

What made Gray come to Scotland is a moot point. One obvious reason could have been that it was a very long way from London and the scandal of Wilde's trial and disgrace, although Gray's name was never mentioned in court. Who would think to connect a simple priest with the life of a dandy poet who once loved 'ponce and Sodomite' Oscar Wilde? And as Gray wrote himself in his 1931 elegy for Wilde: 'I warmed my hands and said aloud, I never knew the man.'

FURTHER INFORMATION: Gray and Raffalovich are both buried at Mount Vernon Cemetery in Edinburgh. Gray is buried in the Priest's Circle, near the centre of the cemetery, where a circular arrangement of graves surrounds a large crucifix. The home of André Raffalovich, from 1907 until his death in 1934, was at 9 Whitehouse Terrace, Morningside.

233 MORNINGSIDE ROAD

St Columba's Hospice Bookshop

The St Columba's Hospice Bookshop opened in November 2001 and has quickly become a popular spot for locals and visitors, who can browse at their leisure and select from a diverse range of books. The books are generously donated by the public and the bookshop is served by dedicated sales staff, a book-sorting team and warehouse back-up in Granton – all volunteers. It has a cheerful, bright interior and the stock is regularly updated. Their window displays are always a talking point, with topical and unusual props to catch the eye of the unsuspecting pedestrian. They also have an efficient 'book request' system and will try to supply special requests for

135

customers. Crime and general fiction are popular, but Scottish and history titles are also in constant demand. They could not survive without the generosity and support of their customers and book donators, and every sale is a gratefully received contribution to the running of the Hospice.

FURTHER INFORMATION: Opening hours: 10 a.m.–4 p.m. Monday to Saturday. Tel: 0131 447 9008.

Email: blamont@stcolumbashospice.org.uk.

210 MORNINGSIDE ROAD

Oxfam Book and Music Shop

Oxfam's strong reputation guarantees this shop enjoys a steady stream of high-quality book and music donations. The variety of donations means that they have constantly well-stocked shelves, and the value for money means turnover is rapid and stock changes daily. Their volunteers take the time to research and identify rare and collectable books and music, so please enquire if you are looking for something in particular. All money made in this shop goes towards funding Oxfam's humanitarian work in the UK and abroad.

FURTHER INFORMATION: Opening hours: 9.30 a.m.–5.30 p.m. Monday to Saturday; 1.30 p.m.–4 p.m. Sunday.

Tel: 0131 446 9169.

Email: oxfamshopf5805@btconnect.com.

390 MORNINGSIDE ROAD

Kay's Bookshop

This is one of Edinburgh's few independent bookshops offering an impressively wide range of new books to suit all tastes. All the usual suspects from the bestseller lists are stocked as well as loved authors old and new, including Scottish books and titles from local authors, children's books, cookery, travel, reference, history, gardening and gift books. Their aim is to offer the widest possible range of books in a small, period-style setting. Also offered in the shop, which has been trading on the south side of the city for the past 50 years, are Ordnance Survey maps, newspapers, magazines, stationery, greetings cards, book tokens and a small stock of videos depicting scenes from Edinburgh's past, including Scottish classics such as *Whisky Galore*, *The Maggie* and *Greyfriars Bobby*. Kay's also offers a book-search service tracking down any out-of-print or

hard-to-find book. All this in the leafy suburb of Morningside – 10 minutes by bus or an entertaining 30–40 minute walk directly south from the west end of Princes Street on the A702.

FURTHER INFORMATION: Opening hours: 7 a.m.–5.30 p.m. Monday to Saturday. Tel: 0131 447 1265. Email: kaysbookshop@btconnect.com.

MORNINGSIDE DRIVE

Morningside Cemetery

Grave of Alison Cunningham (1822–1913)
Devoted nurse of Robert Louis Stevenson

> For the long nights you lay awake
> And watched for my unworthy sake:
> For your most comfortable hand
> That led me through the uneven land:
> For all the story-books you read,
> For all the pains you comforted,
> For all you pitied, all you bore,
> In sad and happy days of yore:–
> My second Mother, my first Wife,
> The angel of my infant life –
> From the sick child, now well and old,
> Take, nurse, the little book you hold!
>
> RLS, 'Dedication to Alison Cunningham from
> her boy', *A Child's Garden of Verses* (1885)

She filled his head with bloodcurdling stories, pumped him full of puritan morals, sang him psalms, made him fear the Devil and was responsible in no short measure for fuelling his guilt-ridden, sin-soaked nightmares, but the ailing child who lay awake 'to weep for Jesus' probably owed his life to the double-edged sword that was Alison Cunningham. Known affectionately as 'Cummy', she was a formidable influence on the early life of RLS, who in adulthood wrote to her saying, 'You have made much that there is in me, just as surely as if you had conceived me.'

RLS's parents had worked their way through a succession of unsuitable nurses for their only child, one of whom had been dismissed for drinking in a public house with her charge. Alison Cunningham, who had probably never entered a pub in her life, let alone tasted alcohol, was hired as his nurse and surrogate mother in the spring of 1852, when he was 18 months old. She was a fisherman's daughter, from the village of Torryburn in Fife, and was brought up on a diet of porridge, Presbyterianism and the Covenanters. Cummy slept in the same room as Louis until he was almost ten years old, nursing him through long nights of endless sickness: nights of hacking coughs, sweats and fevers. 'I remember with particular distinct-

ness,' he recalled in *Memoirs of Himself* (1880), 'how she would lift me out of bed, and take me, rolled in blankets, to the window, whence I might look forth into the blue night starred with street-lamps, and see where the gas still burned behind the windows of other sick-rooms.'

When not stimulating his fears of hell or nursing him back to

health, Cummy would take him for walks – often to the Royal Botanic Garden or the cheery surrounds of Warriston Cemetery. *Cassell's Family Paper* was a regular purchase for them, enabling them to share the next thrilling instalment of their favourite adventure serial. She was friend, mentor and angel of mercy, and RLS never forgot the debt he owed her.

Cummy never married, but it was rumoured she once turned down a proposal of marriage because she was loathe to part from her 'laddie'. She stayed with the Stevensons until 1871, when she left 'to keep her brother's house at Swanston'. In 1893, she lived at 23

Balcarres Street, ending her days with her cousin at 1 Comiston Place, where she died a Victorian icon in July 1913, aged 91.

SEE ALSO: Robert Louis Stevenson, St Giles, RLS Club.

FURTHER INFORMATION: Cummy's grave was restored by the RLS Club in 2004. The cemetery entrance on Morningside Drive is between Ethel Terrace and Dalhousie Terrace. On entering, take the first tree-lined path to the right. Cummy's white tombstone faces the left-hand edge of the path near the large war memorial.

FURTHER READING: A. Cunningham, *Cummy's Diary* (1926).

5 BRAID CRESCENT

Former home of Eugenie Fraser (1905–2002) and where she wrote her classic memoir *The House by the Dvina*

> Bitter would be too small a word. I loathed Communism.
> It destroyed the country, it can never be the same
> again.
>
> Eugenie Fraser

Eugenie Fraser was born Yevgheniya Ghermanovna Scholts in Archangel, Russia, in 1905 to a Russian father and a Scottish mother from Broughty Ferry. In her 80th year, she published her auto-biographical memoirs, *The House by the Dvina*, describing her remarkable childhood at the time of the Russian Revolution, with her vivid recollections of a past which was completely eradicated by the Bolsheviks. To many, she was just a typical respectable Morningside lady with a Russian accent, but her memoirs go much deeper than cream teas, church bazaars and tombolas.

Fraser's father, Gherman Scholts, travelled to Dundee from Archangel in 1903 to learn about the timber trade; there he met and married Nelly Cameron, the daughter of a wealthy flax merchant. He took her back with him to Archangel in 1905, where, shortly afterwards, Eugenie was born in the family house by the Dvina, which she describes in her memoir:

> It was a rambling house built on two levels. The long single storey overlooked the wide expanse of the Dvina. French windows led out into a balcony with wrought-iron railings. There during the long, clear summer nights, friends and members of the family sat talking or listening to the voices carried from the river . . . below our windows, which faced the river front, I

Pre-Revolutionary Archangel.

> saw walking in single file what I took to be six or eight
> dogs . . . We watched in silence as the wolves moved
> towards the gates.

The house was filled with Gherman's large and colourful family, who lived in pre-Revolutionary style, with servants, traditions and a way of life that has long vanished. One of the most dramatic stories in the book is of Fraser's grandmother's desperate journey as a young and pregnant wife across Russia in midwinter by horse-drawn troika, shadowed by wolves, to plead with Tsar Nicholas II for the release of her husband from prison in Siberia. Her mission was successful and she returned to Archangel, where she gave birth to her baby.

The Russian Revolution in 1917 ended the Russia of Fraser's childhood and in 1920 she fled Russia with her brother and mother. Her father remained behind, and she never saw him again. Other family members were imprisoned or executed and the house by the Dvina was bulldozed.

She married Ronald Fraser, a senior administrator in the jute industry, and lived for many years in India and Thailand. When she was 80, she attended creative-writing classes at Edinburgh University and began writing her memoirs. She returned to Archangel in her 80s, visiting the grave of her father and paddling in the Dvina. 'I was glad to go back,' she said. 'I had to go back.' She wrote two other books, *The House by the Hooghly* (1989), about her life in India, and *The Dvina Remains* (1996).

Eugenie Fraser died in the Royal Infirmary of Edinburgh on 20 October 2002. She is buried in Barnhill Cemetery, Broughty Ferry.

Craiglockhart

Napier University Craiglockhart campus, formerly Craiglockhart War Hospital
Where soldier poets Siegfried Sassoon and Wilfred Owen were hospitalised during the First World War

> I am making this statement as an act of wilful defiance of military authority, because I believe the war is being deliberately prolonged by those who have the power to end it. I am a soldier, convinced that I am acting on behalf of soldiers. I believe that this war, upon which I entered as a war of defence and liberation, has now become a war of aggression and conquest. I believe that the purposes for which I and my fellow soldiers entered upon this war should have been so clearly stated as to have made it impossible to change them, and that, had this been done, the objects which actuated us would now be attainable by negotiation.
>
> I have seen and endured the suffering of the troops, and I can no longer be a party to prolong these sufferings for ends which I believe to be evil and unjust. I am not protesting against the conduct of the war, but against the political errors and insincerities for which the fighting men are being sacrificed. On behalf of those who are suffering now I make this protest against the deception which is being practised on them; also I believe that I may help to destroy the callous complacence with which the majority of those at home regard the continuance of agonies which they do not share, and which they have not sufficient imagination to realise.
>
> S. Sassoon, July 1917

Second Lieutenant Siegfried Sassoon (1886–1967) wrote his declaration of 'wilful defiance' whilst on convalescent leave after being wounded in France. He sent a copy of this statement to *The Times* and one to his colonel, fully prepared to accept that his action could result in a court martial. There was no question of cowardice. His war record was exemplary, even to the point of recklessness. His reputation for bravado on the battlefield earned him the nickname 'Mad Jack'. What probably saved him from a

Craiglockhart from Colinton Road.

court martial was his friendship with fellow Welch Fusilier Robert Graves (1895–1985), who got to know Sassoon while serving in France. Graves interceded and persuaded the military authorities to have Sassoon medically referred, and in July 1917 he was sent to Craiglockhart War Hospital, officially suffering from shell shock.

Craiglockhart doctors and nurses during the First World War.

Formerly Craiglockhart Hydropathic, this giant Italianate villa was requisitioned by the Army for use as a military hospital during the First World War. It was at Craiglockhart that Sassoon met poet Wilfred Owen (1893–1918), who was commissioned as a second lieutenant in the 5th Battalion, Manchester Regiment and was suffering from trench fever. Owen edited the hospital magazine *The Hydra* (a pun on Hydro) and nervously approached Sassoon (who was sitting on his bed cleaning his golf clubs) to ask him to sign several copies of *The Old Huntsman*. They soon struck up a friendship and Sassoon became a kind of mentor to Owen, regularly commenting on and criticising his poems. 'Anthem For Doomed Youth', written at Craiglockhart, especially interested Sassoon and his suggested amendments appear in his handwriting on the manuscript.

Siegfried Sassoon.

Nurses relaxing in the staffroom.

While at Craiglockhart, Sassoon was 'treated' by the eminent Army psychologist W.H.R. Rivers (1864–1922), who had a reputation for curing shell-shocked soldiers compassionately. Sassoon's and Rivers's relationship at Craiglockhart was recounted in Pat Barker's acclaimed 1995 novel *Regeneration*, which was filmed in 1997 by Gillies MacKinnon, starring Jonathan Pryce as Rivers. 'Sassoon was the only one in Craiglockhart who didn't have shell shock,' says MacKinnon:

> He'd made this declaration against the war, even though he was an extremely brave and efficient soldier, so they sent him to a mental hospital to avoid having to court martial him. So Rivers has to take somebody who's entirely sane, and make him mad enough to go back and sacrifice himself for a cause he doesn't believe in.

Sassoon was eventually 'discharged to duty' on 26 November 1917 and returned to the front. He never forgot the support and faith Rivers gave him, and his influence on Sassoon can be discerned in the poems 'Revisitation', written after Rivers's death, and 'Repression of War Experience', written in July 1917.

Wilfred Owen arrived back in France on 31 August 1918 and was killed crossing the Sambre Canal on 4 November, a week before the armistice was signed. Only five of his poems were published during his lifetime.

FURTHER INFORMATION: During a fortnight of events marking the 70th anniversary of the signing of the armistice on 11 November 1918, Napier University established the War Poets Collection, a commemorative collection within the library at the Craiglockhart campus, as a tribute to the poets of the Great War. Although the collection is centred on the lives and works of Wilfred Owen and Siegfried Sassoon, it also includes writings by other poets, such as Graves, Brooke and Blunden. The main purpose is to record the poets' work and to set it in its literary, historical and social context. In addition, the collection also encompasses any information that can be gathered regarding individuals who have connections to Craiglockhart at any time during its many and varied histories, particularly the medical and nursing staff of

Wilfred Owen, July 1916.

the war hospital. The collection comprises in excess of 400 items and may be used by all interested readers, as well as members of the University. For further information, or to arrange a guided visit to the War Poets Collection, contact 0131 455 6021. Email: nulis.war@napier.ac.uk.

FURTHER READING: J.M. Wilson, *Siegfried Sassoon: The Making of a War Poet* (Duckworth & Co., 2004); D. Hibberd, *Wilfred Owen* (Weidenfeld & Nicolson, 2002); P. Barker, *Regeneration* (Penguin, 1998). A disguised account of Craiglockhart appears in Sassoon's *Sherston's Progress* (Simon Publications, 2004).

Abbeyhill

Former site of 'Maryfield': childhood home of Scottish novelist Annie Swan (1859–1943)

> I think it beautiful as a work of art, and it must be the fault of a reader if he does not profit by its perusal.
>
> Prime Minister W.E. Gladstone
> praising *Aldersyde*, 16 April 1883

You will not find Annie Swan listed in many literary companions or even biographical dictionaries. Her sentimental novels were not considered great literature, but she is reputed to have written over 150 books, and was immensely popular in her day. She was born in Edinburgh in 1859, where her father was a potato merchant. When she was a small child, her father ran a farm near Coldingham, but the venture failed and the family returned to live in Edinburgh at Maryfield, an old mansion house which stood at the head of Easter Road. 'It was then a lovely country lane,' she recalled in her 1937 autobiography, 'bordered by fields and hedges, white with May bloom, and pink wild roses in summer . . . It was an ideal home for a family of seven "steerin" bairns.' She began writing seriously as a teenager, but never received much encouragement from her father. He did, however, advance the money for her first novel, *Ups and Downs*, and she later won a Christmas short-story competition in *The People's Friend*, which was the start of a long relationship with the magazine. Success came with her novel *Aldersyde* (1883), written when she was 24. The same year, she married schoolmaster James Burnett Smith, who later qualified as a doctor. The success of *Aldersyde* assured her a faithful reading public and she wrote prolifically for the rest of her life, mostly on the themes of sisterly and motherly love and womanly virtues, and typically with happy endings. Novelist Margaret Oliphant, after reviewing *Carlowrie* (1884), accused her of presenting a distorted view of Scottish life, but Annie Swan replied that she wrote only of the life she knew, and once remarked, 'I had stories to tell that would not let me rest till they were told.' She died at Gullane on 17 June 1943.

SEE ALSO: Margaret Oliphant.

FURTHER READING: Annie S. Swan, *My Life* (1934); M.R. Nicoll, *Letters of Annie S. Swan* (1945).

Greenside

PICARDY PLACE

Site of the birthplace of Sir Arthur Conan Doyle (1859–1930)

> The strain was something I could not endure any
> longer. Of course had I continued [to write Sherlock
> Holmes] I could have coined money, for the stories
> were the most remunerative I have written; but as
> regards literature, they would have been mere trash.
>
> Conan Doyle, quoted in Stashower,
> *Teller of Tales* (1999)

Arthur Ignatius Conan Doyle, creator of the world's greatest fictional detective, was born on 22 May 1859, in a small flat at 11 Picardy Place (demolished in 1969). A bronze sculpture of Sherlock Holmes clutching his famous pipe, but minus his hypodermic syringe, now marks the site. Situated beside one of the city's busiest and noisiest road junctions, the gaslit streets, hansom cabs and grubby street urchins of Conan Doyle's era seem as remote as Mars.

Arthur Conan Doyle as a young doctor in Southsea, around 1886, when he wrote 'A Study in Scarlet'.

Doyle is chiefly remembered today for his stories about the great sleuth, which, although they made him a fortune, also became a millstone round his neck. Few people today read his historical romances, the works he most wanted to be remembered for, and his obsession in later life with the occult greatly diminished his reputation and credibility.

Born of Irish-Catholic parentage, he was the second of ten children of Mary Foley and Charles Doyle, an assistant surveyor. Charles came from an artistic family and was himself a talented artist. All three of his brothers prospered in the art world, but Charles, who was an alcoholic and an epileptic, did not. He was involved in designing a fountain at Holyrood Palace and a

The Sherlock Holmes Statue, Picardy Place.

window at Glasgow Cathedral, and did occasional book illustration and sketching, but his career came to nothing. He was eventually institutionalised.

Conan Doyle described his mother in his autobiographical novel, *The Stark Munro Letters*, as having a 'sweet face' and being suggestive of 'a plump little hen'. She was known as 'the Ma'am', and was a voracious reader and storyteller. Conan Doyle recalled in his autobiography that 'as far back as I can remember anything at all, the vivid stories which she would tell me stand out so clearly that they obscure the real facts of life'.

The real 'facts of life' were that he had an alcoholic father to contend with, and life at home was a strain for all. In 1868, when he was nine years old, his wealthy uncles sent him to a Jesuit boarding school in England – a move which may have lifted the stress of home life, but ended up destroying his Catholic faith. He went on to study medicine at Edinburgh, where the uncanny observational powers of his teacher, Dr Joseph Bell, made him the model for Sherlock Holmes. He received his Bachelor of Medicine and Master of Surgery qualifications in 1881, and after a short stint as a ship's medical officer, he set up as a GP in Southsea in 1882.

While still at university, he had his first short story published – 'The Mystery of Sasassa Valley' – in Edinburgh's *Chambers' Journal*, for which he was paid three guineas. Many other stories followed, usually resulting in a rejection slip. Doyle's income after his first year practising in Southsea was a mere £150. Patients were thin on the ground to begin with, and his consulting room was more a place in which to write stories than to consult.

The detective genre in 1886 had only been around for 40 years, and among the role models which were the inspiration for the Holmes character were Poe's Auguste Dupin and Emile Gaboriau's Monsieur Lecoq. On 8 March 1886, he began writing a story called 'A Tangled Skein', which introduced the characters Sherringford Holmes and Ormond Slacker. By April, the title had changed to 'A Study in Scarlet', and the characters had evolved into Sherlock Holmes and Dr Watson. After three rejections, it was accepted by Ward, Lock and Company. Doyle reluctantly sold the copyright for £25 and it was published as the main story in the November 1887 issue of *Beeton's Christmas Annual*. Shortly afterwards, it appeared in book form, with pen and ink drawings by Doyle's father. 'The Sign of Four' followed in 1890, but it wasn't until *The Strand* magazine published 'A

Scandal in Bohemia', and subsequent monthly short stories, that the public developed an insatiable appetite for Sherlock Holmes. And so the legend was born, adding 100,000 copies to *The Strand*'s monthly circulation.

While churning out Holmes stories, Doyle was also busy working on his real love – historical fiction: *Micah Clarke* (1889), *The White Company* (1891), *Brigadier Gerard* (1896), *Rodney Stone* (1896) and *Sir Nigel* (1906). Later came *The Lost World* (1912) and the Professor Challenger stories. Although all these books were extremely competent literary efforts, they never eclipsed the popularity of Sherlock Holmes, much to the dismay of Doyle, who wanted so much to be remembered as a writer of 'quality' fiction.

Eighteen months after the appearance in *The Strand* of his first piece, Doyle was so fed up with his creation that he pitched Holmes over the Reichenbach Falls in 'The Final Problem'. This caused a tremendous public outcry. Doyle may have buried Holmes, but he also buried his bank account along with him. Eight years later, in 1902, he revived them both with *The Hound of the Baskervilles*. Shortly afterwards, the American magazine *Collier's Weekly* offered him a staggering $45,000 for 13 stories. Holmes was back, and he was here to stay.

Doyle stated in his 1924 autobiography, *Memories and Adventures*, that he was giving up his 'congenial and lucrative' writings for the psychic crusade, 'which will occupy, either by voice or pen, the remainder of my life'.

In the *Journal of the Society for Psychical Research*, he claimed he had been contacted by Charles Dickens and asked if he would complete his unfinished novel, *The Mystery of Edwin Drood*. 'I shall be honoured, Mr Dickens,' Doyle replied to his spirit. 'Charles, if you please,' replied the spirit. 'We like friends to be friends.' As far as we know, Doyle never did carry out this project.

After his first wife's death from tuberculosis in 1906, he married Jean Leckie. Doyle died in 1930 and the couple are buried together beneath an oak tree in All Saint's churchyard, Minstead, Hampshire.

SEE ALSO: Grave of Joseph Bell, Palace of Holyroodhouse, Holyrood Park, Rutherford's Howff, *Blackwood's Magazine*, Old College, Conan Doyle pub.

FURTHER INFORMATION: Conan Doyle stayed at various addresses in the city as a young medical student, including 2 Argyle Park Terrace and 32 George Square. Picardy Place is so called because it is the site of the village of Picardy formed by French refugees from the province of that name who came to Edinburgh after the revocation of the Edict of Nantes in 1685. The Franco Midland Hardware Company is an international Sherlock Holmes study group run by Holmesian scholar Phillip Weller, 6 Bramham Moor, Hill Head, Fareham, Hampshire, PO14 3RU. Tel: 01329 667 325.

FURTHER READING: A.C. Doyle, *Memories and Adventures* (Oxford, 1989); J.D. Carr, *Life of Sir Arthur Conan Doyle* (Carroll & Graf, 2003); M. Booth, *The Doctor and the Detective* (Thomas Dunne Books, 2000); D. Stashower, *Teller of Tales* (Penguin, 2001); R.L. Green and J.M. Gibson, *A Bibliography* *of A. Conan Doyle* (Clarendon, 1983); J. Cooper, *The Case of the Cottingley Fairies* (Pocket Books, 1998).

71–3 YORK PLACE

The Conan Doyle Pub

This pub looks interesting enough from the outside but its interior possesses all the personality of a paper cup. Sherlock Holmes fans will be extremely disappointed with this sad little howff which has made little attempt to recreate the world of the great sleuth. Save for a few hanging pictures and period book

spines, there is nothing to connect this place with Conan Doyle. Even its menu lacks imagination. One would like to have tasted a Baskerville Salad, Devil's Foot Soup, or sampled Mrs Hudson's home baking. However, one has to be content with a Conan Doyle Steak Pie. Situated opposite the site of Conan Doyle's birthplace, this pub, with a little imagination, could have created a fascinating shrine for visiting Sherlockians, but as Doyle confirms in *The Valley of Fear*, 'Mediocrity knows nothing higher than itself.'

SEE ALSO: Sir Arthur Conan Doyle, Joseph Bell, Palace of Holyroodhouse, Holyrood Park, Rutherford's Howff, *Blackwood's Magazine*, Old College.

FURTHER INFORMATION: The Conan Doyle, 71–3 York Place, Edinburgh EH1 3JD. Tel: 0131 524 0031.

1 BAXTER'S PLACE

Former home of Robert Stevenson (1772–1850) and birthplace of Thomas Stevenson (1818–87), grandfather and father of Robert Louis Stevenson

> There is scarce a deep sea light from the Isle of May north about to Lerwick, but one of my blood designed it, and I have often thought that to find a family to compare with ours in the promise of immortal memory we must go back to the Egyptian Pharaohs.
>
> Robert Louis Stevenson

Robert Stevenson, RLS's paternal grandfather, was the archetypal Victorian: a pious, right-wing, patriotic, powerhouse of a man, whose skill as an engineer ranks him alongside Brunel. He was involved in the design and construction of 23 Scottish lighthouses, notably the Bell Rock off Arbroath, and was also a consulting engineer for roads, railways, canals, bridges and harbours. He was born in Glasgow to Alan Stevenson, a merchant, and Jean Lillie, a builder's daughter. When he was only two, his father tragically died in the Caribbean, leaving his mother penniless. Thirteen years later, she married Thomas Smith, a ship owner, under-writer and engineer to the fledgling Board of Northern

1–3 Baxter's Place.

Lighthouses. Robert studied engineering in Glasgow and Edinburgh, eventually becoming his stepfather's partner. When he was 27, he married his 20-year-old stepsister, Jean Smith, 'a pious, tender soul' who bore him three sons – Alan, David and Thomas. 'The marriage of a man of 27 and a girl of 20 who have lived for 12 years as brother and sister is difficult to conceive,' wrote RLS.

1 Baxter's Place (now numbered 1–3) was built in 1804 for Thomas Smith, and Robert inherited it on Smith's death, along with the business and his post as engineer to the Board of Northern Lighthouses. Robert died six months before his famous grandson was born, but RLS left us a nostalgic description of Baxter's Place:

> No. 1 Baxter's Place, my grandfather's house, must have been a paradise for boys. It was of great size, with an infinity of cellars below, and of garrets, apple-lofts, etc., above; and it had a long garden, which ran down to the foot of the Calton hill ... There was a coming and going of odd, out-of-the-way characters, skippers, light-keepers, masons, and foremen of all sorts, whom my grandfather, in his patriarchal fashion, liked to have about the house, and who were a never-failing delight to the boys.

'The boys' were all destined to become engineers, and the family became known as 'The Lighthouse Stevensons'. Thomas, RLS's father, was a skilled and creative engineer, who invented the first wave dynamometer. Thomas and his brothers were educated at the Royal High School on Infirmary Street, and later at its new premises on Regent Road. RLS gave the following account of this in his *Memories and Portraits* (1887):

> He never seems to have worked for any class that he attended, and he drifted through school 'a mere

Site of the former stationer's shop on the corner of Antigua Street and Union Street described in 'A Penny Plain and Twopence Coloured' (1887).

consistent idler' . . . he bravely encouraged me to neglect my lessons, and never so much as asked me my place in school. What a boy should learn in school, he used to say, is 'to sit upon his bum.' So were his days bound each to each by this natural suspicion and contempt for formal education.

Despite his loathing for school, Thomas forged himself a successful career in engineering. He never achieved the feats of his father, though, and is remembered more by history for siring his famous son, who wrote of him: 'When the lights come out at sundown along the shores of Scotland, I am proud to think they burn more brightly for the genius of my father!'

SEE ALSO: Howard Place, Inverleith Terrace, Heriot Row, Pilrig House, Colinton Manse, Swanston Cottage, Glencorse Kirk, Rutherford's Howff, New Calton Cemetery, Old Calton Burial Ground, St Giles, Hawes Inn, Rullion Green, W.E. Henley, Alison Cunningham, Henderson's School, Deacon Brodie, The Writers' Museum, *Kidnapped* Statue, RLS Club, Museum of Scotland, George Mackenzie, Martyrs' Monument, Edinburgh Castle, Old College, Parliament Hall, Holyrood Park, Royal College of Surgeons' Museum, R.M. Ballantyne, RLS Memorial, Writers' Corner.

FURTHER INFORMATION: Baxter's Place was sold by the Stevenson family in 1856. The Stevensons' office was at the headquarters of the Commissioners of Northern Lights at 84 George Street. It was here that the map of Treasure Island was redrawn (the original having been lost) for inclusion in the first edition of 1883. The Stevenson family engineering papers are held in the National Library of Scotland, George IV Bridge.

Directly across the street from Baxter's Place, on the corner of Antigua Street and Union Street, there used to be a stationer's shop which RLS was fond of visiting as a child in which 'all the year round, there stood displayed a theatre' and where he would buy plays and sets for his own toy Skelt theatre. In his essay 'A Penny Plain and Twopence Coloured' (1887), Stevenson describes the excitement of his visits there. The shop is now Ferri's restaurant.

FURTHER READING: C. Mair, *A Star for Seamen: The Stevenson Family of Engineers* (J. Murray, 1978); B. Bathurst, *The Lighthouse Stevensons* (Perennial, 2005).

3A, 4A HADDINGTON PLACE

McNaughtan's Bookshop

Established in 1957 and in its present ownership since 1979, McNaughtan's is conveniently situated at the top of Leith Walk opposite another well-known Edinburgh institution – the gastronomical mecca Valvona & Crolla. The bookshop has a large general second-hand and antiquarian stock with prices ranging from pennies to hundreds of pounds. It is organised in separate rooms and alcoves to allow for peaceful browsing. There is a particular emphasis on the fine and applied arts, architecture, children's books, Scottish books and literature. They regularly send well-packed parcels of their books worldwide as required. McNaughtan's is a member of the Antiquarian Booksellers' Association and of the International League of Antiquarian Booksellers.

FURTHER INFORMATION: Opening hours: 9.30 a.m.–5.30 p.m. Tuesday to Saturday. Tel: 0131 556 5897. Email: mcnbooks@btconnect.com. Website: www.mcnaughtansbookshop.com.

Pilrig

Pilrig House
Birthplace of Lewis Balfour, grandfather of Robert Louis Stevenson

> I was thus in the poorest of spirits, though still pretty resolved, when I came in view of Pilrig, a pleasant gabled house set by the walkside among some brave young woods.
>
> David Balfour arrives at Pilrig House in
> *Catriona*, Robert Louis Stevenson (1893)

RLS's grandfather, Lewis Balfour, was born at Pilrig House in 1777, the third son of the second laird of Pilrig. The Balfours were a prosperous landowning family who had fingers in lots of pies, including the ill-fated Darien Company, which attempted colonising and trading in Central America in 1700. When the company collapsed, it left the Balfours almost ruined. In 1719, the government decided to compensate those who had lost their

capital, and with their new-found wealth, James Balfour purchased the estate of Pilrig. James fathered 17 children and the eldest, also named James, was Lewis's father. James Balfour (1705–95) was an advocate, to whom his great-grandson gave immortality when he wove him into the plot of *Catriona*. He was also sheriff-substitute of Midlothian and famously held the chair of moral philosophy at Edinburgh University, denying the post to David Hume, whose religious scepticism ensured he was never in the running.

'Some part of me played there in the eighteenth century,' wrote RLS in *Memories and Portraits* (1887), 'and ran races under the green avenue at Pilrig; some part of me trudged up Leith Walk, which was still a country place . . . All this I had forgotten; only my grandfather remembered and once reminded me.' Lewis

Balfour entered the ministry and married Henrietta Scott Smith. The couple moved to Colinton Manse in 1823, where RLS's mother, Margaret, was born in 1828.

SEE ALSO: David Hume, Howard Place, Inverleith Terrace, Heriot Row, Pilrig House, Colinton Manse, Swanston Cottage, Baxter's Place, Glencorse Kirk, Rutherford's Howff, New Calton Cemetery, Old Calton Burial Ground, St Giles, Hawes Inn, Rullion Green, W.E. Henley, Alison Cunningham, Henderson's School, Deacon Brodie, *Kidnapped* Statue, RLS Club, Museum of Scotland, George Mackenzie, Martyrs' Monument, Edinburgh Castle, Old College, The Writers' Museum, Parliament Hall, Holyrood Park, Royal College of Surgeons' Museum, R.M. Ballantyne, RLS Memorial, Writers' Corner.

FURTHER INFORMATION: Pilrig House, now part of a development for the elderly, was built in 1638 by Gilbert Kirkwood, a wealthy goldsmith who died of the plague. It was built on a ridge over the site of an old peel tower, hence the name Pilrig – the peel on the ridge. The best view of the house is from Pilrig Park, off Pilrig Street, but it can also be approached from the rear via Pilrig House Close. The Balfours worshipped at South Leith Parish Church, 6 Henderson Street, where the family is interred in the churchyard.

West End

St John's Churchyard

St John's Church was erected in 1818 and designed by W. Burn, who copied many of the details from St George's Chapel at Windsor. One of the ministers at St John's was Revd Dean Ramsay, author of *Reminiscences of Scottish Life and Character*.

Grave of Anne Rutherford (1732–1819)
Sir Walter Scott's mother

Described by J.G. Lockhart as 'short of stature . . . and by no means comely', Anne Rutherford was said to be plain-featured like her father, John Rutherford, professor of medicine at Edinburgh University. Her mother's family, the Swintons, were descendants of the Earls of Douglas. In April 1758, Anne married Walter Scott, a young solicitor, with whom she had twelve children, six of whom died in infancy. Her favourite child was 'wee Wattie', born in 1771, to whom she passed on her love of ballads, folk traditions and poetry. 'She was a strict economist,' Scott wrote to Lady Louisa Stuart, 'which she said enabled her to be liberal; out of her little income of about £300 a year she bestowed at least a third in well-chosen charities, and with the rest lived like a gentlewoman, and even with hospitality more general than seemed to suit her age; yet I could never prevail upon her to accept of any assistance.' She died aged 87 at 75 George Street.

SEE ALSO: Birthplace of W.S., childhood home of W.S., townhouse of W.S., Lasswade Cottage, Parliament Hall, Greyfriars Kirkyard, The Heart of Midlothian, Scott Monument, Holyrood Park, The Writers' Museum, High School, Old College, Sciennes Hill House, Assembly Rooms, J.G. Lockhart, Portobello Sands, Canongate Kirkyard, The Edinburgh Walter Scott Club.

FURTHER INFORMATION: Anne Rutherford's grave is marked by a small white stone in the Dormitory Garden at the eastern end of the church.

5 LOTHIAN ROAD

St Cuthbert's Churchyard

The origins of St Cuthbert's are obscure, but in 1127 King David I granted a charter conferring all land below the Castle to St Cuthbert's. The land around the church has been a burial ground for over 1,000 years, but interments ceased at the end of the nineteenth century. In 1738, incidents of grave-robbing were becoming commonplace and the perimeter walls were raised to 8 ft. By 1803, it had become such a scourge that a crenellated watchtower was built to house guards throughout the night; this can still be seen today in the south-west corner of the churchyard.

SEE ALSO: R.M. Ballantyne, Scott Monument.

Grave of Susan Ferrier (1782–1854), 'Scotland's Jane Austen'

Much admired by Walter Scott, Ferrier's novels were as instructive as they were amusing. Although she is often compared to Jane Austen, the penetrating satire in her novels is probably more akin to Tobias Smollett. Her first novel, *Marriage*, published in 1818, tells of the marriage of Juliana to an impoverished Scottish officer. A novel of provincial social manners, it warns against impetuous and foolhardy marriage. Her other two novels are *The Inheritance* (1824) and *Destiny* (1831).

SEE ALSO: Former home of Susan Ferrier.

FURTHER INFORMATION: Susan Ferrier's tombstone is roughly in the centre of the wall opposite the Princes Street side of the church.

Grave of Thomas De Quincey (1785–1859)
Prolific opium-addicted essayist who influenced Edgar Allan Poe, Baudelaire and the French Symbolists

> I have often been asked – how it was, and through what series of steps, that I became an opium-eater. Was it gradually, tentatively, mistrustingly, as one goes down a shelving beach into a deepening sea, and with a knowledge from the first of the dangers lying on that path; half-courting those dangers, in fact, whilst seeming to defy them?
>
> *The Confessions of an English Opium-Eater* (1822)

Thomas De Quincey's life has become synonymous with two words – opium and debt – and outside his bestselling *The Confessions of an English Opium-Eater*, which made his name, little of his work is ever discussed, perhaps because most

De Quincey Cottage, Lasswade.

of it was journalism, written to put bread on the table for his eight children.

He was born into a wealthy family of Manchester textile merchants, the fifth of eight children. His father, who was of Norman descent, died when De Quincey was seven. An extremely bright but unhappy scholar, De Quincey ran away from school when he was 17 and ended up living on the streets of London. In 1804, he studied at Oxford – where he first used opium, as a relief from neuralgia – but left without taking his degree. In 1807, he met Samuel Taylor Coleridge (who also started taking opium for pain relief) in Bath, which led to his becoming acquainted with the Lakeland poets Wordsworth and Southey, and to his forming a close friendship with John Wilson (Christopher North). In 1809, he rented Dove Cottage in Grasmere, where he lived for ten years after it had been vacated by Wordsworth. He experimented with opium while living in the Lake District, but it was a series of illnesses in his late 20s which induced him to take copious doses of the painkiller laudanum, prepared from opium, which turned him into a habitual user.

In 1816, De Quincey married Margaret Simpson, with whom he had had an illegitimate child. By now, he was committed to trying seriously to earn money from his writings, as his family inheritance had dried up. He edited the local *Westmoreland Gazette* and in 1821 moved to London, where he wrote for *Blackwood's Magazine* and the *London Magazine*, publishing *The Confessions of an English Opium-Eater* the following year to great acclaim. His Blackwood's connection, and spiralling debts, prompted the family, which had now swelled to eight children, to move to Edinburgh in 1826. He became encumbered by more and more debt, for which he was eventually imprisoned in 1831, and was convicted twice more in 1833 and three times in 1834, forcing him to take refuge in Edinburgh's Holyrood Abbey Sanctuary. One of his sons died aged two in 1832 and his wife died in 1837. As if this wasn't enough suffering for De Quincey, another of his sons died shortly afterwards fighting, ironically, in the Chinese Opium Wars.

In 1843, he retired with his family to a cottage in Polmont Bank, Lasswade, a village on the River Esk, south-east of Edinburgh, where he finished *The Logic of Political Economy* (1844) and wrote *Suspiria de Profundis* (1845), a sequel to *The*

Confessions. Ralph Waldo Emerson visited him here in 1848. In 1850, he returned to Edinburgh, where he died on 8 December 1859, just as his collected works were about to be published; this knowledge must have brought him great satisfaction after such a tortuous and stressful life.

SEE ALSO: John Wilson, *Blackwood's Magazine*, the Palace of Holyroodhouse and Holyrood Abbey, James Thin.

FURTHER INFORMATION: Entering from Lothian Road, walk straight down the path and turn right up the short steps just before the church. Follow the path round. De Quincey's grave is situated against the centre of the wall facing King's Stables Road. During his 30-odd years in the city, De Quincey resided at various addresses, including 1 Forres Street, 29 Ann Street (home of John Wilson), 9 Great King Street, 113 Princes Street, 71 Clerk Street, 42 Lothian Street (now demolished) and Mavis Bush Cottage, Lasswade.

FURTHER READING: G. Lindop, *Opium Eater: A Life of Thomas De Quincey* (Weidenfeld & Nicolson, 1993); E. Sackville West, *A Flame in Sunlight: The Life and Work of Thomas De Quincey* (Bodley Head Ltd, 1974); H.A. Eaton, *Thomas De Quincey* (1936).

23 RUTLAND STREET

Former home of Dr John Brown (1810–82)
Physician and essayist known as the 'Scottish Charles Lamb'

> They ken your name, they ken your tyke,
> They ken the honey from your byke;
> But mebbe after a' your fyke,
> (The truth to tell)
> It's just your honest Rab they like,
> An' no yoursel'.
>
> Robert Louis Stevenson, from
> 'To Doctor John Brown', *Underwoods* (1887)

Dr John Brown didn't leave the world much to remember his literary talents by, but what little he did leave ranks him amongst the world's foremost essayists. Most of his writings are contained in the three-volume *Horae Subsecivae* (*Leisure Hours*, 1858–82), which includes 'Our Dogs' (1862), 'Marjorie Fleming' (1863), 'Minchmore' (1864) and his masterpiece set in the streets of Edinburgh, 'Rab and his Friends' (1859), one of the best insights into the human nature of dogs ever written.

The son of a minister, he was

Dr Brown (right) with the Clemenses (Samuel Clemens standing) in 1873.

born in Biggar and moved to Edinburgh in 1822, aged 12, where he was educated at the Royal High School and the University of Edinburgh. He qualified as an MD and lived for 60 years in Edinburgh, counting among his friends Francis Jeffrey, Ruskin, Thackeray and Mark Twain.

He became acquainted with Samuel Clemens (Mark Twain) in the summer of 1873 when the Clemenses visited Edinburgh and resided at Veitch's Hotel, 125 George Street. Mrs Clemens took ill on her arrival, and Samuel, who knew of Dr John Brown, obtained his address and consulted him. Under Dr Brown's care, she made a swift recovery and for almost a month the couple were his close companions, accompanying him on his rounds almost daily. The Clemenses would bring along books to read while they waited, and Dr Brown would comment, 'Entertain yourselves while I go in and reduce the population.' Samuel Clemens described Dr Brown as having 'a sweet and winning face, as beautiful a face as I have ever known. Reposeful, gentle, benignant; the face of a saint at peace with all the world and placidly beaming upon it the sunshine of love that filled his heart'. Dr Brown died on 11 May 1882, aged 71.

SEE ALSO: The Scott Monument, the Royal High School, Old College.

FURTHER READING: E.T. Maclaren, *Dr John Brown and his Sister Isabella* (1890); Dr J. Brown (son) and U.W. Forrest, *Letters of Dr John Brown* (1907).

(10 RANDOLPH CRESCENT)

Birthplace of Scottish writer Naomi Mitchison (1897–1999)

> I know I can handle words, the way other people handle colours or computers or horses.
> *Saltire Self-Portraits*

I0 Randolph Crescent.

Socialist, feminist, traveller, birth-control and anti-nuclear campaigner, Naomi Mitchison broke all the rules, wrote over 70 books and lived until she was 101. Her work included poetry, plays, travel writing, children's fiction, short stories and biography, but she will be best remembered for her historical fiction.

She was born on 1 November 1897, the daughter of physiologist John Scott Haldane and suffragist Kathleen Trotter, and was brought up in Oxford. She attended the (boys) Dragon School until she began to menstruate and her education was continued at home with a governess. In 1916, she married her brother's friend, Dick Mitchison. This was a marriage which was reputedly a happy one, but nonetheless an 'open' one. Dick became Labour MP for Kettering, Northamptonshire (1945–64) and was later Lord Mitchison. The couple had seven children.

Inspired by a diary she kept of her dreams and Gibbon's *Decline and Fall*, she wrote her first book, *The Conquered* (1923), set during Caesar's Gallic Wars and mirroring the 1920s situation in Ireland. Her epic historical novel *The Corn King and the Spring Queen* (1931) is set in the Greek city states of Athens and Sparta, and a visit to the Soviet Union in 1932 produced *We Have Been Warned* (1935), depicting a rape, a seduction, an abortion and contraception. She travelled extensively, and in 1963 the Bakgatha of Botswana made her their tribal adviser and 'mother'. During her life, her friends included Neil Gunn, W.H. Auden, Doris Lessing, Aldous Huxley, Stevie Smith and E.M. Forster.

Mitchison was actively involved in Scottish politics and stood as Labour candidate for the Scottish Universities in 1935. In 1937, she bought Carradale, an estate on the Mull of Kintyre, where she was still living and writing 50 years later, commenting, 'so long as I can hold a pencil, let me go on.'

FURTHER READING: Naomi Mitchison published three volumes of autobiography: *Small Talk* (House of Lochar, 2000), *All Change Here* (Bodley Head Ltd, 1975) and *You May Well Ask* (Flamingo, 1986); and two volumes of diaries: *Vienna Diary* (1934), *Among You Taking Notes* (Weidenfeld & Nicolson, 2000).

SEE ALSO: J. Calder, *The Nine Lives of Naomi Mitchison* (Virago, 1997).

8 EGLINTON CRESCENT

Birthplace of Fred Urquhart (1912–95)
Scottish short-story writer and novelist

> Time . . . something that cannot be measured by days or months or by years, for yesterday may not be so clear as a day twenty years ago, and something said five minutes ago can be forgotten, while words spoken when you were young are still ringing in your ears . . .
>
> Fred Urquhart, *Time Will Knit* (1938)

Time Will Knit was the first novel of Edinburgh writer Fred Urquhart, written when he was 26 years old. It tells the story of Mirren and Wattie Gillespie who live in the small, decayed fishing port of Harrisfield on the Forth and who, after 50 years, are about to be evicted from their crumbling cottage in 1929. Although the novel is set in fictional Harrisfield, it is clearly inspired by the Granton of Urquhart's childhood, which is situated to the north of Edinburgh on the Firth of Forth, about a mile west of Newhaven (Forthport in the book), and three miles from the city centre.

In 1919, Urquhart's family moved from his birthplace at 8 Eglinton Crescent in Edinburgh's West End to 37 West Cottages, Granton. Now demolished, the cottages were located opposite Granton Harbour, between the Middle and West Piers. The book was outspoken for its day and didn't flinch when discussing taboo subjects such as homosexuality, premarital sex, the dysfunctional Royal Family and the futility of the First World War, which takes the Gillespies' two sons:

8 Eglinton Crescent.

Medals! . . . You got some satisfaction from seeing the flames lick the coloured red, white and blue ribbons into ashes. You felt as if it really were the men who had started the war who were burning in hellfire. And you laughed as you watched them burn.

Fred Urquhart left school at 15 and worked at various jobs. As well as being employed as a labourer and a tailor's assistant, he did a seven-year stint as a bookseller's assistant at Cairns' Bookshop in Teviot Place. Later, he became a publisher's reader, London scout for Walt Disney and literary editor of *Tribune*. His first published story was 'The Daft Woman in Number Seven', published by Adelphi in 1936. Other novels include *The Ferret Was Abraham's Daughter* (1949), *Jezebel's Dust* (1951) and *Palace of Green Days* (1979). He also published 11 collections of short stories.

4 GRINDLAY STREET

Birthplace of Christina Kay
The original Jean Brodie

Muriel Spark is best known for her 1961 novel, *The Prime of Miss Jean Brodie*, based on her schooldays in the '20s and '30s at James Gillespie's School (the model for the Marcia Blaine School in the novel) where she was taught by the unorthodox Miss Christina Kay, the inspiration for Jean Brodie. Like many other pupils before her, Muriel was fascinated by Miss Kay and fell quickly under her spell, commenting that, 'Miss Kay predicted my future as a writer in the most emphatic terms. I felt I hardly had much choice in the matter.' Miss Kay did not have love affairs with the art master and singing teacher, and was not dismissed for teaching treason and sedition to her students, as was Jean Brodie; the two, however, did share many similar characteristics, such as a love of music, Renaissance painters and exotic travel, and an admiration for Mussolini's Fascisti.

Christina Kay was born at 4 Grindlay Street, off Lothian Road, on 11 June 1878, the only child of Mary McDonald and Alexander Kay, a cabinet maker. She was enrolled at Gillespie's School at the age of five, and, except for two years at training college, there she remained until her retirement in 1943. An article in the school magazine recalls her career the same year:

4 Grindlay Street.

> Many a child has delighted in her vivid descriptions of Italian towns and their picture galleries. From her love of ancient Greece, she pushed home the lesson of the value and beauty of perfection in minute and hidden things, 'for the gods see everywhere'. Through many changes and great progress, Gillespie's ever remained her well-loved 'alma mater' . . .

She lived at Grindlay Street for most of her life, where she often entertained her pupils to tea. She never married, although she lost a lover in the Great War, and died on 25 May 1951 at Midhope, Hopetoun, South Queensferry, of chronic bronchitis and myocarditis, aged 72, unaware of the legend she would become. She is buried in Abercorn Churchyard, near South Queensferry.

SEE ALSO: Muriel Spark.

New Town

ST JAMES SQUARE

Lodgings of Robert Burns on his second visit to Edinburgh during the winter of 1787–8

> If you imagine a Scotch commercial traveller in a Scotch commercial hotel leaning on the bar and calling the barmaid 'Dearie', then you will know the keynote of Burns's verse.
>
> A.E. Housman (1859–1936)

Burns arrived back in Edinburgh at the end of October 1787 after a short tour of Stirlingshire. He changed his digs from Buccleuch Street to the attic of a house owned by William Cruikshank, a schoolmaster at the Royal High School, on the south-west corner of St James Square (now the site of St James Shopping Centre, Leith Street), with the window in the gable looking towards the former General Post Office building. It was here he worked on the lyrics for the second volume of *The Scots Musical Museum*, and also where he was bedridden for six weeks with a dislocated knee, a circumstance which led to the legendary correspondence between Sylvander (Burns) and Clarinda (Nancy McLehose), the inspiration for 'Ae Fond Kiss'.

SEE ALSO: Anchor Close, Buccleuch Street, Burns Monument, White Hart Inn, St Giles, Canongate Kilwinning Lodge, William Smellie, William Creech, The Writers' Museum, Sciennes Hill House, Robert Fergusson, Clarinda, Jean Lorimer, Henry Mackenzie, The Blind Poet pub.

13–14 PRINCES STREET

Waterstone's, East End

Waterstone's is the largest retail bookseller in the UK, with around 200 shops. The chain was founded by Tim Waterstone when he was sacked from WH Smith after losing money trying to launch its US operations. Using the last £6,000 of his redundancy, he established a chain of bookstores which eventually made him a millionaire when WH Smith took a share in 1989. Waterstone sold out to them in 1998, and subsequently Smiths sold the chain on to HMV. Waterstone's are credited with

bringing modern marketing techniques to the sale of highbrow, academic and literary books, providing a 'browser friendly' atmosphere, with knowledgeable booksellers, a wide range of titles and smartly designed shops. There are currently three other branches in Edinburgh, at 83 George Street, 128 Princes Street (West End) and 98–9 Ocean Terminal in Leith.

FURTHER INFORMATION: Opening hours: 9 a.m.–8 p.m. Monday to Friday; 9 a.m.–7 p.m. Saturday; 10 a.m.–7 p.m. Sunday. Tel: 0131 556 3034.

3 ROSE STREET

The Abbotsford
Regular watering-hole of Hugh MacDiarmid (1892–1978) and the poets of the Scottish Renaissance

> I'll hae nae hauf-way hoose, but aye be whaur
> Extremes meet
>
> Hugh MacDiarmid, *A Drunk Man*
> *Looks at the Thistle* (1926)

During the 1950s and early '60s, Hugh MacDiarmid was the centre of a group of Scottish Renaissance poets who met regularly in the city's pubs. Meeting initially in the Café Royal in West Register Street, they later moved along the road to the Abbotsford, then Milnes Bar and latterly the Oxford Bar in Young Street. All are still excellent howffs and little changed, apart from Milnes, which bears no resemblance today to its 'poet's pub' heyday. The Abbotsford, named after Scott's mock-Baronial mansion in the Scottish Borders, was built between 1880 and 1910. It has steadfastly refused to opt for the fashionable tartan tat decor of many city-centre pubs and remains a bastion of traditional ales, malts and good pub grub – hence the attraction for MacDiarmid, Sydney Goodsir Smith, Robert Garioch, Norman MacCaig and many other poets of the Scottish Renaissance.

Regarded as the greatest of twentieth-century Scottish poets and, by many, the greatest of all poets in the Scots tradition,

Hugh MacDiarmid's interpretation of the Scottish consciousness through his baiting and unsentimental verse helped Scotland recognise its true self. He became the catalyst of the Scottish Renaissance, which strove to detach itself from the romantic and nostalgic Scottish literature of the nineteenth century and establish Scottish writing as a contemporary force, and in so doing revitalised Scottish poetry.

MacDiarmid was born Christopher Murray Grieve on 11 August 1892, in Langholm, Dumfriesshire, 'the wonderful little  Border burgh' just a few miles from England. The son of a postman, he attended Langholm Academy, and in 1908 he became a pupil-teacher at Broughton Higher Grade School in Edinburgh. For some years, he worked as a journalist for newspapers in Scotland and Wales. He became active in left-wing politics and in 1915 he joined the RAMC, serving in Salonika, Italy and France. Invalided home with cerebral malaria, he married June Skinner in 1918. On demobilisation, he joined the staff of the *Montrose Review*, and started writing poetry that soon began to be noticed.

Between 1920 and 1922, he edited three volumes of *Northern Numbers*, and in August 1922 he founded the periodical *Scottish Chapbook*, which became a platform for talented Scots poets, including himself, now writing under the pseudonym Hugh MacDiarmid. The *Scottish Chapbook* became dedicated to the furthering of a Scottish Renaissance, using Scots as a serious medium of poetic expression, liberating it from the Kailyard, comic verse and pseudo-Burnsian mawkishness. The 'golden lyrics' of *Sangschaw* (1925) and *Penny Wheep* (1926) were his first collections of mainly Scots poems. In 1926, he published his dramatic masterpiece *A Drunk Man Looks at the Thistle*, a meditation which defines and analyses the state of the Scottish nation. Next came *To Circumjack Cencrastus* (1930), an even longer poem-sequence.

He founded the Scottish Centre of PEN in 1927 and helped to found the National Party of Scotland in 1928. In 1934, he joined the Communist Party, but was expelled in 1938, and only rejoined in 1957 after the Russians invaded Hungary – a time when others were deserting the party. Grieve lived in Montrose until 1929, where he served as a Labour councillor. In 1929, he left for London to edit Compton Mackenzie's doomed radio magazine *Vox*. In 1932, he divorced his first wife and married Cornish girl Valda Trevlyn. Shortly afterwards, they moved to the island of Whalsay in Shetland, where they lived until 1941. During the war, he was a labourer on Clydeside and later entered the Merchant Service. In 1951, the Grieves, together with their only son, moved to Brownsbank Cottage, near Biggar, where, for the next ten years, they lived without water except from an outside pump, without electric light and without kitchen or bathroom. After this, conditions gradually improved, and MacDiarmid lived here until his death in 1978. Towards the end of his life, MacDiarmid evolved into a Scottish institution. His genius was recognised and rewarded, though never financially, and he is now rightly regarded as one of Scotland's greatest poets.

Other publications include the three *Hymns to Lenin* (1931, 1932, 1957), *Scots Unbound* (1932), *Stony Limits* (1934), *A Kist of Whistles* (1947) and *In Memoriam James Joyce* (1955). His autobiography was published in *Lucky Poet* (1943) and *The Company I've Kept* (1966). MacDiarmid's *Complete Poems* was published in 1976.

SEE ALSO: Sydney Goodsir Smith, Robert Garioch, Norman MacCaig, Oxford Bar, Milnes Bar, Edinburgh Park.

FURTHER READING: A. Bold, *Hugh MacDiarmid: A Biography* (Uni. of Massachusetts Press, 1990).

EAST PRINCES STREET GARDENS

The Scott Monument
A memorial to Sir Walter Scott (1771–1832), inventor of the historical and romantic novel

> Sir Walter Scott with his enchantments . . . sets the world in love with dreams and phantoms; with decayed and swinish forms of religion; with decayed and degraded systems of government; with the sillinesses and emptinesses, sham grandeurs, sham gauds, and sham chivalries of a brainless and worthless long-vanished society. He did measureless harm; more real and lasting harm, perhaps, than any other individual that ever wrote.
>
> Mark Twain, *Life on the Mississippi* (1883)

I think we can safely assume that Mark Twain was not the world's number-one Walter Scott fan. He even accuses Scott in the same tirade of being 'in great measure responsible for the [American Civil] war'. It may sound laughable, but he was serious, and Mark Twain's wrath illustrates the enormous extent of Scott's influence and readership. Love him or loathe him, Walter Scott was literary dynamite in his day and Edinburgh wanted to set this fact in stone for all time, lest we forget it.

Following his death in 1832, there was a growing desire that something should be built in the city to commemorate Scott's enormous contribution to Scottish literature. J.G. Lockhart, Scott's biographer and son-in-law, proposed the erection of 'a huge Homeric Cairn on Arthur's Seat – a land and sea mark'. Many other suggestions were mooted, and eventually a competition was organised for the best-designed monument.

Fifty-four plans were submitted, including twenty-two Gothic structures, fourteen Grecian temples, eleven statues, five pillars, an obelisk and a fountain.

The winning design was submitted by Biggar-born draughtsman and self-taught architect George Meikle Kemp (1795–1844), who drew up his plan in five days. Kemp probably thought his humble origins and lack of eminence might prejudice his chances of winning, and shrewdly submitted his design to the selecting committee under the pseudonym John Morvo, the medieval master-mason of Melrose Abbey, from which he admitted that the inspiration for his design 'was in all its details derived'. Tragically, Kemp died before the completion of the monument, when he drowned in mysterious circumstances in the Union Canal at Fountainbridge on the evening of 6 March 1844.

Sir John Steell's sculpture of The Wizard of the North beneath The Scott Monument.

The 200-ft high monument, with two hundred and eighty-seven steps to its pinnacle, incorporating three Scottish monarchs, sixteen poets and sixty-four of Scott's characters into its design, was officially inaugurated fourteen years after Scott's death on 15 August 1846. The twice-life-size statue of Scott at its base was sculpted by Sir John Steell (1804–1901) in white Carrara marble, and is one of the cleverest innovations of the whole structure, skilfully camouflaging the seagull guano deposited daily on his noble brow. Charles Dickens disliked the structure, commenting in 1847 that he was 'sorry to report the Scott Monument a failure. It is like the spire of a Gothic church taken off and stuck in the ground.' John Ruskin was of a similar view in 1873: 'The wise people of Edinburgh built a small vulgar Gothic steeple on the ground, and called it the Scott Monument.'

Mark Twain visited Edinburgh in 1873, residing at Veitch's Hotel, 125 George Street. He must have strolled past the Scott Monument almost daily. One can easily imagine him staring up at Scott's memorial, dwarfed by its Gothic extravagance, and feeling very much the Connecticut Yankee in King Walter's Court.

SEE ALSO: Birthplace of W.S., childhood home of W.S., townhouse of W.S., Lasswade Cottage, Parliament Hall, Greyfriars Kirkyard, St John's Churchyard, The Heart of Midlothian, Holyrood Park, The Writers' Museum, High School, Old College, Sciennes Hill House, Assembly Rooms, J.G. Lockhart, Portobello Sands, Canongate Kirkyard, The Edinburgh Walter Scott Club, Dr John Brown.

FURTHER INFORMATION: George Kemp is buried in St Cuthbert's

Churchyard at the West End of Princes Street, in the plot behind the former Mission Hall. Just across the street from the Scott Monument at 6 South St David Street is the Ivanhoe pub. A few Scott-related prints hang on the wall, but this gloomy little tavern pays little homage to the noble Saxon Wilfred of Ivanhoe, son of Cedric and affectionate friend of Richard Coeur de Lion.

35 HANOVER STREET

Milnes Bar
'The Poets' Pub'

A noticeboard fixed to the pub's wall on Hanover Street stresses the importance of Milnes in Scotland's literary history, and how it became the 'favoured howff for the patriarchs of "Le Group de la Renaissance Ecossaise"', as described in an essay by Denis Saurat in 1924. It also stresses the movement's 'use of broad Scots as a literary language . . . [that was] pioneered by Hugh MacDiarmid, who engaged in lively debate, both political and poetic, with the likes of Sydney Goodsir Smith, Sorley Maclean and Norman MacCaig . . . in a room that came to be hailed as "The Little Kremlin"'.

The pub, however, which held such an attraction to the poets of the Scottish Renaissance, along with others including Alan Bold, Stevie Smith, Dylan Thomas, W.H. Auden and George Mackay Brown, disappeared years ago. Modern refurbishment has totally eradicated the charac-ter and atmosphere which made it so appealing, and all that remains are a few portraits of poets hanging on its sanitised walls. Daddy Milnes is just a memory – the closest you'll get to it is reading the notice-board outside on the street.

SEE ALSO: Hugh MacDiarmid, Sydney Goodsir Smith, Norman MacCaig.

61 PRINCES STREET

John Menzies' first bookshop

> There was a young lady called Menzies
> Who asked, 'Do you know what this thenzies?'
> Her aunt with a gasp
> Replied, 'It's a wasp,
> And you're holding the end where the stenzies.'
> > (Menzies is pronounced Ming-iss, with
> > the primary stress on the first syllable.)

John Menzies was a name synonymous with the book trade in Edinburgh for over 150 years. Born in 1808, he was educated at the Royal High School and, between 1823 and 1830, he was an apprentice with Sutherland the booksellers on Regent Road. Here, he worked a 14-hour day, an 84-hour week and, during the one hour he was granted for lunch, he was not expected to stop work while eating it. After his seven-year apprenticeship, he worked as a bookseller's assistant in London for a couple of years before returning to Edinburgh in 1833 following the death of his father. With fourteen pounds in his pocket, a stepmother and two sisters to support, life didn't promise to be a bowl of cherries.

The safest route would have been to gain regular employment, but instead he took a gamble and rented no. 61, a shop at the corner of Princes Street and Hanover Street (since renumbered) at the centre of the city's bookselling trade, where he became involved in all aspects of the business, most notably as a wholesale distributor of books to the trade. He also began publishing books and engravings, and selling the *Scotsman* newspaper – uniquely for his day, as newspapers were normally obtained by subscription from their publishers. It wasn't long until he prospered, and in 1837 he hired his first employees: a clerk and three apprentices.

By the mid-1800s, the railways covered most of Scotland and passengers were buying books and magazines for their journeys. In 1857, Menzies began acquiring bookstalls on stations, and in 1862, outbidding previous leaseholder William Henry (W.H.) Smith, he offered an annual rent of £180 a year for the Waverley Station bookstall, giving him the right to sell 'books, pamphlets and newspapers' on the understanding that he would 'not sell any book objectionable in its moral character or tendency'.

In 1845, he married Rossie Marr, a Leith merchant's daughter, with whom he had two sons and three daughters. His sons carried on the dynasty, which grew into a sizeable empire with its largest branch at 107

Princes Street employing over a hundred assistants during the 1990s. Since it sold off its retail stores to WH Smith in 1999, John Menzies has ceased to be a familiar high-street name, but still thrives today as a major wholesaler and distributor of newspapers and magazines. John Menzies is buried in Warriston Cemetery.

SEE ALSO: Royal High School.

FURTHER READING: L. Gardiner, *The Making of John Menzies* (Edinburgh Bartholomew, 1983).

32 CASTLE STREET

Birthplace of Kenneth Grahame (1859–1932)
Children's writer and author of *The Wind in the Willows*

Since it was first published in 1908, *The Wind in the Willows* has appeared in over 100 editions and the riverside adventures of Rat, Mole, Badger and Toad now constitute an established children's classic, ranking Kenneth Grahame alongside Lear and Carroll.

Born on the morning of 8 March 1859 at 32 Castle Street, Kenneth had in attendance none other than Queen Victoria's 'beloved professor of chloroform fame', Dr James Simpson. His father was James Cunningham Grahame, an Edinburgh lawyer, and his mother was Bessie Inglis from Lasswade. Kenneth was the third of four children in what was initially a happy and loving family home. In 1860, his father was appointed sheriff-substitute of Argyllshire at Inverary and the family moved to the Highlands. In 1864, after Bessie gave birth to Roland, her fourth child, she contracted scarlet fever and died. Her last words were, 'It's all been so lovely.' As a consequence of Bessie's death,

Kenneth Grahame, aged 60.

Kenneth's father sent all his children to be reared by their maternal grandmother at Cookham Dene, Oxfordshire. From this time onwards, James Grahame's life fell apart through alcoholism and a broken heart. He resigned his post in 1867 and went to live in France for the next 20 years, where he died alone.

Schooled in Oxford, and denied the chance of a university education because of the financial cost, Kenneth began his career, albeit reluctantly, as a gentleman-clerk at the Bank of England, Threadneedle Street, on 1 January 1879. Around this time, he began to jot down quotations, anecdotes, poems and prose in an old bank ledger. London editors first began to publish his essays and articles in 1887. His first known published work was a country essay entitled 'By a Northern

Furrow' which appeared in the *St James's Gazette*. He also contributed to Henry Harland's *The Yellow Book* and various publications edited by W.E. Henley. His first book was a collection of essays and tales, *Pagan Papers* (1893), and he followed this with *The Golden Age* (1895) and *Dream Days* (1898) – collections of classic essays about Victorian childhood.

In 1898, aged 39, he was promoted to the post of secretary of the Bank of England – one of the youngest on record – by which time his literary works had become so popular that he was a household name. In 1899, he married Elspeth Thompson and the following year she gave birth to their only child, Alistair, nicknamed 'Mouse'. Unfortunately, he was born semi-blind due to a congenital cataract of the right eye. *The Wind in the Willows* began as bedtime stories for Mouse around 1904 and later continued as a series of letters to him from spring to autumn of 1907. The story depicts themes close to Grahame's heart: vanishing rural landscapes and the shrinking boundaries of country life provoked by advancing agricultural mechanisation, the railways and the motor car. Grahame based his tale on the stretch of the Thames which runs from Marlow to Pangbourne concentrated around Cookham Dene, where he had spent the golden days of his childhood.

Publishers were sceptical of the finished manuscript. However, after many rejections, it was eventually published by Methuen, who offered no advance but agreed to 'excellent rising royalties'. The reviews on publication were lukewarm, as this example from the *Times Literary Supplement* of 22 October 1908 demonstrates:

> *The Wind in the Willows* (Methuen 6s.) is a book with hardly a smile in it, through which we wander in a haze of perplexity, uninterested by the story itself and at a loss to understand its deeper purpose . . . For ourselves, we lay *The Wind in the Willows* reverently aside.

Fortunately, the reading public made sense of it, as did novelist Arnold Bennett, who summed the book up perfectly: 'The book is an urbane exercise in irony at the expense of the English character and of mankind. It is entirely successful.'

Tragedy struck the Grahames on the night of Friday, 7 May 1920 when Alistair, then an undergraduate at Christchurch, was struck by a train and killed. His body had been decapitated and suicide was suspected, although never proven.

After a short stroll on Tuesday, 5 July 1932, Kenneth Grahame retired to bed with Walter Scott's *The Talisman*. Around 6 a.m. the following morning, he suffered a cerebral haemorrhage from which he never regained consciousness. He is buried in Holywell Churchyard, Oxford. Over the grave is carved an inscription composed by his novelist cousin, Anthony Hope: 'To the beautiful memory of Kenneth Grahame, husband of Elspeth and father of Alistair, who passed the River on 6 July 1932, leaving childhood and literature through him the more blest for all time.'

FURTHER READING: P. Green, *Beyond the Wild Wood: The World of Kenneth Grahame* (Webb & Bower, 1982).

39 NORTH CASTLE STREET

Townhouse of Sir Walter Scott (1771–1832)

> That d—d Sir Walter Scott, that everybody makes such
> a work about! . . . I wish I had him to ferry over Loch
> Lomond: I should be after sinking the boat, if I drowned
> myself into the bargain; for ever since he wrote his
> *Lady of the Lake*, as they call it, everybody goes to that
> filthy hole Loch Katrine, then comes round by Luss, and
> I have had only two gentlemen to guide all this blessed
> season.
>
> Loch Lomond ferryman, after publication
> of Scott's *Lady of the Lake* in 1810

Walter Scott married French émigrée Charlotte Carpenter on
Christmas Eve 1797 and the couple took temporary lodgings
on the second floor of 108 George Street for a few weeks before
moving into 10 South Castle Street, which was soon exchanged
for 39 North Castle Street, where they lived until 1826. Scott,
now in his late 20s, was
beginning to settle down in life.
The income from his Bar
earnings, his wife's allowances,
his father's estate (his father
died in 1799) and his newly
appointed post as sheriff-
deputy of Selkirkshire was
bringing in around £1,000 a
year. In 1796, he published his
translation of Gottfried Burger's
The Chase, and *William and
Helen*, the first publication to
bear his name. His writing
hobby was now absorbing him
more and more, and law was
becoming a chore, but there was
never any question of devoting

39 North Castle Street.

his life entirely to the Muses. His father's advice – that
literature was a good staff but a bad crutch – was wise counsel
not forgotten.

His wanderings in the Border country inspired him to start
collecting the region's ancient and rapidly disappearing ballads,
which he believed would soon be lost forever if not properly
recorded. With the assistance of Border wordsmiths John
Leyden and James Hogg, *The Minstrelsy of the Scottish Border*
appeared in 1802–3, printed in Kelso by Scott's old schoolfriend
James Ballantyne.

Between 1799 and 1805, Charlotte gave birth to two sons and
two daughters. In the autumn of 1804, the family moved to
Ashiestiel, near Clovenfords, the sheriff being bound by statute
to reside for part of the year in the Borders. North Castle Street
was kept on as a winter residence. It was at Ashiestiel that Scott
wrote the works which turned him into a celebrated poet: *The*

Lay of the Last Minstrel (1805), *Marmion* (1808) and *The Lady of the Lake* (1810).

In 1806, he became principal clerk to the Court of Session in Edinburgh, which meant he no longer needed to practise as an advocate. In 1809, he became a secret partner in James Ballantyne's printing business, a rash move for which he would later pay dearly.

Byron was beginning to eclipse Scott as a poet, and, wisely, Scott turned his talents to novel-writing. *Waverley*, his first

novel, was published by Constable anonymously on 7 July 1814, and was staggeringly successful, much to Scott's surprise. The impact the novel had on the literary world at that time is difficult to take in today, but it was a literary phenomenon which caused a sensation around the world. With one book, Scott had established the form of the historical novel, a genre which did not exist before, and, perhaps more importantly, he gave the novel prestige. In the early nineteenth century, the novel was an extremely questionable form of literature, and far beneath the dignity of a clerk of the Court of Session. Scott knew the legal establishment would not have approved so, rather than jeopardise his career, he published anonymously.

An engraving of Walter Scott from a painting by T. Lawrence.

After the success of *Waverley*, Scott turned into a virtual novel-writing machine, producing some of his best work over the next five years, all without giving up the day job and all published anonymously, including *Guy Mannering* (written in six weeks in 1815), *The Antiquary* (1816), *Old Mortality* (1816), *Rob Roy* (1818), *The Heart of Midlothian* (1818), *The Bride of Lammermoor* (1819) and *Ivanhoe* (1820).

In 1811, he bought a small farm near Melrose called Cartley (nicknamed Clarty Hole) which he renamed Abbotsford, and began building himself what can only be described as a fake castle. In 1823, Maria Edgeworth visited Abbotsford and afterwards wrote, 'All the work is so solid you would never guess it was by a castle-building romance writer and poet.'

Scott was created a baronet in 1820 and did not publicly admit authorship of his novels until 1827. In 1826, disaster struck when he became insolvent after the failure of his printer, James Ballantyne, and his publisher Archibald Constable. As a partner of Ballantyne's, he was liable for debts of over £100,000. His wife Charlotte died the same year.

Most men would have buckled under this enormous burden, but all Scott asked of his creditors was time to write his way out of debt. After his death six years later in 1832, his creditors were paid in full; the novel-writing machine had ground to a halt, leaving Scottish literature more riches than it had ever known. He died at Abbotsford and his remains were laid by the side of those of his wife in the sepulchre of his ancestors in the ruins of Dryburgh Abbey. Lockhart quotes a fitting epitaph from the *Iliad*: 'There lay he, mighty and mightily fallen, having done with his chivalry.'

SEE ALSO: Birthplace of W.S., childhood home of W.S., Lasswade Cottage, The Heart of Midlothian, Greyfriars Kirkyard, Scott Monument, Holyrood Park, St John's Churchyard, The Writers' Museum, High School, Old College, Sciennes Hill House, Assembly Rooms, James Hogg, J.G. Lockhart, Portobello Sands, Archibald Constable, Canongate Kirkyard, The Edinburgh Walter Scott Club.

FURTHER INFORMATION: 39 North Castle Street is not open to the public. James Ballantyne's printing office – Old Paul's Work – was in old Leith Wynd, now the lower end of Cranston Street, off the Canongate. Abbotsford House, situated two miles east of Galashiels, is open to the public from March to October. Tel: 01896 752 043.

Website: www.scottsabbotsford.co.uk.

Three miles away, the Scott's Selkirk weekend festival takes place every December in the Border town of Selkirk, when this royal and ancient burgh celebrates the work of Scott with two days of readings, dramatisations, re-enactments, processions and general mayhem. No one at Scott's Selkirk is a spectator: everyone joins in the fun. www.scottsselkirk.com.

FURTHER READING: W. Elliot, *The Walter Scott Trail* (2001); J. Millgate, *Walter Scott: The Making of the Novelist* (Uni. of Toronto Press, 1987); E. Quayle, *The Ruin of Sir Walter Scott* (Hart-Davis, 1968); Sir W. Scott and W.E.K. Anderson (ed.), *The Journal of Sir Walter Scott* (Oxford Uni. Press, 1972); Sir W. Scott and H.J.C. Grierson (ed.), *The Letters of Sir Walter Scott* (Oxford, Clarendon Press, 1979).

60 GEORGE STREET

Lodgings of Percy Bysshe Shelley (1792–1822)
English lyric poet and writer

> Lift not the painted veil which those who live
> Call Life.
>> Percy Bysshe Shelley, 'Sonnet' (1824)

One of the major English Romantics, Shelley was born in Horsham in Sussex and educated at Eton and Oxford, from where he was expelled in 1810 for contributing to a pamphlet called 'The Necessity of Atheism'. The summer of the same year, he eloped to Edinburgh with 16-year-old Harriet Westbrook, the daughter of a coffee-house proprietor, and they were married at the home of Revd Joseph Robertson at 225 Canongate on 28 August. They stayed for five weeks in the city in a two-storey flat (a third storey was added later) at 60 George Street, the ground floor of which is now a shop.

Novelist and poet Thomas Love Peacock (1785–1866), a close friend of Shelley's, described Harriet as 'fond of her husband, and accommodated herself in every way to his tastes. If they mixed in society, she adorned it; if they lived in retirement, she was satisfied; if they travelled, she enjoyed the change of scene.' Shelley and Harriet had two children, but their marriage collapsed in 1814 when Shelley fell in love with 16-year-old Mary Wollstonecraft Godwin, whom he described as 'a dream from heaven'. In December of 1816, Harriet drowned herself in the Serpentine, and in the same month Shelley and Mary Godwin were married. After Harriet's death, her family brought a petition before the courts which effectively deprived Shelley of the custody of his children, making them wards of the court.

An eccentric and a nomad, Shelley, when not writing masterpieces like *Prometheus Unbound* (1820), spent his short life dodging creditors, speaking in public or writing on subjects such as political reform, democracy and vegetarianism. The pressure of creditors and being ostracised socially eventually drove him abroad. In 1818, the Shelleys left England for good and settled in Italy, where Shelley was drowned when the schooner *Ariel* sank in a violent summer squall off the coast near Livorno in August 1822. Mary returned to England in 1823 with her son Percy. She lived until the age of 53 and is best remembered not for marrying Percy Shelley, but for her first, ground-breaking novel, *Frankenstein* (1818).

FURTHER INFORMATION: Fleeing their ever-present creditors, the Shelleys returned to Edinburgh in 1813 and lodged fleetingly at 36 Frederick Street.

Frankenstein's, a themed pub (based more on the films than the novel), is situated at 26 George IV Bridge.

FURTHER READING: K.N. Cameron, *Shelley: The Golden Years* (Harvard Uni. Press, 1974) and *The Young Shelley: Genesis of a Radical* (Gollancz, 1951); R. Holmes, *Shelley: The Pursuit* (Weidenfeld & Nicolson, 1974); T.L. Peacock, *Memoirs of Shelley* (Hart-Davis, 1970).

57 GEORGE STREET

Ottakar's
Named after the Tintin title *King Ottakar's Sceptre*, this chain began in 1987 when James Heneage and Philip Dunne raised venture-capital finance to open three branches in Brighton, Banbury and Salisbury. Growing slowly to begin with, its successful formula attracted backers, and in 1998 the company floated on the London Stock Exchange. In 2002, it acquired eight branches of Edinburgh's James Thin's Booksellers, and today its George Street shop occupies the site of the old Edinburgh Bookshop. The shop offers a huge selection of children's books and educational toys, a comprehensive range of Scottish titles and a growing stationery department. If they don't have it, chances are

they can get it in a couple of days or so depending upon availability. Brodies Coffee Shop is upstairs, and they even have a lift.

FURTHER INFORMATION:

Opening hours:
9 a.m.–7 p.m. Monday, Wednesday and Friday;
9.30 a.m.–7 p.m. Tuesday; 9 a.m.–8 p.m. Thursday;
9 a.m.–6 p.m. Saturday; 11.30 a.m.–5.30 p.m. Sunday.
Tel: 0131 225 4495. Email: george.street@ottakars.co.uk.

54 GEORGE STREET

The Assembly Rooms
Where Sir Walter Scott first publicly admitted the authorship of the Waverley novels

> The novel was not the form of literature in the best repute, and a Clerk of Court, who had hopes of the Bench, and whose name had so far only been associated with the responsible roles of poet, critic and antiquary, might well seek an incognito when he appeared in the character of a popular entertainer.
>
> John Buchan, *Sir Walter Scott* (1932)

Many literary legends have given readings in the Assembly Rooms, including Charles Dickens and William Thackeray, but probably its most memorable literary event happened at a Theatrical Fund dinner on 23 February 1827, when Sir Walter Scott, after 13 years of the public's postulation and conjecture, finally admitted that he was the author of the Waverley novels. It had long been an open secret, and when Lord Meadowbank, who had been asked to propose a toast, took him aside, he asked him if the time had not come to own up to their parentage. Scott smiled, and said, 'Do just as you like – only don't say much about so old a story.' (Lockhart's *Life*.) When Meadowbank made his announcement, the 300 diners stood up on their chairs and tables, and their applause was said to be deafening. Scott, known as 'The Wizard of the North', replied, 'The wand is broken and the book buried.'

Scott desired anonymity initially because the novel at that time was judged to be of low moral and artistic status, and he didn't want to jeopardise his reputation. But there was also another reason. What a lark it must have been to have written successive bestsellers signed simply, 'By the author of *Waverley*', while critics and the public were kept guessing year after year. It was also slightly fashionable to publish anonymously, but it's more likely he just loved playing at being a literary Scarlet Pimpernel.

SEE ALSO: Birthplace of W.S., childhood home of W.S., townhouse of W.S., Lasswade Cottage, Parliament Hall, Greyfriars Kirkyard, St John's Churchyard, The Heart of Midlothian, Holyrood Park, The Writers' Museum, Old College, Sciennes Hill House, Scott Monument, High School, J.G. Lockhart, Portobello Sands, The Edinburgh Walter Scott Club.

FURTHER INFORMATION: Scott's novels sold in enormous numbers in the USA, but largely in pirated editions. A copy of *Quentin Durward* was received by an American printer in 1823 and within 28 hours pirate copies had been printed and bound and were ready for sale.

The Assembly Rooms, designed by John Henderson, was built in 1782–7 by public subscription, and its chandeliers and mirrored walls have played host to dinners, balls, conferences and concerts for over 200 years. The arcaded Doric portico overhanging the pavement was added in 1818.

45 GEORGE STREET

Offices of *Blackwood's Magazine* from 1830 to 1972

> Ever since the days of John Keats, to be bludgeoned by
> Blackwood has been the hallmark of an author of ideas.
> Thomas Hardy, 1907

Blackwood's Magazine, the monthly periodical known affectionately as 'The Maga', was launched by Edinburgh bookseller and publisher William Blackwood (1776–1834) from his bookshop at 17 Princes Street in 1817 as a Tory rival to the Whig-dominated *Edinburgh Review*. It began as the *Edinburgh Monthly Magazine*, but within six months it changed its title to *Blackwood's Edinburgh Magazine*, and from 1906 onwards became *Blackwood's Magazine*.

The witty satirical journalism of its early editors John Wilson and John Gibson Lockhart set the tone of *The Maga* as it praised and pilloried leading literary figures of the day. Depending on your point of view, you either rolled about in hysterics or contacted your lawyer. 'How I have longed for their utter extinction!' wrote Gerard Manley Hopkins in 1863.

Many of the literary greats of the nineteenth and early twentieth century were published in *Blackwood's*, notably Sir Walter Scott, Anthony Trollope, Joseph Conrad, James Hogg, Thomas De Quincey, John Galt, Susan Ferrier, Henry James, Oscar Wilde, Elizabeth Barrett Browning, R.D. Blackmore, John Buchan, Walter de la Mare, J.B. Priestley, Neil Munro and Hugh MacDiarmid. The talents of the unknown George Eliot were not lost on *Blackwood's*, who serialised her first fictional work, *The Sad Fortunes of Amos Barton*, in 1857, and went on to publish all her works except *Romola*.

Blackwood's failed, however, to detect genius when they rejected a short story entitled 'The Haunted Grange of Goresthorpe' submitted by an 18-year-old Edinburgh medical student in 1877. The story was filed by *Blackwood's* and was never returned to the student because he failed to supply a stamped addressed envelope. It lay forgotten until the Blackwood archives were presented to the National Library of Scotland in 1942. The story was written by Arthur Conan Doyle, and although the names are different, the characters in the tale are clearly blueprints of Sherlock Holmes and Dr Watson.

The magazine ceased publication in December 1980 after more than 180 years, a victim of changing taste and style, an ageing readership and falling advertising revenue.

SEE ALSO: William Blackwood, John Wilson, J.G. Lockhart, John Buchan, James Hogg, Thomas De Quincey, Sir Walter Scott, Susan Ferrier, Oscar Wilde, John Galt, Neil Munro, Hugh MacDiarmid.

FURTHER INFORMATION: The Blackwood archives can be consulted at the National Library of Scotland, George IV Bridge.

FURTHER READING: F.D. Tredrey, *The House of Blackwood, 1804–1954* (W. Blackwood & Sons, 1954); M. Oliphant, *Annals of a Publishing House* (W. Blackwood & Sons, 1897).

CORNER OF ST COLME AND NORTH CHARLOTTE STREET

The Catherine Sinclair Monument

> All play of imagination is now carefully discouraged, and books written for young persons are generally a mere record of dry facts.
>
> From the preface of *Holiday House* (1839)

At the western end of Queen Street stands the Catherine Sinclair Monument, an imperious Gothic memorial designed by architect David Bryce (1803–76) for novelist and philanthropist Catherine Sinclair (1800–64), best known for her classic children's novel *Holiday House*.

Born in Edinburgh, she was the fourth daughter of agrarian reformer Sir John Sinclair, and at the age of 14 she became her father's secretary until his death in 1835. After her father's demise, she started writing and evolved into a prolific writer of travel, biography, children's books, novels and essays. Unlike most Victorian children's books, which guaranteed a predictably moralising tale, Sinclair's *Holiday House* attempted to reverse the trend, and was an enormous success with young readers. Apart from writing, she also immersed herself in philanthropic works, namely setting up workers' canteens, funding street fountains and benches, and founding a Volunteer Brigade for boys in Leith. She is buried close by at St John's Churchyard at the west end of Princes Street.

FURTHER INFORMATION: Catherine Sinclair is often credited as being the first person to guess the identity of the author of *Waverley*, published anonymously by Sir Walter Scott in 1814. This seems unlikely, as it became an open secret at the time, and a fairly well known one, although Scott only 'officially' admitted authorship in 1827.

SEE ALSO: The Assembly Rooms.

8 YOUNG STREET

The Oxford Bar

Wullie Roose's Coxfork in Bung Strait
Sydney Goodsir Smith, *Carotid Cornucopius* (1947)

Today this pub is synonymous with Ian Rankin and Inspector Rebus, who both regularly drink here. You may, therefore, catch a glimpse of Ian Rankin, but the closest you'll get to Rebus is by ordering a beetroot-filled 'Rebus Roll'. The Oxford Bar has always

been a popular watering hole for Scottish writers and artists, especially those of the Scottish Renaissance, who frequented it when it was run by the late and legendary Willie Ross. Ian Rankin gave a colourful description of Ross in *Guardian Unlimited* in October 2002:

> He left in 1979, just before I started drinking there . . . You weren't allowed to hit on women because no women were allowed in. There was no women's toilet. If you were English, you weren't allowed in. If you were a student, you weren't allowed in. If you asked for food, like a packet of crisps, he dragged you outside, pointed at the sign and said, 'Does that say bar or fucking restaurant?' Some people have got great stories about him. He sounds like a terrible man to me, but a character, and you need characters.

Although Willie Ross is now part of the pub's history, there is no shortage of colourful characters at the Oxford Bar and, as one local commented, 'It's the only pub I know with an emergency entrance.'

SEE ALSO: The Abbotsford, Milnes Bar, Sandy Bell's.

FURTHER INFORMATION: The Oxford Bar, 8 Young Street, Edinburgh EH2 4JB. Tel: 0131 539 7119.
Website: www.oxfordbar.com.

(1 QUEEN STREET)

Scottish National Portrait Gallery

> Is the painting famous? Yes! Think of all the people who
> have carefully spared one minute of their lives to stand
> in front of it.
>
> Jeanette Winterson, *Art Objects* (1995)

Countless portraits of wordsmiths are entombed within the
trappings of this hallowed Gothic shrine, perpetually dangled
for the delight of the literary pilgrim. There's something slightly
eerie about staring at portraits, a bit like gawking at the dead,
but portraits can be uncannily alive and a painting reveals so
much more than a photograph. Hugh MacDiarmid looks as if he
is definitely gagging for a wee dram, Compton Mackenzie's
haemorrhoids were clearly acting up that day and J.M. Barrie
resembles an assassin on his day off. Other faces behind the nib
worth tracking down include Alexander Naysmith's classic
portrait of Robert Burns, which has graced many a shortbread
tin, Raeburn's Sir Walter Scott, and portraits of James Boswell,
Thomas Carlyle, Robert Fergusson, Susan Ferrier, Alasdair Gray,
Eric Linklater, Robert Garioch, Naomi Mitchison, Thomas De
Quincey, Muriel Spark, Margaret Oliphant, Neil Gunn and many
more. The portraits are continually rotated as the collection is
too vast to display in its entirety. The building is also home to
the National Collection of Photography, which features many
literary figures. The photography collection can be viewed by
appointment in the Print Room, which also houses a large
collection of engravings and drawings.

FURTHER INFORMATION: The Gallery is close to St Andrew Square
Bus Station and a few minutes from the east end of Princes
Street. Admission is free, although a charge is made for some
exhibitions.

FURTHER INFORMATION: Opening times: daily 10 a.m.–5 p.m. Late
night Thursday until 7 p.m. Extended hours during the
Edinburgh Summer Festivals. Closed 25 and 26 December
and restricted hours over New Year. Tel: 0131 332 2266.
Website: www.nationalgalleries.org.

The National Galleries of Scotland Picture Library can
supply copies of works from the collections as photographs
or prints on canvas. For details, call: 0131 624 6258/6260.

36 INDIA STREET

Site of 'Cocky' Henderson's School
Former school of Robert Louis Stevenson (1850–94)

> Here we suffer grief and pain
> Under Mr Hendie's cane
> If you don't obey his laws
> He will punish with his tawse
> Robert Louis Stevenson

Schooling for the young Louis Stevenson was always an unpredictable and erratic experience due to his chronic ill health, which meant he was often absent for long periods at a time. His

first school was at Canonmills (on the hill between Warriston Road and Broughton Road, now a Baptist Church), where he was reputedly teased and generally given a rough time of it. He next attended Thomas Henderson's School, a preparatory establishment in India Street, health permitting, from 1857 to 1861. Rosaline Masson, in her *Life of Robert Louis Stevenson* (1923), writes that the neighbours observed

36 India Street.

'young Mrs Stevenson running the little fellow up and down sunny Heriot Row after breakfast to warm him before his school hours'. In later life, Louis met someone who had also attended Mr Henderson's School, commenting, 'Oh, shades of Cocky Henderson and the companions of my palmy days! I too was at this school in the days of my misspent youth.' Between 1861 and 1862, he briefly attended Edinburgh Academy on Henderson Row, where his 'customary place' was 'pretty well down in the class', according to fellow pupil G.M. Stuart's reminiscences in Masson's *I Can Remember Robert Louis Stevenson* (1922).

SEE ALSO: Howard Place, Inverleith Terrace, Heriot Row, Pilrig House, Colinton Manse, Swanston Cottage, Baxter's Place, Glencorse Kirk, Rutherford's Howff, New Calton Cemetery, Old Calton Burial Ground, St Giles, Hawes Inn, Rullion Green, W.E. Henley, Alison Cunningham, Deacon Brodie, *Kidnapped* Statue, RLS Club, Museum of Scotland, George Mackenzie, Martyrs' Monument, Edinburgh Castle, Old College, Parliament Hall, Holyrood Park, Royal College of Surgeons' Museum, R.M. Ballantyne, RLS Memorial, Writers' Corner.

17 HERIOT ROW

Former home of Robert Louis Stevenson (1850–94)

> For we are very lucky with a lamp before the door,
> And Leerie stops to light it as he lights so many more;
> And O! before you hurry by with ladder and with light,
> O Leerie, see a little child and nod to him tonight!
>
> RLS, from 'The Lamplighter',
> *A Child's Garden of Verses* (1885)

Thomas Stevenson, engineer to the Northern Lighthouse Board, was prospering, and his new house reflected it. The Stevensons moved to Heriot Row in 1857, a Georgian street in Edinburgh's New Town which today still exudes affluence and pedigree. Built between 1802 and 1806, this large terraced house overlooking Queen Street Gardens is spacious enough to billet a boy-scout troop. For the three Stevensons and a couple of servants, it must have seemed positively Brobdingnagian. Looking at no. 17 from the street, Louis's bedroom was situated on the top floor on the far right, overlooking the gardens. These were the windows from which the sickly Louis would have observed Leerie, 'The Lamplighter', and heard the coarse cries of the carters as they wound their way up from Stockbridge to the town.

Thomas Stevenson had hoped that his son would follow in his footsteps and become an engineer, but Louis gave up his engineering studies in favour of law, passing his Bar exams in 1875. Louis the advocate, however, was never a serious proposition. What he really wanted to be was a writer, an artist and a free spirit. In appearance and lifestyle, he was already halfway there, wandering around the Old Town in his famous velvet jacket, carousing with the city's underbelly and sowing his wild oats. And, like all good bohemians, he doubted the existence of God (which infuriated his father), became seriously depressed, wrote and abandoned novels, fell in love with an older woman and yearned to travel.

In France in 1876, he met his future wife, Fanny Osbourne, and in the same year he canoed through Belgium and France with his friend Walter Simpson, a journey which inspired the creation of his first book, *An Inland Voyage* (1878). In 1878, he tramped across the Cévennes with his obstreperous donkey Modestine, which resulted in *Travels with a Donkey* (1879). He travelled to California in pursuit of Fanny in 1879, a trip which nearly killed him. The literary outcome of this was *The Silverado Squatters* (1883). After marrying Fanny, who was ten years his senior, Stevenson and his new wife returned to Britain in 1884

A youthful Louis.

and settled in Bournemouth for three years. His short stories, essays and travel writings were now appearing regularly in magazines and in 1883 he published *Treasure Island*, his first full-length work of fiction. *The Strange Case of Dr Jekyll and Mr Hyde* (1886) and *Kidnapped* (1886) followed, establishing his reputation as a master storyteller.

Following his father's death in May 1887, he returned home for the funeral. However, he was too ill on the day of the service to attend. This was to be his last visit to Heriot Row before departing for the South Seas in 1888.

Flora Masson recalled his departure from Edinburgh in *I Can Remember Robert Louis Stevenson* (1922):

> An open cab, with a man and a woman in it, seated side by side, and leaning back – the rest of the cab piled high with rather untidy luggage – came slowly towards us . . . As it passed us, out on the broad roadway . . . a slender, loose garbed figure stood up in the cab and waved a wide-brimmed hat.
> 'Good-bye!' he called to us. 'Good-bye!'

Searching for the climate that he hoped would prolong his life, Stevenson eventually settled in Samoa. In his exile, he still wrote prodigiously, notably *Island Nights Entertainments* (1893) and his unfinished masterpiece *Weir of Hermiston* (1896). Not even an island paradise, however, could prolong his life. He died of a brain haemorrhage shortly after 8 p.m. on 3 December 1894 and is buried on the summit of Mount Vea in Samoa.

SEE ALSO: The Edinburgh Book Lovers' Tour, Howard Place, Inverleith Terrace, Pilrig House, Colinton Manse, Swanston Cottage, Baxter's Place, Glencorse Kirk, Rutherford's Howff, New Calton Cemetery, Old Calton Burial Ground, St Giles, Hawes Inn, Rullion Green, W.E. Henley, Alison Cunningham, Henderson's School, Deacon Brodie, The Writers' Museum, *Kidnapped* Statue, RLS Club, Museum of Scotland, George Mackenzie, Martyrs' Monument, Edinburgh Castle, Old College, Parliament Hall, Holyrood Park, Royal College of Surgeons' Museum, R.M. Ballantyne, RLS Memorial, Writers' Corner.

FURTHER INFORMATION: 17 Heriot Row is not open to the public, but it does operate as a bed and breakfast, and is available to hire for dinners, weddings or any other special occasions. Accommodation consists of one double bedroom and one twin bedroom at the rear of the house with a view of Fife. The double bedroom used to be the bedroom of RLS's parents, with the en suite bathroom being the original

Stevenson installation. Contact John and Felicitas Macfie on 0131 556 1896. Email: mail@stevenson-house.co.uk. Website: www.stevenson-house.co.uk.

For literary dinners at 17 Heriot Row, see the Edinburgh Book Lovers' Tour. An information panel, erected by the RLS Club, can be seen opposite the house on the railings of Queen Street Gardens.

FURTHER READING: RLS, *Edinburgh: Picturesque Notes* (Pallas Athene, 2003); R. Masson (ed.), *I Can Remember Robert Louis Stevenson* (1922); E.B. Simpson, *Robert Louis Stevenson's Edinburgh Days* (Kessinger, 2005); J. Calder, *Stevenson and Victorian Scotland* (Edinburgh Uni. Press, 1984).

(4 NELSON STREET)

Former home of Robert Garioch (1909–81)
Scottish satirical poet and translator

> But truth it is, our couthie city
> has cruddit in twa parts a bittie
> Robert Garioch, from 'To Robert Fergusson' (1950)

Garioch's poem 'To Robert Fergusson' was addressed to a poet with whom he felt a special kinship. Both wrote in Scots and had a passion for Edinburgh – the city that 'speaks twa tongues' – which they observed and celebrated throughout their lives, memorialising the city, warts and all, in their own 'coorse and grittie' verse.

Born Robert Garioch Sutherland on 9 May 1909, he was educated at the Royal High School and Edinburgh University. During the Second World War, he was a POW for four years, an experience he recounted in his only prose work, *Two Men and a Blanket*, written in 1945 but not published until 1975. A shy, retiring man, he spent most of his life as a schoolmaster, teaching in Scotland and London. Although Garioch wrote comic verse, it would be wrong to dismiss him as a comic lightweight, for his poetry has great depth, and had he not chosen to write mainly in Lallans (a distinctive Scottish literary form of English, based on standard older Scots), there is no

4 Nelson Street.

doubt he would have had a wider audience. Scottish literature is, nonetheless, much the richer for it. Whether in the informal style of 'Fi'baw in the Street' and 'Heard in the Cougate', or the formal language of poems like 'The Muir' and 'The Wire', his poetry has universal appeal. He undertook Scots versions of George Buchanan's Latin tragedies, *Jepthah and The Baptist*, and also produced translations from the Roman sonnets of Guiseppe Belli. His first book of poetry, *17 poems for 6d: in Gaelic, Lowland Scots and English* (1940), was published jointly with Gaelic poet Sorley Maclean (1911–96). His last individual volume was *Doktor Faust in Rose Street* (1973) and his long-awaited *Complete Poetical Works* was published in 1983. He died on 26 April 1981, aged 71.

Poet Donald Campbell recalled in 1981 that 'if I learned anything at all from Robert Garioch, it was to do the work as well as I could do it and not worry too much about either the applause of success or the obscurity of failure.'

SEE ALSO: Robert Fergusson, Old College.

3 ABERCROMBY PLACE

Birthplace of Marie Stopes (1880–1958)
Birth-control pioneer and author of *Married Love* (1918)

> Jeanie, Jeanie, full of hopes,
> Read a book by Marie Stopes.
> Now, to judge by her condition,
> She must have read the wrong edition
>   Children's playground chant, London, 1924

Condemned by the Catholic Church and denounced as a worse enemy of the Empire than Hitler or Goebbels, Marie Stopes's pioneering work on sex education and birth control freed countless women from the anguish of sexual ignorance and accidental pregnancy. She wrote over 70 books, including volumes of plays, novels and poetry, but it is her works on parenthood, birth control and sexual fulfilment within marriage, notably *Married Love*, for which she will be remembered. *Married Love* was written by Stopes during the

Marie Stopes in 1915.

185

First World War after her first unhappy and unconsummated marriage, and discusses frankly the then sacred mystery of mating, arguing that marriage should be an equal relationship between husband and wife. It caused an outcry on publication and was declared obscene in the USA, where it was promptly banned. Despite the controversy, the book was an immediate success, selling two thousand copies in two weeks. By the end of the year, it had been reprinted six times and it was later translated into fifteen languages.

Marie Charlotte Carmichael Stopes was the daughter of English engineer, architect and fossil collector Henry Stopes and Edinburgh native Charlotte Carmichael, daughter of landscape painter J.F. Carmichael. In 1898, she won a science scholarship to University College, London, and in 1901 achieved a double first in botany and geology. In 1904, she was awarded a doctorate in Munich for her work on fossilised plants. She also became a passionate supporter of the women's suffrage campaign. In 1911, her marriage to Reginald Gates was a union which proved to be both antagonistic and sexless. Gates was impotent and Stopes was so sexually ignorant it took her three years to comprehend the fact. The marriage was annulled in 1916 and Stopes began writing *Married Love*, stating in the preface to the first English edition that in 'my first marriage I paid such a terrible price for sex-ignorance that I feel that knowledge gained at such a cost should be placed at the service of humanity'.

She first became interested in birth control after a meeting in London with American campaigner and former nurse Margaret Sanger, who fled America after being charged with publishing an 'obscene and lewd' birth-control article. In 1918, Stopes wrote her contraception guide, *Wise Parenthood*, and in 1921 she founded the Society for Constructive Birth Control.

Her second husband was aircraft manufacturer Humphrey Roe, and with his help and money she opened the Mothers' Clinic in Holloway, North London – Britain's first birth-control clinic – on 17 March 1921, offering a free service to women. A small network of clinics soon followed and today the Marie Stopes International Global Partnership works in 37 countries.

Margaret Pyke, chair of the Family Planning Association, commented in 1962, 'In a final estimate, Marie Stopes may well prove to have been one of the most important and outstanding influences of the twentieth century – a judgement with which, one feels sure, she would be in complete agreement.'

FURTHER READING: R. Hall, *Marie Stopes* (Deutsch, 1977); M. Box, *The Trial of Marie Stopes* (Femina Books, 1967).

25 DRUMMOND PLACE

Former home of Sydney Goodsir Smith (1915–75)
Poet, dramatist, novelist and critic

> A most lovable, unpretentious and compassionate man who, as poet, translator, literary critic, art critic, dramatist, and editor displayed a record of versatility hardly any of his contemporaries come near equalling.
>
> Hugh MacDiarmid

Although born in Wellington, New Zealand, it was 'the auld toon o' Edinburgh' that was Sydney Goodsir Smith's spiritual home. He wrote about what he saw in the city, often fused with the common speech of his favourite Edinburgh howffs, in lively and humorous Lallan lyrics. Regarded as one of Scotland's leading literary scholars and a major figure in the Scottish Renaissance, he

25 Drummond Place.

was also a well-known broadcaster, dramatist, novelist and critic, but he will be best remembered as a poet who invoked and upheld the spoken tradition of Scottish verse in the essence of Dunbar and Fergusson. His greatest achievement was *Under the Eildon Tree* (1948), now acknowledged as one of the masterpieces of Scottish poetry.

He arrived in Edinburgh in 1927 when his father became professor of forensic medicine at Edinburgh University. He studied medicine at Edinburgh University, but abandoned it to read history at Oriel College, Oxford. He started writing poetry in Scots in the 1930s and during the Second World War taught English to Polish troops.

Writing poetry in a language which is not one's native tongue can be problematic for an audience. Stanley Roger Green attempted to explain this enigma in his 1975 'Appreciation' of Smith:

> At first, like most people who knew him, I was puzzled by the apparent paradoxes in his nature. A life-long socialist with aristocratic tastes: a New Zealander educated mainly in England who became one of our greatest modern patriots: a man with a gentlemanly 'English' accent who carried Lallans to heights of virtuosity which few have emulated . . . Only when I came to know him better did I realise that here was one of those outstanding people who are too richly varied, too kaleidoscopic in character to be constrained by

ordinary definitions, and that analysis of such a person
is almost an impertinence.

Smith's interests and talents were wide-ranging. As a
playwright, he wrote the verse play *The Wallace* in 1960. As a
novelist, he penned *Carotid Cornucopius* in 1947, in which
Carotid, the Caird o' the Cannon Gait, visits the well-known
watering holes of 'Sunday Balls in Fairest Redd' (Sandy Bell's),
'the Abbotsfork in Low Street' (The Abbotsford), 'Doddie
Mullun's' (Milnes Bar) and 'Wullie Roose's Coxfork in Bung
Strait' (the Oxford Bar). Hugh MacDiarmid described *Carotid*

Cornucopius as 'doing
for Edinburgh no less
successfully   what
Joyce did for Dublin in
Ulysses'.   His   first
collection of   poetry
was   *Skail   Wind*,
published   in   1941.
Other works include
The   Deevil's   Waltz
(1946), *So Late Into the
Night* (1952), *Figs and
Thistles* (1959), *Kynd
Kittock's Land* (1965)
and   *Gowdspink   in
Reekie* (1974).

Sydney Goodsir Smith with Norman MacCaig.

Sydney   Goodsir
Smith lived for many years in 'Schloss Schimdt' at 50 Craigmillar
Park and in later life at 25 Drummond Place. He died a relatively
young man, aged 59, in 1975 and is buried in Dean Cemetery.
Scottish poet Tom Scott attended his funeral and recorded his
last farewell in the *Scotia Review*, April 1975:

> On the Sunday, after the funeral at which strong men
> grat and some less strong were feart to greet, I went to
> the cemetery to spend a last half hour with him. The
> roses were already frost-bitten, and on impulse I cut
> one off, took it home, kept it in a whisky bottle till it
> faded, then buried the calyx deep in our rose-bed here.
> Silly, but I FELT so relieved.

SEE ALSO: Sandy Bell's, The Abbotsford, Oxford Bar, Milnes Bar.
FURTHER READING: H. MacDiarmid, *Sydney Goodsir Smith*
(Hamilton, 1963); E. Gold, *Sydney Goodsir Smith's* Under the
Eildon Tree (Akros, 1975).

31 DRUMMOND PLACE

Home of Compton Mackenzie (1883–1972)
Novelist, biographer, essayist, poet, travel writer, journalist and secret agent

> Many romantic pages have been written about the sunken Spanish galleon in the bay of Tobermory. That 4,000-ton steamship on the rocks off Little Todday provided more practical romance in three and a half hours than the Tobermory galleon has provided in three and a half centuries. Doubloons, ducats, and ducatoons, moidores, pieces of eight, sequins, guineas, rose and angel nobles, what are these to vaunt above the liquid gold carried by the *Cabinet Minister*?
>
> Compton Mackenzie, *Whisky Galore* (1946)

Mackenzie based *Whisky Galore* on actual events which occurred in 1941 when the 4,000-ton cargo ship SS *Politician* ran aground

31 Drummond Place.

in treacherous seas in the Sound of Eriskay, off the coast of Barra. Her cargo included pianos, bicycles, Jamaican banknotes and 22,000 cases of whisky. Mackenzie was commander of the Home Guard on Barra at the time, and got his fair share of the 'liquid gold', unlike the pompous Captain Waggett in his novel. When working on the final draft for the script of the 1949 Ealing Studios film adaptation, Mackenzie grumbled, 'Another of my books gone west.' Producer Monja Danischewsky seemed of the same opinion, commenting, 'Well, I don't know . . . all I can see is a lot of elderly Scotsmen sitting by the fire and saying "och aye".' History has proved them both wrong. The film became an Ealing classic and the novel is now ranked amongst the great Highland comedies.

For a successful writer, praised by Henry James and acknowledged as a major influence on Scott Fitzgerald, Compton Mackenzie is today curiously neglected. His main desire was to entertain his readers, and his portraits of couthy Highlanders are uproarious subtle parodies that never patronise.

He was born in West Hartlepool in 1863, the son of actor Edward Compton, and was educated at St Paul's School and Magdalen College, Oxford. He studied for the English Bar, but abandoned law in 1907 to write his first play, *The Gentleman in Grey*. His first novel, *The Passionate Elopement*, was published in 1911. *Carnival* (1912) followed, but it was the publication of

Whisky Galore script conference on Barra, 1948: Compton Mackenzie, Monja Danischewsky (producer) and Alexander Mackendrick (director).

Sinister Street (1913) which won him acclaim. During the First World War, he was recruited into the British Secret Service in Greece, an experience he later recounted in *Greek Memories* (1932). The book was immediately withdrawn, however, and all remaining copies destroyed. Mackenzie was charged with breaching the Official Secrets Act and fined £100.

After the war, he returned to novel writing, producing *Rich Relations* (1921) and two novels about lesbian love, *Vestal Fire* (1927) and *Extraordinary Women* (1928). Between 1937 and 1945, he published the sextet *The Four Winds of Love*, and between 1963 and 1971 he produced his massive ten-volume autobiography, *My Life and Times.*

Mackenzie was a staunch nationalist and a founder member of the Scottish National Party. He was also literary critic of the *Daily Mail* during the 1930s and was the founder editor of *Gramophone* magazine, now the oldest surviving record magazine in the world. He lived for a period in Capri after the war and in 1934 built a house on the island of Barra. He was knighted in 1952.

He died in Edinburgh on 30 November 1972 and is buried at Eoligarry on Barra. During his burial service, piper Calum Johnston, an old friend of Mackenzie, collapsed and died after playing a lament.

FURTHER READING: A. Linklater, *Compton Mackenzie: A Life* (Chatto & Windus, 1987).

(SCOTLAND STREET)

Setting for Alexander McCall Smith's 'daily novel', *44 Scotland Street*

> We hear that Irvine Welsh might be buying a flat in Scotland Street for the next series and will his arrival alter the tone of the place?
> A question from the audience at a special charity reading of *44 Scotland Street*, June 2004

Scotland Street is an unassuming New Town street which does not quite possess the class of Heriot Row or Abercromby Place.

Nevertheless, it is the setting for one of Edinburgh's most famous fictional addresses: no. 44 Scotland Street (the street exists but no. 44 does not). This celebrity status is due to Alexander McCall

Smith's daily novel of the same name which appeared in *The Scotsman* during 2004. To write weekly instalments of a novel for the press is a daunting enough prospect, but to write daily ones is a feat only a novel-writing machine like McCall Smith – who can

polish off 3,000 words before lunch – can tackle. 'In the last three weeks,' he told *The Scotsman* in May 2004, 'I've written episodes at Palm Springs in the Californian desert, in Hollywood and New York, and on the plane between Las Vegas and Virginia. I wrote two the other day, coming up on the train from London.'

McCall Smith – Sandy to his friends – grew up in Zimbabwe, then Rhodesia, and was educated there and in Scotland. He became a law professor and is currently professor of medical law at Edinburgh University. He also helped set up a new law school at the University of Botswana, is an international authority on genetics, and advisor to UNESCO and the UK

Alexander McCall Smith.
(© Graham Clark)

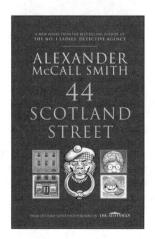

government on bioethics. How he has found the time to write more than 50 books over the past 20 years is anybody's guess.

Although he's written specialist academic titles, children's books and short-story collections, it was his 1998 detective novel, *The No. 1 Ladies' Detective Agency*, which introduced his heroine Mma Ramotswe, Botswana's finest – and only – female detective, which shot him to literary super-stardom. More than four million copies of the books in the series have been sold in the English-speaking world, and they have been translated into 26 other languages from Catalan to Estonian. He also created Isabel Dalhousie, a respectable lady detective who inhabits genteel Merchiston, in *The Sunday Philosophy Club*, in which a young man plunges to his death from the gods in Edinburgh's Usher Hall.

When not on gruelling American book tours, McCall Smith lives in Edinburgh with his wife and two daughters. He plays the bassoon with 'The Really Terrible Orchestra', but dislikes 'the very high notes'. And by the way, not only is no. 44 Scotland Street fictitious, but its residents are too, so if you're after the blood of Bruce, the vain surveyor, you'll have to vent your wrath on someone else.

14 CUMBERLAND STREET

Former student lodgings of J.M. Barrie (1860–1937)
Scottish novelist and dramatist

> Oh, for an hour of Herod.
> Anthony Hope's comment after watching a
> performance of *Peter Pan*.

Chiefly remembered today as the creator of *Peter Pan*, James Matthew Barrie rose from humble origins to become one of the most praised and successful dramatists of his day. Wealth and fame, however, failed to bring him happiness, and he spent much of his life trying to win the love denied him as a child. His generosity could be overwhelming, his affection intense and possessive. Small in stature, shy, secretive and with unpredictable moods, Barrie was an odd and complex genius.

14 Cumberland Street.

He was born on 9 May 1860 in Kirriemuir, the ninth child of Margaret Ogilvy and David Barrie, a hand-loom weaver. They had ten children in all: seven daughters and three sons. David, his mother's favourite son, died tragically in a skating accident aged fourteen, when James was six. His mother was 'always delicate from that hour', he recalled, and constantly thinking of her boy who was gone. She never recovered from her loss and throughout his childhood James tried desperately to replace him, yearning for his mother's love.

He attended Glasgow Academy, Dumfries Academy and the local school in Kirriemuir. When he was 18, he entered Edinburgh University, the fees for which were paid by his elder brother, Alec, with whom he shared lodgings at the top of a house at 14 Cumberland Street. His father sent him an allowance, which he supplemented by writing theatre reviews for the *Edinburgh Courant*. He lived frugally and kept pretty much to himself. A fellow student described him as 'a spare, short figure in a warm-looking Highland cloak'. In 1882, he received his degree and had his photograph taken in cap and gown, with 'hair straggling under the cap as tobacco may straggle over the side of a tin when there is difficulty in squeezing down the lid'.

He was writing regularly by this time, but apart from a few articles written for the *Courant*, no one was interested in publishing his work. In 1883, more in desperation than as a career move, he started work as a leader writer for the *Nottingham Journal*, eventually moving to London in 1885, where he began freelancing. In 1888, he published the first of his Kailyard stories, *Auld Licht Idylls* (1888), followed by *A Window in Thrums* (1889) and *The Little Minister* (1891). His first play, *Richard Savage*, was performed in London in 1891, and from this point onwards he wrote mainly for the theatre. J.M. Barrie was becoming a talent to be reckoned with.

In 1894, he married 32-year-old actress Mary Ansell, who discovered on her wedding night that Barrie was impotent; consequently their marriage was never consummated. Barrie refused to discuss his problem or seek medical advice. Mary made the best of it, but effectively they ended up living separate lives, eventually divorcing in 1909.

Between 1901 and 1920, Barrie produced his most successful plays, including *Quality Street* (1901), *The Admirable Crichton* (1902), *Peter Pan* (1904), *What Every Woman Knows* (1906), *Dear Brutus* (1917) and *Mary Rose* (1920).

In 1897, he began a curious infatuation with Sylvia Llewelyn Davies and her young sons, to whom he became an oppressive and domineering guardian, lavishing gifts, holidays, money and counsel. Sylvia and her husband died young and Barrie unofficially adopted the five children; they became literally the 'Lost Boys'. One of them, Michael, photographed by Barrie in 1906, was the original inspiration for the Peter Pan statue in Kensington Gardens. Another of the boys, Peter, once described *Peter Pan* as 'that terrible masterpiece'.

The 'little Scotchman' died on 19 June 1937 and is buried in the town cemetery, Kirriemuir.

SEE ALSO: Old College, Rutherford's Howff, W.E. Henley.

FURTHER INFORMATION: J.M. Barrie also lived at 3 Great King Street and 20 Shandwick Place. His birthplace at 9 Brechin Road, Kirriemuir, is now a museum containing manuscripts, diaries, photographs and Barrie's own writing desk. The National Library of Scotland contains his university notebooks. Barrie bequeathed the perpetual rights of *Peter Pan* to the Great Ormond Street Hospital for Sick Children.

FURTHER READING: J. Dunbar, *J.M. Barrie, The Man Behind the Image* (Collins, 1970); C. Asquith, *Haply I May Remember* (1950), *Portrait of Barrie* (Barrie, 1954); V. Meynell (ed.), *Letters of J.M. Barrie* (London, 1942).

6 GLOUCESTER PLACE

Christopher North House Hotel, former home of John Wilson (1785–1854)
Scottish critic, novelist, essayist and editor of *Blackwood's Edinburgh Magazine*, who wrote under the pseudonym Christopher North

> I like to abuse my friends
>
> John Wilson

Damning wit and a mastery of the art of the spoof catapulted John Wilson to the centre stage of early-nineteenth-century literary Edinburgh when he became co-editor, along with John Gibson Lockhart, of *Blackwood's Edinburgh Magazine* in 1817.

Born in Paisley, the son of a wealthy gauze manufacturer, he was educated at Glasgow and Oxford, where he built up a reputation as a poet and an athlete. After graduating, he bought an estate in Windermere, where he befriended Wordsworth, Coleridge, Southey and De Quincey. Through an uncle's mismanagement, he lost his estate. He moved to Edinburgh, where he qualified as an advocate, but never practised. His writings were relatively successful, but it was his connection with *Blackwood's Edinburgh Magazine* which established the literary reputation for which he is remembered.

6 Gloucester Place.

William Blackwood's '*Maga*', a direct challenge to the Whig-dominated *Edinburgh Review*, got off to a shaky start when it first appeared on 1 April 1817. After six monthly issues, it was clearly no match for the *Edinburgh Review* and looked like ending up a costly failure. Blackwood acted swiftly, sacking its editors and giving editorial control to Wilson and Lockhart. It was the appearance of the 'Translation from an Ancient Chaldee Manuscript' in the October 1817 issue – a biting satire on literary and political Edinburgh written in the language of the Old Testament, the first draft of which was reputedly written by James Hogg – which overnight transformed *Blackwood's Magazine* from a lethargic rag into a flagship of satirical journalism. Nobody was immune from the sting of Wilson's pen, not even his close circle of friends, and no subject was sacrosanct.

A few years later, together with James Hogg, Wilson (writing as Christopher North) created 'Noctes Ambrosianae' for *Blackwood's*: fictional dialogues of alcohol-fuelled evenings spent at Ambrose's Tavern in Gabriel's Road (now demolished, but reputed to have stood on the site of New Register House at the east end of Princes Street).

In 1820, the Tory Town Council elected Wilson to the chair of moral philosophy at Edinburgh University. This was a subject on which he knew next to nothing, but such was the excellence of his oratory that his lectures proved a popular and instructive entertainment for generations of students.

He published a series of rural short stories, collectively entitled *Lights and Shadows of Scottish Life* (1822), and two novels, *The Trials of Margaret Lyndsay* (1823) and *The Foresters* (1825). His *Works* (1855–8) were edited by his son-in-law, James Ferrier, nephew of Susan Ferrier. Wilson lived at various addresses in the city, including his mother's house at 53 Queen Street (where the 'Chaldee' MS was concocted), 29 Ann Street (where De Quincey called one evening and ended up staying for a year) and 6 Gloucester Place, where he lived from 1826 until his death in 1854.

SEE ALSO: James Hogg, Sir Walter Scott, J.G. Lockhart, Thomas De Quincey, *Blackwood's Magazine*, the *Edinburgh Review*, James Thin, Susan Ferrier.

FURTHER INFORMATION: The Christopher North House Hotel, 6 Gloucester Place, Edinburgh EH3 6EF. Tel: 0131 225 2720. Website: www.christophernorth.co.uk.

A statue to John Wilson can be seen at the western end of East Princes Street Gardens.

FURTHER READING: E. Swann, *Christopher North* (1934).

Stockbridge

(**26 NORTH WEST CIRCUS PLACE**)

Stockbridge Bookshop

Opened in April 1981 by Nigel Tranter, Stockbridge Bookshop is the oldest bookstore owned by David Flatman Ltd, better known on the high street as BW! and Bookworld, now the largest Scottish-based bookstore chain. Stock-  bridge Bookshop was originally promoted by Flatman himself pedalling round Edinburgh on a bicycle towing a trailer with the shop advertised on it. The shop stocks a wide range of titles, including many with big discounts. Favourites are fiction, travel, cookery, biography, non-fiction and Scottish titles. They can also order any title in print in Britain, often in as little as 48 hours. They hold regular events, signings and exhibitions, and recently they have been a Fringe venue for Rebus Tours. It's a pity Inspector Rebus was not around to help in their moments of excitement – over the years, they've had two hold-ups, but nobody was injured! Don't let that deter you from visiting – a warm welcome awaits you.

FURTHER INFORMATION: Opening hours: 8.30 a.m.–8 p.m. Monday, Tuesday, Wednesday, Friday and Saturday; 8.30 a.m.–9 p.m. Thursday; 11 a.m.–7 p.m. Sunday. Tel: 0131 225 5355. Email: sbridge@flatman.co.uk.

ST STEPHEN STREET

**Setting for the novels of Joan Lingard (1932–)
Scottish novelist**

Joan Lingard.

When writing about Edinburgh, I place my characters in the parts of the city that I myself have lived in, or else know well, those being the Southside, Marchmont in particular, where I lived as a student, and the New Town/Stockbridge area where I live now and have done for the past 30 years.

Stockbridge has made an appearance in a number of my books, such as the novels *After Colette* (1993) and *The Kiss* (2003), and the children's books *Rags and Riches* (1988), *Odd Girl Out* (1979) and *Me and My Shadow* (2001). *The Kiss* is set partially in Paris but also in the Colonies at Glenogle by the Water of Leith. *Me and My Shadow* opens on the bridge at Stockbridge and moves up the hill to a street reminiscent of Ann Street. In *After Colette*, the central character, Aimée, lives in St Stephen Street, while *Rags and Riches* centres around a second-hand clothes shop in a street which is very similar, though not named. I find the narrow street has an atmosphere of its own, with its mixture of flats, second-hand shops, hairdressers, pubs, restaurants, an art gallery and even a dancing school.

Encarnita's Journey (2005), while being set mostly in Spain, opens and closes in Edinburgh. Encarnita and her daughter, Concepcion, having arrived in Edinburgh, take a taxi from the airport:

Entering Princes Street they caught a brief glimpse of Edinburgh's famous castle sitting high up on its rock before the driver turned off. They speeded up a little now and rattled over cobbles, past imposing squares and dripping green gardens guarded by black, wrought-iron railings until, finally, they entered a small grey street.

This is St Stephen Street. I seem to find it difficult to get away from it.

The setting for my latest children's book, *The Sign of the Black Dagger*, is the Royal Mile – my association with that goes back a long way! I was born in the Canongate, in a taxi cab, to be exact. *The Sign of the Black Dagger* operates on two levels, today and 1796, at the time when Holyrood Abbey with its precincts was a sanctuary for debtors – the three brass letters SSS marking the boundary can still be seen on the roadway – and the Comte D'Artois came from France seeking refuge from his creditors. The children, both present and past, live in the same house in Advocate's Close opposite St Giles Cathedral.

I am currently writing a novel set in 1924 on the Southside, around the Tollcross and Fountainbridge areas – where my mother was born and bred – called *Give Mother My Love*. Willa lives in a tenement flat at Tollcross with the mother of her husband, who is away at sea and sends back missives from exotic places:

From up here she could look down on the intersection, the meeting of the ways, and the traffic coming from four different directions. It was a hub, maybe not of the world, but of the city, and she enjoyed seeing folk out and about on their business and the trams as they came rattling around the clock.

As a writer, I find Edinburgh a stimulating place in which to live, with it being a city of contrasts, both architecturally and socially, and each district having a definite character of its own.

Joan Lingard, 2005

SEE ALSO: Holyrood Abbey, Advocate's Close.

25 ANN STREET

Birthplace of R.M. Ballantyne (1825–94)
Writer of adventure stories and author of *Coral Island*

Roving has always been, and still is, my ruling passion, the joy of my heart, the very sunshine of my existence.

Ralph Rover, *Coral Island* (1857)

One Sunday in 1866 after morning service outside St Cuthbert's Church in Edinburgh's West End, an admiring, thin, long-haired stranger of 16 years approached Ballantyne and invited him to dinner. Unfortunately, he had to decline due to another engagement, and a teenaged Robert Louis Stevenson lost his only chance of making acquaintance with his boyhood hero. Although they never met again, Stevenson acknowledged Ballantyne's influence on his own adventure stories.

Robert Michael Ballantyne was born in Edinburgh in 1825 at 25 Ann Street, Stockbridge, the son of a newspaper editor, and was educated at Edinburgh Academy (1835–7) and privately. Bad financial investments caused the family's fortunes to topple and Ballantyne's life changed dramatically. Between the ages of 16 and 22, he was employed in Canada by the Hudson Bay Company, trading with local Indians in remote areas. In 1847, he returned to Scotland, where he became a clerk at the North British Railway Company in Edinburgh for two years, later working for paper-makers Alexander Cowan and Company. From 1849 to 1855, he was a junior partner at Thomas Constable and Company, a printing house.

Ballantyne had started writing about his adventures while

25 Ann Street.

stationed at the desolate outposts of the Hudson Bay Company and, in 1848, *Hudson's Bay, Every-day Life in the Wilds of North America* was published. An autobiographical work, the book depicts his youth and adventures in Canada. From 1856, he devoted himself entirely to freelance writing and giving lectures.

Annoyed by a mistake he made in *Coral Island* (1858), Ballantyne subsequently travelled widely to gain first-hand knowledge and to thoroughly research the backgrounds of his embryonic stories. He spent three weeks on Bell Rock, near Arbroath, to write *The Lighthouse* (1865) and joined the London Fire Brigade to write *Fighting the Flames* (1867); for *Deep Down* (1868) he lived with the tin miners of St Just for over three months. Experiences as a fireman on board the tender of the London to Edinburgh Express and weeks on the Gull Lightship also provided material for his subsequent novels. Ballantyne was especially careful with the details of local flora and fauna, giving believable settings to his dramatic adventures, whether they entailed capture and escape, shipwrecks or other colourful events.

He became every schoolboy's hero and his lighthearted descriptions of the slaughter of fauna and natives in *Coral Island*, the book for which he will be best remembered, then passed without comment. His 'ripping yarns', although well written and meticulously researched, now belong to that other age when most of the world map was pink and the British Empire shone like an unquestioned beacon. Ballantyne's narrative skills remain nonetheless supreme. During his career, Ballantyne wrote over 80 books. In 1866, he married Jane Grant; they had four sons and two daughters. After 1883, the family lived in Harrow, Middlesex. Ballantyne died in Rome on 8 February 1894.

SEE ALSO: *Kidnapped* Statue, James Ballantyne.

25 RAEBURN PLACE

Oxfam Bookshop

A short walk north from Princes Street and across the Water of Leith will bring you to leafy Stockbridge and the Raeburn Place Oxfam Bookshop. This well-established and friendly shop is renowned for the wide variety and high quality of its books. Oxfam is the UK's largest second-hand bookseller and its good reputation guarantees a constant stream of donations. The shelves of this shop are always full and reasonable prices mean turnover is rapid. What's more, all

the money made in the shop funds Oxfam's humanitarian projects in the UK and abroad. As well as a wide range of contemporary, crime and science fiction, they have a large selection of literature and classics, academic (including history, psychology, archaeology and foreign language) and non-academic (including travel, art, leisure and Scottish interest) books. They take time to identify first editions and rare/collectable books, so if you are seeking something in particular, do ask.

FURTHER INFORMATION: Opening hours: 9.30 a.m.–5.30 p.m. Monday to Saturday; 1 p.m.–5 p.m. Sunday. Tel: 0131 332 9632. Email: f5817oxfambookshop@hotmail.com.

106A RAEBURN PLACE

Shelter Books

In addition to a comprehensive range of fiction, this shop has large sections dedicated to history, politics, sport, travel, sci-fi and fantasy, DIY and crafts, gardening and cooking. It also boasts an impressive children's section plus a rapidly expanding selection of vintage and antiquarian books. The well-organised shelves are continually updated with good-condition books. The shop owes its success to a team of well-trained and helpful volunteers, and to a regular supply of donated books and magazines. Shelter shops are located throughout the UK and raise funds for Shelter's work

with homeless and badly housed people from the sale of second-hand goods and new products. Shelter is Britain's leading housing charity: it believes everyone should have a home and helps 100,000 people a year fight for their rights, get back on their feet, and find and keep a home. It also tackles the root causes of Britain's housing crisis by campaigning for new laws, policies and solutions.

FURTHER INFORMATION: Opening hours: 9 a.m.–5.30 p.m. Monday to Friday; 9 a.m.–6p.m. Saturday; 12 p.m.–5 p.m. Sunday. Tel: 0131 315 0221.

Comely Bank

Former home of Thomas Carlyle (1795–1881) and Jane Carlyle (1801–66)
Historian and essayist Thomas Carlyle and his wife, Jane, were amongst the best and most copious letter writers in the English language

> It was very good of God to let Carlyle and Mrs Carlyle marry one another and so make only two people miserable instead of four.
>
> Samuel Butler, letter to Miss
> Savage, 21 November 1884

Much has been made of Thomas Carlyle's melancholy and Jane Carlyle's frustration in the role of the 'Lion's wife' during their tempestuous 45-year relationship, but had they not met, the world would have been denied the bounteous correspondence of this high Victorian thinker and his ingenious, caustic wife, who between them wrote thousands of letters, of which over nine thousand still survive, describing everything from revolutionary Europe to dinner parties at Charles Dickens's house, which Jane recounted in 1849:

> The dinner was served up in the new fashion – not placed on the table at all – but handed round – only the des[s]ert on the table and quantities of artificial flowers, but such an overloaded des[s]ert! – pyramids of figs raisins oranges – ach!

Thomas Carlyle was born in Ecclefechan, Dumfriesshire, the son of a stonemason. He arrived in Edinburgh for the first time in 1809, barely 14 years of age, to study at the University for a general Arts degree. He left in 1813, without taking his degree, and took up teaching at his old school in Annan. He returned to Edinburgh again in 1817 to begin theological training, but religious doubts and disaffection with the Church put an end to his intended career in divinity. Miserable and suffering from chronic dyspepsia, he commented, 'I was entirely unknown in Edinburgh circles . . . a prey to nameless struggles and miseries.'

He first met 19-year-old Jane Welsh, the only child of Dr John Welsh and his wife, Grace, at her parents' home in

21 Comely Bank.

Haddington in 1821. After a frenetic courtship, they married in October 1826. He was 31, careerless, possibly impotent and would not achieve fame until middle age. Their first home was at 21 Comely Bank, an unpretentious Georgian terraced house on the north-east edge of the New Town, described by Jane as 'quiet and light and dry', with 'a pretty tree before the door'.

Carlyle's early efforts at trying to make a living from his pen included writing entries for *Brewster's Encyclopaedia*. He also tutored and began penning articles for the *Edinburgh Review*. As a writer and historian, he became influenced by German philosophy and literature, and in 1824 he published a translation of Goethe's *Wilhelm Meister*. In 1833–4, *Sartor Resartus*, his first major work on social philosophy, was published in instalments in *Fraser's Magazine*. His best-known work remains his *History of the French Revolution* (three volumes, 1837), the first of which had to be rewritten after a servant accidentally burnt the draft. Described by Dickens as 'that wonderful book' – which he claimed in a letter in 1851 to be reading 'for the 500th time' – it was, no doubt, a major influence on his own *A Tale of Two Cities* (1859).

Jane Carlyle, by Samuel Laurence, 1849.

The Carlyles left Edinburgh in May 1828 to live at Jane's family farm at Craigenputtoch in Dumfriesshire in an attempt to reverse Thomas's declining health, moving to London in 1834, where they were to spend the rest of their lives. In 1841, when Thomas's phenomenal success as a historian and social prophet was at its height, the possibility of returning to Edinburgh loomed on the horizon. Jane swiftly discounted it, writing to her mother, 'No, no, we are done with Edinburgh. He owes it no gratitude for any recognition he ever found there. It is only now when London and the world have discovered his talent that they are fain to admit it. As for me, I would as soon go back to Craigenputtock as to that poor, proud, formal, "highly respectable" city.'

The Carlyles settled in Chelsea at 5 Cheyne Row (now renumbered 24) in June 1834, where they lived together for 32 years until Jane's death. In 1848, William Thackeray told his mother, 'Tom Carlyle lives in perfect dignity' in a little house in Chelsea, 'with a snuffy Scotch maid to open the door, and the best company in England ringing at it'.

Thomas Carlyle, by Robert Tait, 1856.

Jane died on 23 April 1866, and is buried with her father in the nave of the old Abbey Kirk, Haddington. Thomas survived Jane by nearly 15 years, dying on 4 February 1881, aged 85, and is buried beside his parents in Ecclefechan churchyard. Although Thomas is the more renowned of the two – his reputation is secure as one of the great historians – Jane's talents were also formidable. Had she written in the novel form, she might well have achieved the fame of Eliot, Sand or Brontë. After her death, Thomas dated and annotated her letters, which he thought 'among the cleverest ever written'; in contrast to Dickens, who burned most of his, or George Eliot, who took her partner's letters to her grave, the letters of Mr and Mrs Carlyle are preserved for posterity, warts and all.

SEE ALSO: Old College, the *Edinburgh Review*, National Library of Scotland, St Giles, James Boswell, James Thin.

FURTHER INFORMATION: The largest collection of letters, journals and related material is in the National Library of Scotland, George IV Bridge. The second largest collection is in the Houghton Library, Harvard University.

FURTHER READING: J.A. Froude, *Thomas Carlyle: A History of the First Forty Years of his Life* (Uni. Press of the Pacific, 2002); R. Ashton, *Thomas and Jane Carlyle: Portrait of a Marriage* (Pimlico, 2003). Collections of Jane's letters have been published by J.A. Froude (1883), L. Huxley (1924) and T. Scudder (1931).

Dean Village

DEAN PATH

Dean Cemetery

Grave of Dr Joseph Bell (1837–1911)
Sir Arthur Conan Doyle's inspiration for Sherlock Holmes

> Doyle was always making notes. He seemed to want to copy down every word I said. Many times after the patient had departed my office, he would ask me to repeat my observations so that he would be certain he had them correctly.
>
> Dr Joseph Bell

When Arthur Conan Doyle was a young unknown medical student in the late 1870s at Edinburgh University, his most memorable teacher was Dr Joseph Bell, whose talent for making

lightning diagnoses, combined with his acute powers of observation, inspired Doyle in later life to use him as the model for the world's greatest consulting detective: Sherlock Holmes.

Bell was a noted surgeon of the time, who practised at the Royal Infirmary and who also passed on his knowledge and skills through lectures to medical students. Besides studying under Bell, Doyle was also appointed as his clerk for a time – a duty which was regularly given to students – thereby allowing Doyle even more intimacy with the eminent physician. They only had contact with each other for a couple of years, but the impression was a lasting one which planted the seeds for the great sleuth in Doyle's imagination. In an interview published in *The Bookman* in May 1892, Doyle stated that:

> Sherlock Holmes was the literary embodiment of my memory of a professor of medicine at Edinburgh

> University, who would sit in the patients' waiting room, with a face like a Red Indian, and diagnose the people as they came in, before even they had opened their mouths. He would tell them their symptoms. He would give them details of their lives, and he would hardly ever make a mistake.

Bell later wrote to Doyle praising the stories and denied that he had been 'more than a minor influence on them'. Doyle replied:

> It is most certainly to you that I owe Sherlock Holmes although, in the stories, I have the advantage of being able to place him in all sorts of dramatic positions, I do not think that his analytical work is in the least an exaggeration of some of the effects which I have seen you produce in the outpatient ward.

Bell's dramatic and arrogant diagnosing style may have seemed like the inspired guesswork of a show-off lecturer to some, but in the 1870s there were no X-rays or scans to help make up a physician's mind. Everything rested on what they saw, what they felt, what they smelt and what they heard with their stethoscope.

Joseph Bell.

Born the eldest of nine children in Edinburgh in 1837, Joseph Bell came from a medical family which spanned four generations. Educated at Edinburgh Academy and Edinburgh University, qualifying as an MD in 1859, he began his surgical career as a house surgeon at the Royal Infirmary in Lauriston Place. In 1887, he became the first chief surgeon at the fledgling department of surgery in the Royal Hospital for Sick Children in Sciennes Road. In 1863, he became a fellow of the Royal College of Surgeons of Edinburgh, becoming its president in 1887.

In 1865, he married Edith Murray, with whom he had three children. When Edith died of puerperal peritonitis in 1874, Dr Bell's black hair is said to have turned white almost overnight. Following his death on 4 October 1911, a staggering number of people attended his funeral, while thousands more lined the streets.

SEE ALSO: Sir Arthur Conan Doyle.

FURTHER INFORMATION: Joseph Bell's grave is marked by a white marble cross situated roughly midway along the northern wall bordering Ravelston Terrace. The Joseph Bell Archive can be viewed at the library of the Royal College of Surgeons of Edinburgh, 18 Nicolson Street, Edinburgh. Tel: 0131 527 1600.

Grave of Lord Cockburn (1779–1854)
Advocate, biographer and memorialist

> The exemption of Scotch claret from duty, which
> continued (I believe) till about 1780, made it till then the
> ordinary beverage. I have heard Henry Mackenzie and
> other old people say that, when a cargo of claret came
> to Leith, the common way of proclaiming its arrival was
> by sending a hogshead of it through the town on a cart,
> with a horn; and that anybody who wanted a sample, or
> drink under pretence of a sample, had only to go to the
> cart with a jug, which, without much nicety about its
> size, was filled for sixpence.
>
> Dinner hours and customs;
> from *Memorials of His Time*

Henry Cockburn is best remembered today for *Memorials of His Time* (1856), a rich and amusing memoir of a vanished Edinburgh, and his *Life of Jeffrey* (1852). The son of a lawyer, Henry Cockburn was educated at the old Royal High School and Edinburgh University. As an advocate, he defended Thomas Burke's wife in the Burke and Hare trial of 1828, eventually becoming solicitor general for Scotland. A passionate Whig, he contributed legal and political articles to the *Edinburgh Review*, which fondly described him as 'rather below the middle height, firm, wiry and muscular, inured to active exercise of all kinds, a good swimmer, an accomplished skater and an intense lover of the breezes of heaven. He was the model of a high-bred Scotch gentleman.'
SEE ALSO: The *Edinburgh Review*.

Grave of Francis Jeffrey (1773–1850)
Judge, critic and editor of the Edinburgh Review

> [You combine] the force and nature of Scott in his
> pathetic parts, without his occasional coarseness and
> wordiness, and the searching disclosure of inward
> agonies of Byron, without a trait of his wickedness.
>
> Letter from Jeffrey to Charles Dickens, 1847

Francis Jeffrey, along with the Reverend Sydney Smith, Henry Brougham and Francis Horner, founded the *Edinburgh Review* in 1802, an enormously successful quarterly magazine which became renowned for its highly influential views and savage criticism. Jeffrey, who became its first editor, was also an advocate and an MP. In 1830, he was appointed lord advocate.
SEE ALSO: The *Edinburgh Review*.
FURTHER READING: H. Cockburn, *Life of Jeffrey* (Lexden, 2004).

Canonmills

(5 TANFIELD)

Duncan & Reid

After 15 years dealing solely in books, Duncan & Reid combined their business with antiques in 1993. Their stock contains some antiquarian volumes, a good selection of books on art, literature (fiction and biography), some fashion and feminism, and a Scottish section. They also keep a small quantity of illustrated children's books, and usually stock some Jessie M. King items. Many of their book customers take an equal interest in their eighteenth- and nineteenth-century ceramics and glass, while antique-hunters may find books on the objects they are interested in collecting.

FURTHER INFORMATION: Opening hours: 11 a.m.–5 p.m. Tuesday to Saturday. Tel: 0131 556 4591.

(6 TANFIELD)

Aurora Books

Aurora Books is situated opposite the birthplace of Robert Louis Stevenson and just down the road from the site of Tanfield Hall, scene of the Great Disruption of 1843. You'll find books on both these subjects in the shop, as well as thousands of books on dozens of others: everything from art, antiques, arts and crafts, biography, business, children's, fiction, food and drink, and history to modern firsts, reference, Scottish, transport and travel, via humanities, language, law, literature, media and popular culture. Much of the inventory is online and orders can be taken via the Web as well as by phone, fax or email for shipment worldwide. The shop is accessible from the Water of Leith Walkway by walking east from Stockbridge and turning right where it becomes the Rocheid Path and meets Inverleith Row. It's

Tom Chambers of Aurora Books.

also on bus routes 23, 27 and 8, and is on the way to the Royal Botanic Garden from town.

FURTHER INFORMATION: Opening hours: 10 a.m.–6 p.m. Monday to Saturday. Tel: 0131 557 8466. Email: aurorabooks@btconnect.com. Website: www.aurorabooks.co.uk.

9 HOWARD STREET

Second Edition

Established in 1978, this family business run by Maureen (who started the shop) and Bill Smith is one of the largest and longest-established antiquarian and second-hand bookshops in Edinburgh. Primarily a collector's stock, it has a very wide range of good-quality and good-condition hardback books. Each book is purchased individually: no auction lots to be found here. The stock is well-organised, clearly labelled and systematically arranged. There are over 2,000 Scottish books covering history, topography and literature; over 1,000 art and applied-art books; about 1,000 travel books; and some 1,000 modern first editions, from Buchan (including many scarce titles) to P.G. Wodehouse. Smaller (but

Bill Smith of Second Edition.

significant) stocks of children's/illustrated, science and medicine, philosophy/religion, literature and books of many other categories are also held. All this with mainstream and melodic jazz as a background. What more could you ask for? . . . Well, you could always read one of Bill's entertaining essays, which are frequently displayed in the window. Lots of people do!

FURTHER INFORMATION: Opening hours: 10 a.m.–5.15 p.m. Monday to Saturday. Tel: 0131 556 9403.
Website: www.secondeditionbookshop.co.uk.

2 SUMMER PLACE

T&B Bookcrafts

T&B Bookcrafts is a newly established bookshop with a very distinctive difference. Housed below the stocked bookshelves on the ground floor is a basement with a fully equipped craft bookbinding workshop, offering the Edinburgh book scene classic-style bindings, specialist book restoration and contemporary binding work to order. Situated in an area of Edinburgh regarded as the new 'book corner', T&B also offers a selection of second-hand and rare antiquarian books, including many fine bindings and a good Scottish section.

FURTHER INFORMATION: Opening hours: 9.30 a.m.–5.30 p.m. Friday; 9.30 a.m.–5.30 p.m. Saturday; 12.30 p.m.–4.30 p.m. Sunday. Tel: 0131 556 7857. Email: T_Bbooks@fireflyuk.net.

8 HOWARD PLACE

Birthplace of Robert Louis Stevenson (1850–94)
Scottish writer who became a legend in his lifetime

> A fractious little fellow . . . though decidedly pretty.
> A description of the baby RLS by
> one of his mother's bridesmaids

Robert Lewis Balfour Stevenson was born on 13 November 1850 and was named after his grandfathers, Robert Stevenson and the Reverend Lewis Balfour. His parents, Thomas Stevenson and Margaret Balfour, married in 1848 and set up their first home at 8 Howard Place, a relatively new Georgian terrace situated just beyond the northern rim of the New Town. Their only child was christened by his grandfather at Howard Place, and the family nicknamed him 'Smout', after the Scots word for salmon fry.

The universal image of RLS is synonymous with that of chronic ill health, but for the first two of years of his life Smout was a healthy child, with no signs of the purgatory to come. Like many Victorians, his parents worried about the family's health, perhaps overly so, but for the time being Smout was in no danger. When he was 18 months old, his nurse, Alison Cunningham, entered his life. 'Cummy' was from Torryburn, in Fife, and her zealous devotion to her young charge, coupled with her strict Calvinism and 'blood-curdling tales of the Covenanters', had a profound and lasting influence on RLS for the rest of his life. It was Cummy to whom he dedicated *A Child's Garden of Verses* in 1885.

Howard Place was small, and a little too close for comfort to

the dampness of the Water of Leith, which in those days conveyed sewage, secretions from local mills and their hovering stench towards the sea. Hence the move in 1853 to a house at 1 Inverleith Terrace, which, although just across the street, was a larger and, it was hoped, a healthier one.

SEE ALSO: Inverleith Terrace, Heriot Row, Pilrig House, Colinton Manse, Swanston Cottage, Baxter's Place, Glencorse Kirk, Rutherford's Howff, New Calton Cemetery, Old Calton Burial Ground, St Giles, Hawes Inn, Rullion Green,

8 Howard Place.

W.E. Henley, Alison Cunningham, Henderson's School, Deacon Brodie, The Writers' Museum, *Kidnapped* Statue, RLS Club, Museum of Scotland, George Mackenzie, Martyrs' Monument, Edinburgh Castle, Old College, Parliament Hall, Holyrood Park, Royal College of Surgeons' Museum, R.M. Ballantyne, RLS Memorial, Writers' Corner.

FURTHER INFORMATION: From 1926 to 1963, 8 Howard Place was an RLS museum and HQ of the RLS Club. It was sold in 1964 and its exhibits can now be seen in The Writers' Museum, Lady Stair's Close. Poet and critic W.E. Henley (1849–1903), friend, collaborator and ultimately antagonist of RLS, lived at 11 Howard Place between 1889 and 1891, when he was editor of the *Scots Observer*.

FURTHER READING: J.C. Furnas, *Voyage to Windward* (Faber, 1952); I. Bell, *Dreams of Exile: Robert Louis Stevenson – A Biography* (Mainstream, 1992); J. Calder, *RLS: A Life Study* (Hamish Hamilton, 1980); C. Harman, *Robert Louis Stevenson: A Biography* (Harper Collins, 2005).

34 HOWARD PLACE

Former home of Lewis Spence (1874–1955)
Scottish poet and folklorist

> O wad this braw hie-heapit toun
> Sail aff like an enchanted ship,
> Drift owre the warld's seas up and doun
> And kiss wi' Venice lip to lip
>> Lewis Spence, 'The Prows o' Reekie'

Born in Broughty Ferry, near Dundee, he came to Edinburgh in 1892 to study dentistry, but ended up as a sub-editor on *The Scotsman* and later the *British Weekly* (1905–09). Along with Hugh MacDiarmid, he was one of the founders of the Scots Literary Renaissance, the purpose of which was to 'bring Scottish literature into closer touch with current European tendencies in technique and ideation'. Written in classical Scots, his collections of poetry included *The Phoenix* (1924) and *Weirds and Vanities* (1927). An ardent nationalist, he was one of the founders of the Scottish Nationalist Party in 1929, and in the same year became the first nationalist to stand for election. He was also a leading authority on ancient folklore and wrote many books on the subject, including the *Dictionary of Mythology* (1913), *Encyclopaedia of Occultism* (1920) and *The Magic Arts in Celtic Britain* (1945).

SEE ALSO: Hugh MacDiarmid.

Inverleith

Childhood home of Robert Louis Stevenson (1850–94)

> Whenever the moon and stars are set,
> Whenever the wind is high,
> All night long in the dark and wet,
> A man goes riding by.
> Late in the night when the fires are out,
> Why does he gallop and gallop about?
>
> RLS recalling his fear of stormy nights at
> Inverleith Terrace, from 'Windy Nights',
> *A Child's Garden of Verses* (1885)

On 27 June 1853, when RLS was two years six months old, the Stevenson family moved from 8 Howard Place to 1 (now no. 9)

9 Inverleith Terrace.

Inverleith Terrace, conveniently situated just across the road. This larger three-storey house was, at first glance, more salubrious, but in reality it proved to be the opposite, and was draughty, damp and mildewed. Whether Inverleith Terrace was a catalyst for RLS's decline in health around this time is debatable, but it sounds likely. Both his parents had bronchial complaints, so his respiratory problems would probably have been inherited anyway, but a combination of 'one of the vilest climates under heaven', dampness, air pollution and chronic chest

trouble doesn't bode well. Tuberculosis of the lungs is a diagnosis which is often put forward but cannot be confirmed, as there were no blood tests or X-rays available in the nineteenth century.

RLS wrote of Inverleith Terrace in *Notes of Childhood* (1873):

> All this time, be it borne in mind, my health was of the most precarious description. Many winters I never crossed the threshold, but used to lie on my face on the nursery floor, chalking or painting in water-colours the pictures in the illustrated newspapers; or sit up in bed, with a little shawl pinned about my shoulders, to play with bricks or whatnot.

When he was well, his devoted nurse Cummy took him for walks to the Royal Botanic Garden and nearby Warriston Cemetery. 'Do you remember, at Warriston, one autumn Sunday,' he wrote to Cummy in 1883, 'when the beech-nuts were on the ground, seeing Heaven open? I would like to make a rhyme of that, but cannot.' His spirits were lifted in October 1856 when cousin Bob, his uncle Alan's son, came to spend the winter. 'This visit of Bob's was altogether a great holiday in my life,' wrote RLS in *Memoirs of Himself* (1880). 'We lived together in a purely visionary state. We had countries; his was Nosingtonia, mine Encyclopaedia; where we ruled and made wars and inventions . . . We were never weary of dressing up. We drew, we coloured our pictures; we painted and cut out figures for a pasteboard theatre; this last one of the dearest pleasures of my childhood.'

Louis and his father, Thomas Stevenson.

In 1856, the Stevensons moved to their new south-facing home at 17 Heriot Row in the middle of the New Town – a move that reflected Thomas Stevenson's thriving career and would, it was hoped, improve little Lou's health.

SEE ALSO: Howard Place, Heriot Row, Pilrig House, Colinton Manse, Swanston Cottage, Baxter's Place, Glencorse Kirk, Rutherford's Howff, New Calton Cemetery, Old Calton Burial Ground, St Giles, Hawes Inn, Rullion Green, W.E. Henley, Alison Cunningham, Henderson's School, Deacon Brodie, *Kidnapped* Statue, The Writers' Museum, RLS Club, Museum of Scotland, George Mackenzie, Martyrs' Monument, Edinburgh Castle, Old College, Parliament Hall, Holyrood Park, Royal College of Surgeons' Museum, R.M. Ballantyne, RLS Memorial, Writers' Corner.

FURTHER READING: R. Woodhead, *The Strange Case of R.L. Stevenson* (Luath Press, 2001).

Fairmilehead

The Tusitala Restaurant and The Pavilion Bar

Situated at Fairmilehead, The Tusitala Restaurant and the Pavilion Bar are a short distance from Swanston Village, where

Stevenson lived for a number of summers to obtain respite from the polluted air of 'Auld Reekie'. The premises were built in 1989 on land originally owned by the water board. Stevenson would have been very familiar with this area in his youth. The owners were well aware of the history of the area and when the premises were built they decided to reflect Stevenson's association with it, naming the bar after his short story 'The Pavilion on the Links', an adventure story set in the blowing sandhills of the East Coast. Ten years later, when a new restaurant extension was built with views over the Pentland Hills towards Swanston Village, the

connection with Stevenson was further cemented by the choice of 'Tusitala' as the name of the new restaurant, meaning 'the teller of tales', the name by which RLS was known in Samoa.

Each year, a McGonagall supper is held at The Pavilion Bar and Tusitala Restaurant. This supper loosely takes the format of a Burns Supper, but with the difference that the programme is followed in reverse order. Unlike a Burns Supper, the prime dish is a Dundee Scotch pie, in recognition of McGonagall's association with the city. A light-

Samoan chief with Tusitala.

215

hearted approach is taken to McGonagall that reflects his standing with the students in Dundee, who privately mocked his poetry yet would attend his poetry readings and give false praise. Should Burns's name be inadvertently mentioned at the supper, the guests are expected to respond with calls of derision, Burns being regarded as a masquerader, the true 'Bard of Scotland' being McGonagall.

The proceedings are organised by the Heidyin Tragedian and the highlight of the evening is the enactment and recital of McGonagall's most famous poem, 'The Tay Bridge Disaster'. Reflecting McGonagall's epic journey to Balmoral, the loyal toast is made to HRH Queen Victoria. Although this is meant to be a fun evening, the participants do gain an appreciation of some of the poetry of McGonagall, which they might not otherwise encounter.

FURTHER INFORMATION: Tel: 0131 445 2233.

Swanston

Swanston Cottage
Summer retreat of the Stevenson family

> The cottage was a little quaint place of many rough-cast gables and grey roofs. It had something of the air of a rambling infinitesimal cathedral, the body of it rising in the midst two storeys high, with a steep-pitched roof, and sending out upon all hands (as it were chapter-houses, chapels, and transepts) one-storeyed and dwarfish projections. To add to this appearance, it was grotesquely decorated with crockets and gargoyles, ravished from some mediaeval church. The place seemed hidden away, being not only concealed in the trees of the garden, but, on the side on which I approached it, buried as high as the eaves by the rising of the ground.
>
> RLS's description of Swanston
> Cottage in *St Ives* (1897)

Swanston is the most romantic of Stevenson's Edinburgh haunts. A rural idyll, it is conveniently situated at Edinburgh's back door, only a two-hour walk from Heriot Row with the Pentlands on its doorstep. It was a place where Stevenson could lose himself walking in the hills and write undisturbed save for 'the whaup's wild cry on the breeze'. The steep slopes of Allermuir and Caerketton Hill rose before him with Glencorse, Rullion Green and the Covenanter's graves beyond. 'The hills are close by across a valley,' he wrote in *Picturesque Notes*, 'Kirk Yetton, with its long, upright scars visible as far as Fife, and Allermuir, the tallest on this side, with wood and tilled field running high upon their borders, and haunches all moulded into glens and shelvings and variegated with heather and fern. The air comes briskly and sweetly off the hills.'

'The place in the dell' first entered his heart in 1867 when his father decided to rent Swanston Cottage as a summer retreat, an arrangement which lasted 14 years. Built in 1761, the cottage was given a second storey about 1835, and in 1867 the Stevensons built an extension on its west side.

In 1871, the census records that Swanston village had 22

Swanston Cottage.

houses with 72 residents. Stevenson befriended many of them, including the farmers and shepherds, notably John Todd, the 'Roaring Shepherd', who features in his essay 'Pastoral', in *Memories and Portraits* (1887):

> In the ripeness of time, we grew to be a pair of friends, and when I lived alone in these parts in the winter, it was a settled thing for John to 'give me a cry' over the garden wall as he set forth upon his evening round, and for me to overtake and bear him company.

Stevenson used the hen-house at Swanston Cottage as the basis for his fictional place of refuge for the fugitive Monsieur le Vicomte de Saint-Yves during his daring escape from Edinburgh Castle in *St Ives*, his unfinished novel which was completed by Arthur Quiller-Couch in 1897.

Today, Edinburgh is steadily creeping towards Swanston like volcanic lava, and one day it will swallow it. They say a Scotsman never thinks of hills but he hears a whaup (a curlew), but if the wind is in the right direction at Swanston, the drone of the city bypass is more likely to reach your ears than a peewee. Stevenson was thankfully spared this pollution and, writing from his tropical exile in Samoa to S.R. Crockett, the Pentlands were set in aspic as his 'Hills of Dream':

> Be it granted me to behold you again in dying,
> Hills of home! and to hear the call,
> Hear about the graves of the martyrs the peewees
>   crying,
> And hear no more at all.

SEE ALSO: Howard Place, Inverleith Terrace, Heriot Row, Pilrig House, Colinton Manse, Baxter's Place, Glencorse Kirk, Rutherford's Howff, New Calton Cemetery, Old Calton Burial Ground, St Giles, Hawes Inn, Rullion Green, W.E. Henley, Alison Cunningham, Henderson's School, Deacon Brodie, The Writers' Museum, *Kidnapped* Statue, RLS Club, Museum of Scotland, George Mackenzie, Martyrs' Monument, Edinburgh Castle, Old College, Parliament Hall, Holyrood Park, Royal College of Surgeons' Museum, R.M. Ballantyne, RLS Memorial, Writers' Corner.

FURTHER INFORMATION: To get to Swanston, approach it from Swanston Road, off Oxgangs Road. If coming from the city bypass, exit at Lothianburn for Oxgangs Road. Swanston Cottage is off to the right behind Swanston Farm. It is not open to the public. Parking is available just beyond the Golf Club sign. A bench near the gate at the south end of the village leading to the Pentlands is dedicated to the memory of Edwin Muir, who often visited Swanston and enjoyed its peace and tranquillity.

Swanston Farm Holiday Cottages: Tel: 0131 445 5744.

Website: www.swanston.co.uk.

Recommended map: OS Explorer 344.

Pentland Hills Regional Park: 0131 445 3383.

Email: ranger@phrangerservice.demon.co.uk.

Website: www.pentlandhills.org.

FURTHER READING: D.G. Moir, *Pentland Walks: Their Literary and Historical Associations* (Bartholomew, 1977); R.A. Hill, *Pure Air and Fresh Milk: Robert Louis Stevenson at Swanston* (privately printed, 1995).

Colinton

Former home of Dorothy Dunnett (1923–2001)
Scottish novelist

> A historical novel without humour, like passion without
> humour, is a very dull thing.
>
> Dorothy Dunnett

Author of the Lymond Chronicles and the House of Niccolò
series of historical novels, Dorothy Dunnett was a prolific writer
whose meticulous research into the fifteenth and sixteenth
centuries created a series of novels which attracted a worldwide
readership.

Born Dorothy Halliday in 1923 in Dunfermline, Fife, she was
educated at James Gillespie's High School for Girls in Bruntsfield,
Edinburgh — the model for the
Marcia Blaine School in the novel
The Prime of Miss Jean Brodie. From
1940 to 1955, she worked with the
Civil Service as a press officer and in
1946 she married the journalist
Alastair Dunnett. Her writing career
began in the late 1950s, but her first
novel was rejected by five British
publishers. Not unduly perturbed
by this, her husband sent the
manuscript to his American friend
Lois Cole, the agent who discovered
Gone with the Wind by Margaret
Mitchell. *Game of Kings* was
subsequently published by Putman
in the USA in 1961, and its romantic
hero, the sixteenth-century soldier
of fortune Francis Crawford of
Lymond, made the first of his many

Dorothy Dunnett. (© Betty Cooper)

appearances. Five more volumes of the Lymond Chronicles
followed over the next fifteen years, together with her Johnson
Johnson detective novels. In 1986, she began a second historical
series: the eight-volume House of Niccolò, set during the
Renaissance. Dunnett was also an accomplished portrait painter
and exhibited at the Royal Scottish Academy. In 1992, she was

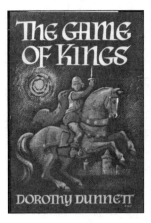

awarded the OBE for services to literature. Dorothy Dunnett lived for more than 40 years at Colinton Road and wrote most of her books there, writing in a converted garage at the back of the house. She died of cancer on 9 November 2001 in an Edinburgh hospice.

SEE ALSO: St Giles, Heart of Midlothian.

FURTHER READING: E. Morrison, *The Dorothy Dunnett Companion, Volumes I and II* (Vintage, 2001, 2002).

DELL ROAD

Colinton Manse
Former home of Robert Louis Stevenson's maternal grandparents and birthplace of his mother

> For long ago, the truth to say,
> He has grown up and gone away,
> And it is but a child of air
> That lingers in the garden there.
>
> RLS, from 'To Any Reader',
> *A Child's Garden of Verses* (1885)

Stevenson's 'rhymes' and 'jingles', as he called his poems in *A Child's Garden of Verses*, were written when he was in his early 30s. Some were written in the intervals of writing *Treasure Island*, at Braemar, and the rest were written in his sickbed at Hyères. Many of the poems are recollections of his childhood days spent with his grandparents at Colinton Manse, which he fondly recalls in *Memoirs of Himself* (1880):

> I have not space to tell of my pleasures at the manse. I have been happier since; for I think most people

Colinton Manse.

Colinton Parish Church.

exaggerate the capacity for happiness of a child; but I have never again been happy in the same way. For indeed, it was scarce a happiness of this world, as we conceive it when we are grown up, and was more akin to that of an animal than of that of a man. The sense of sunshine, of green leaves, and of singing of birds, seems never to have been so strong in me as in that place. The deodar upon the lawn, the laurel thickets, the mills, the river, the church bell, the sight of people ploughing, the Indian curiosities with which my uncles had stocked the house, the sharp contrast between this place and the city where I spent the other portion of my time, all these took hold of me, and still remain upon my memory.

Stevenson's grandfather, Lewis Balfour, was born in 1777, the third son of the laird of Pilrig, and was described by his grandson as 'the noblest looking old man I have ever seen . . . one of the last, I suppose, to speak broad Scots and be a gentleman'. He entered the ministry in 1806 and his first parish was at Sorn, in Ayrshire, where he met and married minister's daughter Henrietta Scott Smith in 1808. The couple moved into Colinton Manse in 1823, and on 11 February 1828 Margaret Isabella Balfour (RLS's mother) was born. Maggie, 'the Minister's white-headed lassie', was the twelfth of thirteen children and the fourth and youngest daughter. After a chance meeting on a train, she was courted by engineer Thomas Stevenson, whom she married in

The Balfour tomb.

1848. He was 30 and she was 19. The newly-weds moved into 8 Howard Place at Canonmills, and on 13 November 1850 their son, and only child, Robert Lewis Balfour Stevenson was born.

The Balfour tomb, the last resting place of RLS's

grandparents and family, including four of their children who died in infancy, can be seen at the north end of the churchyard near the church door. Robert Louis Stevenson and his wife Fanny are entombed on the summit of Mount Vea in Samoa, 1,300 feet above sea level, but RLS longed to be buried in Scotland, perhaps in Colinton Kirkyard, close to the manse and garden he loved so dearly.

SEE ALSO: Howard Place, Inverleith Terrace, Heriot Row, Pilrig House, Swanston Cottage, Baxter's Place, Glencorse Kirk, Rutherford's Howff, New Calton Cemetery, Old Calton Burial Ground, St Giles, Hawes Inn, Rullion Green, W.E. Henley, Alison Cunningham, Henderson's School, Deacon Brodie, *Kidnapped* Statue, RLS Club, Museum of Scotland, George Mackenzie, Martyrs' Monument, Edinburgh Castle, Old College, Parliament Hall, Holyrood Park, Royal College of Surgeons' Museum, R.M. Ballantyne, RLS Memorial, Writers' Corner.

FURTHER INFORMATION: Colinton Parish Church, Dell Road (at the foot of Spylaw Street), Edinburgh EH13 0RJ. Tel: 0131 441 2232.

The Church Rooms, opened in 1998, house The Swing Café, which opens Monday–Friday 10 a.m.–2 p.m. The café is named after RLS's poem 'The Swing' in *A Child's Garden of Verses*, and outside the east window stands the yew tree that RLS's original swing hung from. The 'dark brown' river in 'Where Go the Boats?' in *A Child's Garden of Verses* is the Water of Leith, which RLS would have accessed through the water door (now just a gap) behind the graveyard wall to the rear of the manse.

Leith

> ## 2 WELLINGTON PLACE

Former Home of Irvine Welsh (1958–)
Hibs supporter and author of *Trainspotting*

> Somebody said, 'There's too many f***s and too many
> c***s in the book.' I says, 'Well, how many is enough
> and how much is too many?'
>
> Irvine Welsh

Born in Leith and brought up in Muirhouse, Irvine Welsh became
a household name in 1993
when his novel *Trainspotting*,
about a group of heroin
addicts living in Leith,
exploded with the shock and
impact of a thunderbolt and
saw Welsh acknowledged as
the voice of 1990s British
youth culture. Danny Boyle's
1996 film reached an even
wider audience, securing
Welsh's place in Scotland's
literary hall of fame – or
infamy, depending on your
taste. Today, the controversy
and outrage has all but
evaporated and *Trainspotting*
sits comfortably on bookshop

Irvine Welsh. (© Rankin)

shelves beside the Waverley novels, where Leith meets the Heart
of Midlothian (why did Scott never write a book about the Hibs?).

A controversial figure, who has a love–hate relationship with
his native city, Welsh is never afraid of expressing his opinions
in vernacular expletives. There have been many media 'claims'
about Welsh's background. The word 'shrouded', for example,
is often used when referring to his roots, but there's nothing
sinister about a man who wants to keep his past from the muck-
rakers. Personally, I would respect his privacy and enquire no
further, mainly because Welsh himself would probably tell me
to 'F**k off, ya plukey-faced wee hing-oot.'

We both went to the same secondary school – Ainslie Park in
Pilton Avenue (now the North Campus of Telford College) – but we

2 Wellington Place (second floor/left).

never met. Our council estates were virtually next door to each other, and my Auntie Lizzie lived in sunny Leith, where her window looked directly onto the bleak stone wall of Leith Central Station, from which Welsh derived his title 'Trainspotting', an ironic reference to the fact that trains no longer stop there, Leith now being a community ignored and forgotten.

Welsh was reputedly born in 1958 and left school aged 16 to serve his time as an apprentice TV repair man. He later moved to London, where he had various jobs, got involved in the punk scene and ended up working in the offices of Hackney Council. He returned to Scotland and was employed as a training officer with Edinburgh City Council from 1986 to 1994, during which time he took computer studies at Heriot Watt University.

Trainspotting began appearing in 1991 in the London-based low-budget magazine *DOG* and also in Glasgow's *West Coast Magazine* and *Scream, If You Want to Go Faster: New Writing Scotland No. 9*, edited by Hamish Whyte and Janice Galloway. Early drafts of *Trainspotting* also appeared in the first edition of the Edinburgh-based *Rebel Inc.* in April 1992, and in Duncan McLean's *Clocktower Booklet: A Parcel of Rogues*. It was McLean who recommended Welsh to Robin Robertson, editorial director of Secker & Warburg, who decided to publish *Trainspotting*.

Following the book's success, Welsh gave up his day job and turned to full-time writing. Stories proliferate that he peaked with his debut and begot the craze for lad-lit, but he did reach a vast audience who understood where he was coming from and recognised a language they could tune into. Welsh continues to produce some startling work. *Porno* (2002) continues the story of the principal characters of *Trainspotting* ten years on, where Sick Boy is now a director of porno movies and Spud is writing a history of Leith, though still an addict. Other works include *The Acid House* (1994), *Marabou Stork Nightmares* (1995), *Ecstasy* (1996), *Filth* (1998) and *Glue* (2001).

Literary travellers searching

225

out the sites of *Trainspotting* will need to move fast as the city's landscape is forever changing. The bookmaker's in Muirhouse's Pennywell Road where Renton lost and had to recover his drugs in the 'worst toilet in the world' is now no more, and the 'jigsaw' flats off West Granton Road where Tommy died of Aids have been demolished. Deacon Brodie's pub in the Royal Mile, visited by Renton and his pals, and Begbie's regular boozer, the Central Bar at the foot of Leith Walk, are still going strong. Welsh's favourite Leith bar, the Boundary Bar at 379 Leith Walk, is now called City Limits.

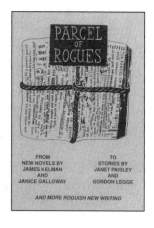

According to Ron McKay of *The Observer* (4 February 1996), not everyone in Muirhouse is a fan:

> 'Ah ken that Irvine Welsh,' said the scarfaced barman in the Penny Farthing pub. 'He's a sad f**king case, he is. He's a f**king Hibee . . .' One woman defended him stoutly, 'Ah don't care what they say, naebody's ever written aboot Muirhouse before,' but, asked whether she'd actually read any of his books, she said, 'Ah'll get roon tae them when they're on offer at Kwik Save.'

SEE ALSO: The Trainspotting Tour.

FURTHER INFORMATION: Muirhouse can be reached by the intrepid literary pilgrim by jumping on a no. 37 bus outside Fraser's department store at the west end of Princes Street or by catching a northbound no. 27 bus in Hanover Street. From Leith, take a westbound no. 32 from Bernard Street.

JUNCTION OF BERNARD STREET AND CONSTITUTION STREET

Statue of Robert Burns (1759–96)

This imposing bronze figure of Burns was erected by the Leith Burns Club in 1898 and sculpted by D.W. Stevenson. On each of the four faces of the plinth there is a bronze plaque bearing the following inscriptions respectively:

> South: The priest like father reads the sacred page. From scenes like those old Scotia's grandeur springs, that makes her loved at home, revered abroad.
>
> East: When Vulcan gies his bellows breath an' plowmen gather wi' their graith.

West: In order on the clean hearth staine, the luggies
   three are ranged.
North: I there wi' something did forgather that pat me in
   an eerie swither.

SEE ALSO: Anchor Close, St James Square, Buccleuch Street, Burns Monument, Canongate Kilwinning Lodge, White Hart Inn, St Giles, William Smellie, William Creech, The Writers' Museum, Sciennes Hill House, Robert Fergusson, Clarinda, Jean Lorimer, Henry Mackenzie, The Blind Poet pub.

Portobello

Former home of J.G. Lockhart (1794–1854)
Novelist, critic, essayist and biographer of Sir Walter Scott

> You can't know Burns unless you hate the Lockharts
> and all the estimable bourgeois and upper classes as
> he really did – the narrow-gutted pigeons . . . Oh, why
> doesn't Burns come to life again, and really salt them?
> D.H. Lawrence, letter to Donald Carswell (1927),
> after reading Lockhart's *Life of Burns*.

John Gibson Lockhart is best remembered today for his biographies
of Napoleon and Robert Burns, and his monumental seven-volume
magnum opus on the life of his
father-in-law, Sir Walter Scott.
He was born at Cambusnethan
in Lanarkshire, where his
father was a Church of
Scotland minister. He grew up
in Glasgow, studying at the
University and later at Oxford.
In 1815, he moved to
Edinburgh to practise as an
advocate and in 1817, along
with John Wilson, began
editing the new monthly
Blackwood's Magazine, where
his powers of derision and
parody gained him a
reputation as a vicious critic.
James Hogg, who joined forces
with the two editors, described
Lockhart as:

37 Bellfield Street.

> a mischievous Oxford puppy, for whom I was terrified,
> dancing after the young ladies, and drawing
> caricatures of every one who came into contact with
> him . . . I dreaded his eye terribly; and it was not without
> reason, for he was very fond of playing tricks on me, but
> always in such a way, that it was impossible to lose
> temper with him.

Such was the hostility between *Blackwood's Magazine* and its competitor, the *London Magazine*, that Lockhart in 1821 challenged its editor John Scott to a duel in which Scott was fatally wounded by Lockhart's second (his assistant). In 1819, Blackwood published Lockhart's *Peter's Letters to His Kinfolk*, in which he lampooned leading Edinburgh figures.

Lockhart was a handsome young blade and demands for locks of his hair from young ladies were such that he once remarked that 'it threatened me with premature baldness'. He was also slightly deaf, which tended to make him appear stand-offish. In 1820, he married Sir Walter Scott's daughter, Sophia. They moved to London in 1825, where Lockhart edited the *Quarterly Review*. His pen name, The Scorpion – he 'who delighteth to sting the faces of men' – was a fitting nom de plume.

In 1827, the Lockharts occupied 37 Melville Street (now Bellfield Street), Portobello, a two-storey house on the east side of the street which was next to the grounds of Melville House (now the site of Vernon Villas). This visit appears to have been primarily for the sake of their children's health, and especially for their ailing eldest child. On 9 June 1827, Scott noted in his journal:

> When I came home from Court, I found that John Lockhart and Sophia were arrived by the steamboat at Portobello, where they have a small lodging. I went down with a bottle of champagne and a flask of maraschino, and made buirdly cheer with them for the rest of the day.

Here Scott regularly visited his grandchildren, who Lockhart tells us were 'a source of constant refreshment to him . . . for every other day he came down and dined with them, and strolled about afterwards on the beach'.

Lockhart wrote four novels – *Valerius* (1821), *Adam Blair* (1822), *Reginald Dalton* (1823) and *Matthew Wald* (1824) – about which George Saintsbury commented in his *Essays in Literary Criticism*, 'Lockhart had every faculty for writing novels, except the faculty of novel writing.' Be that as it may, no one can deny that Lockhart's *magnum opus*, *The Life of Sir Walter Scott* (seven volumes, 1837–8), is an outstanding work of biography, arguably second only to Boswell's *Life of Johnson*.

He died at Abbotsford, Scott's former home in the Scottish Borders, which Sophia had inherited, on 25 November 1854, and is buried at nearby Dryburgh Abbey, at Sir Walter's feet.

SEE ALSO: *Blackwood's Magazine*, Sir Walter Scott, John Wilson, James Hogg.

FURTHER INFORMATION: Lockhart lived at various addresses in Edinburgh, including 23 Maitland Street and 25 Northumberland Street.

PORTOBELLO SANDS

Where Walter Scott rode with the 'soor dooks'

> It was not a duty with him, or a necessity, or a pastime, but an absolute passion, indulgence in which gratified his feudal tastes for war . . .
>
> Lord Cockburn on Scott's military zeal in *Memorials of his Times* (1856)

The Battle of Puerto Bello took place off the Panama coast in 1739, and George Hamilton, a sailor who fought in it, built himself a cottage on a stretch of coast on the Firth of Forth which he named the Portobello Hut. Over the years, Portobello and its picturesque beach grew into a favourite resort. During the Napoleonic Wars, Portobello Sands was used by the Volunteer Cavalry Regiment, known as the Edinburgh Light Horse, for exercising and practising drills. Prevented from joining the infantry because of his lameness, Walter Scott joined this new cavalry corps in 1797, the headquarters of which were at Musselburgh, and became its quartermaster. The 'soor dooks', as the regiment was nicknamed for its members' surly demeanour, became his passion and he could often be seen galloping through the surf of Portobello Sands on his black horse, or practising with his sabre at charging a turnip stuck on top of a staff, bellowing, 'Cut them down, the villains, cut them down!' Once, in Paris, the Tsar of Russia asked him in what battles he'd been engaged. 'In some slight actions,' he replied, 'such as the battle of the Cross Causeway and the affair of Moredoun Mill.'

SEE ALSO: Birthplace of W.S., childhood home of W.S., townhouse of W.S., Lasswade Cottage, Parliament Hall, Greyfriars Kirkyard, St John's Churchyard, The Heart of Midlothian, Holyrood Park, The Writers' Museum, High School, Old College, Sciennes Hill House, Assembly Rooms, Dr John Brown, Scott Monument, J.G. Lockhart, The Edinburgh Walter Scott Club.

Portobello Sands.

Newcraighall

Borders

The chain began as a small shop selling used books on the campus of the University of Michigan by Tom and Louis Borders in 1971. The Kinnaird Park shop was the second Borders store in Scotland after one in central Glasgow, and is now the largest single-floor bookstore in Scotland, covering 20,000 sq. ft. Borders offers a selection of around 200,000 book, music and DVD titles, plus the UK's largest selection of magazines – currently over 2,000 different titles. Borders at Fort Kinnaird is ideally placed, being

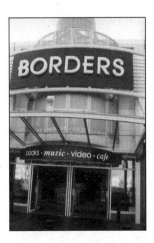

only a 10-minute drive from Edinburgh city centre and moments away from the A1(M). Borders' browsing ethos means longer opening hours, designed to suit people who work locally as well as visitors and tourists to the capital. Starbucks is now in all of Borders' branches, supplying hot and cold beverages as well as a variety of snacks. The shop also hosts regular events, including author signings, readings and musical events. Children's events are particularly successful, ranging from story time to favourite author signings as well as frequent theme days including Harry Potter and Star Wars. Fort Kinnaird also offers free parking to over 2,000 vehicles. There is no doubt customers benefit from the Borders experience: 'I just came in for the toilet,' remarked one customer, 'and ended up in Pompeii for three hours!'

FURTHER INFORMATION: Opening hours: 9 a.m.–10 p.m. Monday to Saturday; 9 a.m.–8 p.m. Sunday. Tel: 0131 657 4041.

Corstorphine

Statue of David Balfour and Alan Breck
Heroes in Robert Louis Stevenson's *Kidnapped*

> We came the by-way over the hill of Corstorphine; and when we got near to the place called Rest-and-be-Thankful, and looked down on Corstorphine bogs and over to the city and the castle on the hill, we both stopped, for we both knew without a word said that we had come to where our ways parted.
>
> The parting of David Balfour and Alan Breck in
> *Kidnapped* (1886)

Stevenson began writing his tale of the Forty-five Rebellion, begun 'partly as a lark, partly as a potboiler', in March 1885 at Skerryvore, his house in Bournemouth. Breck and Balfour represent a Scotland divided: Breck the romantic Highlander and follower of the Young Pretender; Balfour the steadfast Lowlander faithful to the Hanoverian cause. In bringing these two protagonists together, Stevenson created his first and best Scottish historical novel.

Three years in the making and sculpted in bronze by Alexander Stoddart, this 15-ft statue was unveiled by another Scots exile, Sean Connery, in 2004. Commissioned by Scottish & Newcastle brewers, the sculpture is situated at Corstorphine Road and Western Corner.

SEE ALSO: Robert Louis Stevenson, Old Calton Burial Ground, Hawes Inn, Pilrig House, RLS Club, R.M. Ballantyne.

FURTHER INFORMATION: It's ironic that Robert Louis Stevenson was known to be no great lover of statues. He

The statue on the cover of Ian Nimmo's *Walking With Murder: On the Kidnapped Trail* (Birlinn, 2005).

was once asked to contribute towards a statue for his boyhood hero, R.M. Ballantyne, to which he responded thus: 'Mr Ballantyne would, I am sure, be vastly more gratified if we added to the prosperity of his wife and family than if we erected to him the tallest monument in Rome.'

The viewpoint of 'Rest and be Thankful' is on the Ravelston side of Corstorphine Hill and can be accessed from Ravelston Dykes Road. Breck's pub is at 110–14 Rose Street, but apart from a few painted scenes from *Kidnapped*, there is nothing of interest here for the Stevenson fan.

FURTHER READING: I. Nimmo, *Walking With Murder: On the* Kidnapped *Trail* (Birlinn, 2005).

South Gyle

EDINBURGH PARK

Herms of Scottish Poets

The *New Oxford Dictionary of English* defines a herm as 'a square stone pillar with a carved head on top (typically of Hermes), used in ancient Greece as a boundary marker or signpost'. In ancient Athens, they were placed on street corners and further afield they were used as milestones. In Edinburgh, we placed ours in a park wedged between the city bypass and an industrial estate. Edinburgh may well be the 'Athens of the North', but I don't think we're quite ready yet for the street-corner herm which would predictably be daily adorned with the traffic bollard, Hibs scarf and chewing-gum in the eye. The bronze sculptures in the award-winning Edinburgh Park celebrate twentieth-century Scottish poetry, depicting the heads of Liz Lochhead, Edwin Morgan, Hugh MacDiarmid, Iain Crichton Smith, Tom Leonard, Sorley Maclean, Douglas Dunn, Hamish Henderson and others. The columns display biographical information and extracts of the poets' work. Edinburgh Park's public art programme has won much acclaim, especially its poetry bus shelter, which won the Jeu d'Esprit category in the Royal Fine Arts Commission Building of the Year Awards 2001.

SEE ALSO: Hugh MacDiarmid, Hamish Henderson.

Turnhouse

RAF Turnhouse
Former headquarters of No. 603 (City of Edinburgh) Squadron –
legendary squadron of Richard Hillary (1919–43), Battle of
Britain fighter pilot and author of *The Last Enemy*

> The fighter pilot's emotions are those of the duellist –
> cool, precise, impersonal. He is privileged to kill well.
> For if one must either kill or be killed, as now one must,
> it should, I feel, be done with dignity. Death should be
> given the setting it deserves; it should never be a
> pettiness; and for the fighter pilot it never can be.
>
> Richard Hillary, *The Last Enemy*

When Richard Hillary's bestselling book *The Last Enemy* was published in 1942, it joined the ranks of the classic literature of the Second World War. It is not just another tale of combat reminiscences; it is a book which has given future generations a real understanding of what life was like for 'The Few' who died during the Battle of Britain.

Born in Sydney, Australia, in 1919, he was sent to boarding school in England in 1927. He later attended Shrewsbury and entered Trinity College, Oxford, in 1937, where he joined the University Air Squadron. When war broke out, he joined the RAF Volunteer Reserve, which led in July 1940, after initial training, to a posting to 'B' Flight of No. 603 (City of Edinburgh) Fighter Squadron, then based at Montrose.

On 16 October 1939, 603 Squadron shot down the first enemy aircraft over the UK and by November 1940 it had shot down its 100th. Shortly after Hillary joined them, the squadron headed south to RAF Hornchurch and into the cauldron of the Battle of Britain. After a week of relentless combat, he was hit during an aerial attack at 25,000 feet. Bailing out of his blazing Spitfire, he was plucked out of the sea by the Margate Lifeboat. Suffering from horrific burns to his face and hands, his life hung in the balance. Miraculously, he survived and he later underwent extensive plastic-surgery treatment.

During his lengthy convalescence, he visited the USA in 1941 on a propaganda tour, as did many of the British war-wounded, to try to persuade Americans to join the war effort, but ironically his mutilated face and claw-like hands were thought to convey too much of the horror of war and most of his tour was cancelled. It was at this time, during a three-month period in New York, that he wrote his book, published first in America under the title *Falling Through Space*. In June 1942, it was published in Great Britain by Macmillan as *The Last Enemy* and within a few weeks it had sold out of its run of 15,000 copies. The book was more than just an account of a fighter pilot's experience of war. His biographer, Lovat Dickson, described it as the story of 'a spoilt young man who had gone into the war *pour le sport*, who had mocked at everything, not least at himself and his own class, and came in the end humbly to accept humanity'.

He returned to operational flying in November 1942 and was posted to a night fighter squadron at RAF Charterhall in the Scottish Borders. On 8 January 1943, Richard Hillary finally met his last enemy ('The last enemy that shall be destroyed is death' – I Corinthians XV.26) when his converted bomber crashed during a night-training exercise shortly after take-off, killing Hillary and a crew member. Had he lived, his career as a writer would have been assured, because Richard Hillary was a writer who was a fighter pilot, not a fighter pilot who could write, and although his life was short, *The Last Enemy* – his only book – turned him into a legend.

FURTHER INFORMATION: In 2001, a memorial was erected in memory of Hillary and all who died at Charterhall during the Second World War. There were 85 deaths. Charterhall is situated in the Borders, east of Greenlaw on the B6460.

Sadly, much of RAF Turnhouse has now disappeared and what remains is in a sad state of disrepair. Edinburgh Airport was built on the south side of the airfield, opposite the original site, which was, in the early days of 603 Squadron, a small grass airfield. The first hard runway was not built until late 1939 and early 1940. The RAF badges have disappeared from the main gates, although the gates themselves still exist and the concrete gate pillars are still adorned with the RAF eagles, simply because they are part of the concrete moulding. The air-traffic-control tower still exists, although it has been modernised. An air-freight ferry depot has based itself in this location. One of the original hangars is still standing, although many buildings, including the officers' mess, have been demolished. The wartime operations room (bunker) is still where it was during the Second World War. Richard Hillary and friends would frequently visit the Maybury, a nearby art-deco watering-hole on Maybury Road, now a casino.

FURTHER READING: D. Ross, *Richard Hillary* (Grub Street, 2003); L. Dickson, *Richard Hillary* (Macmillan, 1950); A. Koestler, 'The Birth of a Myth', first published in *Horizon*, April 1943 (reprinted in his book of essays *The Yogi and the Commissar*, 1945); E. Linklater, 'Richard Hillary', an essay in *Art of Adventure* (Macmillan, 1947).

Lasswade

CHURCH ROAD

Lasswade Old Kirkyard

Grave of William Drummond of Hawthornden (1585–1649)
Scottish poet

> I long to kiss the image of my death.
> William Drummond, from the sonnet
> 'Sleep, Silence Child' (1614)

In an age of confrontation and dispute, the poet William Drummond was no radical, but a royalist who desired peace and the seclusion of his idyllic castle 'far from the madding worldling's

Tomb of William Drummond.

hoarse discords', to compose his mournful and highly stylised poetry. Born at Hawthornden Castle in the parish of Lasswade, he was educated at Edinburgh University and studied law in France, returning to his estate on the death of his father *c.*1610. He is best remembered today for his meeting with Ben Jonson, who visited him at Hawthornden for Christmas in 1618, when they reputedly greeted each other in rhyme: 'Welcome, welcome, royal Ben,' – 'Thank ee, thank ee, Hawthornden.' Jonson thought that Drummond's poetry 'smelled too much of the schools', and Drummond recorded their spirited dialogue in his book *Conversations of Ben Jonson and William Drummond.*

He is best known for his pastoral lament *Teares on the Death of Moeliades* (1613); *Poems, Amorous, Funereall, Divine, Pastorall in Sonnets, Songs, Sextains, Madrigals* (1614); and *Flowers of Sion and Cypresse Grove* (1623). He also wrote the *History of Scotland 1423–1524* and a *History of the Five Jameses*, posthumously published in 1655.

Melancholic to the end, Drummond wrote his own epitaph, which reads:

> Here Damon lies, whose song did sometimes grace
> The wandering Esk; may roses shade the place.

SEE ALSO: Edinburgh University Library.

FURTHER INFORMATION: William Drummond's grave is situated in what was a small arched aisle in the remains of the old parish church, but no stone marks the exact spot. A memorial was erected to him here in 1893. Hawthornden Castle lies on the banks of the River North Esk about a mile east of Roslin. Since 1982, it has been a writer's retreat. It is not open to the public.

FURTHER READING: F.R. Fogle, *A Critical Study of William Drummond of Hawthornden* (1952).

WADINGBURN ROAD

Barony House, formerly Lasswade Cottage
Summer house of Sir Walter Scott and family

> . . . and it was amidst these delicious solitudes that he did produce the pieces which laid the imperishable foundations of all his fame . . .
>
> J.G. Lockhart, *Memoirs of the Life of Sir Walter Scott, Bart.* (1839)

Walter and Charlotte Scott rented Lasswade Cottage on the western edge of Lasswade village (the 'Gandercleugh' in *Tales of my Landlord*) every summer from 1798 to 1804. Lockhart describes its picturesque charm in his *Life*:

> It is a small house, but with one room of good dimensions, which Mrs Scott's taste set off to advantage at very humble cost – a paddock or two – and a garden (commanding a most beautiful view) in which Scott delighted to train his flowers and creepers. Never, I have heard him say, was he prouder of his handiwork than when he had completed the fashioning of a rustic archway, now overgrown with hoary ivy, by

Lasswade Cottage.
(© Midlothian Council
Library Service)

238

way of ornament to the entrance from the Edinburgh
road. In this retreat they spent some happy summers,
receiving the visits of their few chosen friends from the
neighbouring city, and wandering at will amidst some of
the most romantic scenery that Scotland can boast.

In the summer of 1798, Walter Scott was beginning to feel
settled in life: a steady income, a new wife of six months and a
pen that wouldn't stop writing. The Scotts' townhouse was at 39
North Castle Street, bang in the city centre – wonderful if you
need to be at the pulse of things, but not so good if you want
peace to write. Lasswade Cottage, therefore, was the perfect
retreat – a rural idyll only six miles from Edinburgh.

Scott wrote his translation of Goethe's *Götz von Berlichingen*
here, the first substantial publication to bear his name, and also
his ballad 'The Gray Brother' and the opening stanzas of the
poem which made him famous, *The Lay of the Last Minstrel*.

Visiting literati included James Hogg (the 'Ettrick
Shepherd'), and William and Dorothy Wordsworth during their
tour of Scotland in 1803. His near neighbours were Henry
Mackenzie, the Duke of Buccleuch and Lord Melville. Life was
sweet and fame was just around the corner.

SEE ALSO: Birthplace of W.S., childhood home of W.S.,
townhouse of W.S., Parliament Hall, Greyfriars Kirkyard, St
John's Churchyard, The Heart of Midlothian, Holyrood Park,
The Writers' Museum, Old College, Sciennes Hill House,
Scott Monument, High School, The Assembly Rooms, J.G.
Lockhart, Portobello Sands, Canongate Kirkyard, The
Edinburgh Walter Scott Club.

FURTHER INFORMATION: Barony House is not open to the public.
In *c.*1781 it was extended from an existing eighteenth-
century cottage by the addition of a thatched, bowed
drawing room and tree-trunk porch. In 1865, it was
converted into a dower house with unbecoming baronial
dormers and crowstepped gables. Lasswade lies on the River
North Esk, six miles south-west of Edinburgh, between
Dalkeith and Loanhead.

Pentland Hills

RULLION GREEN

Site of the Covenanters' first battle and inspiration for Stevenson's 'The Pentland Rising'

> Those who sacrificed themselves for peace, the liberty, and the religion of their fellow-countrymen, lay bleaching in the field of death for long, and when at last they were buried by charity, the peasants dug up their bodies, desecrated their graves, and cast them once more upon the heath for the sorry value of their winding sheets!
>
> Robert Louis Stevenson, 'The Pentland Rising' (1866)

The Pentland Rising and the Battle of Rullion Green in 1666 is a significant event in Covenanting history, as it was the first time that Covenanters had banded together as a force to be reckoned with to protest against the outlawing of their religion. On 28 November, 900 Covenanters were intercepted by 3,000 professional troops, who, after a bloody battle, left 50 Covenanters dead on the slopes of Turnhouse Hill overlooking the valley of the Glencorse Burn. Many of the wounded died in the hills and about 30 prisoners were hanged at the Mercat Cross in Edinburgh. After their execution, their right hands were cut off and nailed to the prison door at Lanark and their severed heads displayed in their home towns and villages: a severe lesson to others thinking of sacrificing themselves 'for peace, the liberty, and the religion of their fellow-countrymen'.

Stevenson grew up with tales of the Covenanters resounding in his ears and was surrounded by their bloody history during his summers at Swanston. In 1866, aged only 16, he wrote and published anonymously 'The Pentland Rising: a page of History, 1666'. This 16-page 'slim green pamphlet', of which only 100 copies were printed, is now a collector's item. His father, however, wasn't impressed, as his Aunt Jane Balfour recollected in 1866:

> I was at Heriot Row . . . and Louis was busily altering 'The Pentland Rising' then to please his father. He had made a story of it, and by so doing, had, in his father's opinion, spoiled it. It was printed not long after in a

small edition, and Mr Stevenson very soon bought all the copies in, as far as was possible.

This, his first published work, never seemed to find a fond corner in his memory and he described it in later life as 'an absurdity written by a schoolboy'. Maybe so, but Louis always loved a lost cause, and the Covenanters would surely have been honoured.

SEE ALSO: Howard Place, Inverleith Terrace, Heriot Row, Pilrig House, Colinton Manse, Swanston Cottage, Baxter's Place, Glencorse Kirk, Rutherford's Howff, New Calton Cemetery, Old Calton Burial Ground, St Giles, Hawes Inn, W.E. Henley, Alison Cunningham, Henderson's School, Deacon Brodie, The Writers' Museum, *Kidnapped* Statue, RLS Club, Museum of Scotland, George Mackenzie, Martyrs' Monument, Edinburgh Castle, Old College, Parliament Hall, Holyrood Park, Royal College of Surgeons' Museum, R.M. Ballantyne, RLS Memorial, Writers' Corner.

FURTHER INFORMATION: Rullion Green lies about eight miles south of Edinburgh on the slopes of the Pentland Hills. Recommended map: OS Explorer 344. To visit Rullion Green, turn off the A720 city bypass at the Lothianburn Junction, heading south on the A702. Park at the Flotterstone Ranger and Visitor Centre about four miles further on. Walk along the pavement by the A702 for about 20 minutes, then turn right at Rullion Green Cottage into the hills. The Martyrs' Memorial is about half a kilometre from the A702 on the south-east slopes of Turnhouse Hill, and is marked on OS Explorer 344.

Pentland Hills Regional Park. Tel: 0131 445 3383.
Email: ranger@phrangerservice.demon.co.uk.
Website: www.pentlandhills.org.

FURTHER READING: D.G. Moir, *Pentland Walks: Their Literary and Historical Associations* (Bartholomew, 1977).

LITTLE SPARTA

Home and garden of Ian Hamilton Finlay, Scottish artist, poet and writer

In 1966, Ian Hamilton Finlay moved to an abandoned croft in the Pentland Hills where, over the years, he has created a unique garden fusing poetry and sculpture. Acknowledged by many as one of the most important gardens in the UK, its works of art range in theme from the French Revolution to fishing fleets and the sea. A 'must see' for all literary pilgrims.

FURTHER INFORMATION: Take the A702 from Edinburgh to Dolphinton and turn right for Dunsyre. Little Sparta is a mile beyond the village.

OPENING HOURS: 2.30 p.m.–5 p.m. Friday and Sunday, June–September.

Tel: 01556 640 244. Website: www.littlesparta.co.uk.

Glencorse

KIRK BRAE

The Old Kirk of Glencorse
Favourite haunt and inspiration of Robert Louis Stevenson (1850–94)

> Do you know where the road crosses the burn under Glencorse Church? Go there, and say a prayer for me: *moriturus salutat*. See that it's a sunny day . . . stand on the right-hand bank just where the road goes down into the water, and shut your eyes, and if I don't appear . . . well, it can't be helped, and will be extremely funny.
>
> RLS to S.R. Crockett, from Samoa, 17 May 1893

Built in 1699, with a steep slate roof and a wooden steeple, this little kirk and kirkyard was one of Robert Louis Stevenson's favourite haunts. When he stayed at Swanston Cottage, Stevenson would go to services there with his father and listen to old Mr Torrance preach ('over eighty and a relic of times forgotten, with his black thread gloves and mild old foolish face'). Glencorse is also the church featured in his prose poem 'Sunday Thoughts':

Old Glencorse Kirk.

> A plague o' these Sundays! How the church bells ring up the sleeping past! I cannot go into sermon: memories ache too hard; and so I hide out under the blue heavens, beside the small kirk whelmed in leaves. Tittering country girls see me as I go past from where they sit in the pews, and through the open door comes the loud psalm and the fervent solitary voice of the preacher.

242

Napoleonic prisoner-of-war grave.

The grave-robbing scene in his 1884 'crawler' 'The Body Snatcher' was set in the old kirkyard:

The coffin was exhumed and broken open; the body inserted in the dripping sack and carried between them to the gig; one mounted to keep it in its place, and the other, taking the horse by the mouth, groped along by wall and bush until they reached the wider road by the Fisher's Tryst.

He also placed scenes from *Weir of Hermiston* (1896) here and it is highly likely that one of the tombstones ignited the inspiration for his Napoleonic prisoner-of-war novel, *St Ives* (1897): 'Ici repose Charles Cotier de Dunkerque. Mort le 8 Janvier 1807.' 'I suppose he died prisoner in the military prison hard by,' noted Stevenson.

He remembered Glencorse with affection and missed it dearly, lamenting from his tropical Samoan paradise that he 'shall never take that walk by the Fisher's Tryst and Glencorse; I shall never see Auld Reekie; I shall never set my foot again upon heather. Here I am until I die, and here will I be buried.'

SEE ALSO: Howard Place, Inverleith Terrace, Heriot Row, Pilrig House, Colinton Manse, Swanston Cottage, Baxter's Place, Rutherford's Howff, New Calton Cemetery, Old Calton Burial Ground, St Giles, Hawes Inn, Rullion Green, W.E. Henley, Alison Cunningham, Henderson's School, Deacon Brodie, the Writers' Museum, *Kidnapped* Statue, RLS Club, Museum of Scotland, George Mackenzie, Martyrs' Monument,

'Where the road crosses the burn'.

Edinburgh Castle, Old College, Parliament Hall, Holyrood Park, Royal College of Surgeons' Museum, R.M. Ballantyne, RLS Memorial, Writers' Corner.

FURTHER INFORMATION: Unfortunately, Old Glencorse Kirk is on private land and is not open to the public. For many years, the kirk was a roofless ruin, but recent restoration has returned it to its former glory. RLS's description of the location 'where the road crosses the burn' in his letter to S.R. Crockett (see above) refers to a spot about half a mile westward from the gates of Glencorse House, where the public road crosses Glencorse Burn, and is on a double bend. Glencorse Kirk is signposted in Milton Bridge, opposite the Fisher's Tryst pub on the A701. This signpost refers to the new Glencorse Kirk, but the old kirk and 'where the road crosses the burn' are on the same road.

Penicuik

PEEBLES ROAD

Penicuik South Church
Former church of Scottish novelist S.R. Crockett (1860–1914)

> 'Janet,' said the minister to his housekeeper, 'I am to preach tonight at Cauldshaws on the text, "Whatsoever thy hand findeth to do, do it with thy might."'
>
> 'I ken,' said Janet, 'I saw it on yer desk. I pat it ablow the clock for fear the wun's o' heevin micht blaw it awa' like chaff, an' you couldna do wantin' it!'
>
> 'Janet MacTaggart,' said the minister, tartly, 'bring in the denner, and do not meddle with what does not concern you.'
>
> The Lammas Preaching, from *The Stickit Minister and Some Common Men* (1893)

Born the illegitimate son of a dairymaid at the farm of Little Duchrae, Balmaghie, Kircudbrightshire in 1860, Samuel Rutherford Crockett was a leading exponent of the Kailyard school, which typified a sentimental and romantic image of Scottish rural life. Written in a cosy vernacular, his books were frequently bestsellers, but are little read today. Educated at the Free Church School at Castle Douglas, he won a bursary to Edinburgh University, where legend has it he lived on meals of oatmeal, penny rolls and milk.

S.R. Crockett.

In 1886, he was appointed Free Church minister at Penicuik. With the success of *The Stickit Minister*, published in 1893, he abandoned the ministry in 1895 and became a full-time writer. *The Raiders* and *The Lilac Sunbonnet* followed in 1894, and 40-odd novels later he had accrued vast fame and fortune.

Robert Louis Stevenson admired his book of poems, *Dulce Cor*, published in 1887. They became friends, and in 1893 Crockett dedicated *The Stickit Minister* to him.

Stevenson reciprocated with the poem 'To S.R. Crockett', written in Samoa and permeated with a yearning to return to Scotland.

Crockett lived at Bank House in Penicuik Estate on the banks of the River Esk. The former Free Church (now Penicuik South Church) is still standing on the Peebles Road at Alder Bank. Crockett moved to Torwood Villa, near Peebles, in 1906, and died suddenly in Tarascon in France in 1914.

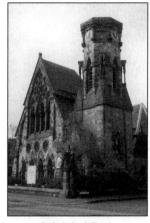

Penicuik South Church.

SEE ALSO: Swanston, Old College, W.E. Henley, Glencorse Kirk.

FURTHER READING: I.M. Donaldson, *Life and Work of S.R. Crockett* (Mercat Press, 1989).

South Queensferry

The Hawes Inn
Sixteenth-century inn featured in Robert Louis Stevenson's
Kidnapped

> Some day, I think, a boat shall put off from the Queen's
> Ferry, fraught with a dear cargo.
> Robert Louis Stevenson, 'A Gossip on Romance' (1882)

The romantic setting of the Hawes Inn first appealed to Sir Walter Scott, who had Lovel and Jonathan Oldbuck dining there in *The Antiquary* in 1816, but it was Robert Louis Stevenson who secured its immortality when he wove it into the plot of *Kidnapped* (1886), his tale of the Jacobite rising of 1745 and its sad aftermath. 'There it stands,' he wrote, 'apart from the town, beside the pier, in a climate of its own, half inland, half marine – in front, the ferry bubbling with the tide and the guardship swinging to her anchor; behind, the old garden with the trees.'

Although altered and extended over the years, the Hawes Inn still retains some of the backdrop, and perhaps a little of the spirit, in which old Ebenezer arranged the kidnap of his nephew David Balfour with the assistance of Captain Hoseason in 'a small room, with a bed in it, and heated like an oven by a great

fire of coal'. The unsuspecting David Balfour later boards the brig *Covenant*, moored at South Queensferry, where he is kidnapped and destined to be sold as a slave in the Carolinas.

Stevenson was a regular visitor to Queensferry in his youth, rambling along the shores of Cramond and canoeing in the Forth with Walter Simpson, his companion in *An Inland Voyage*. Since 1890, the Hawes Inn has been dwarfed by the adjacent Forth Railway Bridge, a spectacular feat of Victorian engineering that Stevenson never saw. The ferry disappeared in the early 1960s with the opening of the Forth Road Bridge.

SEE ALSO: Sir Walter Scott, Howard Place, Inverleith Terrace, Heriot Row, Pilrig House, Colinton Manse, Swanston Cottage, Baxter's Place, Glencorse Kirk, Rutherford's Howff, New Calton Cemetery, Old Calton Burial Ground, St Giles, Rullion Green, W.E. Henley, Alison Cunningham, Henderson's School, Deacon Brodie, *Kidnapped* Statue, RLS Club, Museum of Scotland, George Mackenzie, Martyrs' Monument, Edinburgh Castle, Old College, Parliament Hall, Holyrood Park, Royal College of Surgeons' Museum, R.M. Ballantyne, RLS Memorial, Writers' Corner.

FURTHER INFORMATION: The Hawes Inn, Newhalls Road, South Queensferry. Tel: 0131 331 1990.

In *Catriona* (1893), the sequel to *Kidnapped*, David Balfour is imprisoned on the Bass Rock, opposite North Berwick, about 20 miles east of Edinburgh. Stevenson visited North Berwick for holidays as a young boy and set his essay 'The Lantern-Bearers' (1887) there.

FURTHER READING: I. Nimmo, *Walking With Murder: On the Kidnapped Trail* (Birlinn, 2005).

Appendices

LITERARY TOURS

The Edinburgh Book Lovers' Tour

A guided walking tour with travel writer Allan Foster, author of *The Literary Traveller in Edinburgh* – the book you hold in your hands.

To discover literary Edinburgh, you have to walk it, defying Robert Louis Stevenson's 'bleak winds' and exploring Dorothy Wordsworth's 'passes of dark stone', simply because there is no

Sandy Bell's – one of the watering holes on the Edinburgh Book Lovers' Tour.

Allan Foster.

other way of penetrating the ancient wynds, closes and creeper-ridden burial grounds of this city, whose literary past is written on its dark and hoary face. This book recounts many lives and tales, but to squeeze 500 years of literary Edinburgh into one single volume is an impossible task. There is so much more to tell, and so much more to see. Having travelled the length and breadth of Edinburgh researching and photographing the sites featured in the book, I can assure you the pickings are rich, the locations diverse and stimulating, and with over 500 years to choose from, everybody's reading taste is catered for – from Robert Burns to J.K. Rowling. So why not accompany me (and a strolling player or two) on a book lovers' odyssey around the Old Town to explore more of literary Edinburgh's fascinating and never-ending story, complete with commentary, readings, dramatisations and lots of laughter.

FURTHER INFORMATION: The tour lasts approximately two hours with refreshment stops.

For tour dates, departure points, times, prices and bookings, phone 07866 276 952/01573 223 888

or consult www.edinburghbookloverstour.com.

Email: allanfoster@movietraveller.co.uk.

Group bookings welcome.

Dine at the Stevenson House

An exclusive tour of 17 Heriot Row, followed by dinner, with readings and dramatisations from the life and works of Robert Louis Stevenson.

Felicitas Macfie outside 17 Heriot Row.

Have you ever wondered what it is like to dine in the historic home of Robert Louis Stevenson? Or to climb the broad staircase to the elegant drawing room and look through the same windows as did the sickly young Louis, while waiting expectantly for 'Leerie the Lamplighter' to pass by? This is the house with which RLS is most associated, and where he spent his youth, adolescence and early adulthood from 1857: a house full of stories and legends waiting to be told. The Stevenson House is a typical Georgian New Town house which has always been in private ownership and is still used as a family home. It has never been a museum and is not open to the public, but exclusive admission is now available to the literary pilgrim through the Edinburgh Book Lovers' Tour.

SEE ALSO: 17 Heriot Row.

FURTHER INFORMATION: For dates, times, prices and bookings, phone 07866 276 952/01573 223 888

or consult www.edinburghbookloverstour.com.

Email: allanfoster@movietraveller.co.uk.

Group bookings welcome.

The *Trainspotting* Tour

When Irvine Welsh was writing his loosely connected pieces on the drugs scene of his native Leith in the mid-'80s, he made no attempt to disguise where the action took place. He also made little attempt to conceal the identities of the individuals who inspired his fictional characters, and many people in Leith recognise themselves in the pages of his novels.

This tour is a combination of literature and history, both funny and telling. The tour combines *Trainspotting* (1993) and its sequel *Porno* (2002), set almost 10 years later, when Sick Boy has acquired a pub called Port Sunshine – the Port o' Leith Bar, where the tour starts and finishes. Stand in the car park where the enigmatic word 'trainspotting' was uttered and see with your own eyes the environs of the drug addict and the wino. Neither Welsh, nor the tour, glamorises the danger of drugs, and

Tim Bell with Mary Moriarty, landlady of the Port o' Leith.

the pure crudities in the language come so thick and fast that by the end of the tour you'll hardly notice them.

SEE ALSO: Irvine Welsh.

FURTHER INFORMATION: The tour departs from the Port o' Leith Bar, 58 Constitution Street, Leith, and lasts around two hours with a refreshment stop. For programme dates and times, contact Tim Bell on 0131 555 2500 or consult www.leithwalks.co.uk. Not suitable for children. By arrangement, there is an extended tour available which takes the same bus route Renton took on his trip to Mikey Forrester and the worst toilet, from there to the Sheriff Court, Deacon Brodie's and other up-town scenes. The extended tour depends on buses, so precise timing is impossible, but allow a morning.

Rebus Tours

Since its launch in 2000, Rebus Tours has attracted thousands of Rebus fans from all over the world. Led by the erudite John Skinner, this tour has the approval of Ian Rankin, who once commented that 'John knows more about Rebus than I do.'

Each year, Ian Rankin and John Skinner stage a special Rebus Tour event to raise funds for one of Ian's chosen charities, mainly to do with children with special needs.

The tour route, called 'Body Politic', starts at The Royal Oak pub on Infirmary Street, just off South Bridge near to the Royal Mile. The route leads past the city morgue, past the historic Flodden Wall into Holyrood Road and up hidden closes to the Canongate, with its kirk and kirkyard, the resting place of many famous Scots. After a refreshment stop, the walk goes past the front of the new Scottish Parliament and up towards the graceful Regency terraces beside Calton Hill (with stunning views of the Old Town and Arthur's Seat), ending very near the east end of Princes Street and close to the Balmoral Hotel. Politics and corruption is the theme – contrasting the time of the Act of Union in 1707 with the present day! Readings include passages from *Knots and Crosses*, *Set in Darkness*, *Strip Jack*, *The Falls* and *Dead Souls*. The tour lasts about two hours.

SEE ALSO: Ian Rankin, Oxford Bar, Holyrood Park, Fopp.

FURTHER INFORMATION: The tour season runs from Easter to the end of August but group bookings are welcome throughout the year. The tours run every day during the Edinburgh

Fringe Festival in August and have won a 'Sell Out Show' Award from the Fringe Festival. During the Fringe, tickets are only available from the Fringe Box Office (0131 226 0000; www.edfringe.com). Outwith the Fringe, tickets can be reserved on www.rebustours.com or by emailing info@rebustours.com.

The tour departs from The Royal Oak, 1 Infirmary Street, and will normally be led by John Skinner or Colin Brown, who took part in the Rebus TV adaptation of *Dead Souls* (with John Hannah in the title role). Other specialist walking tours of Edinburgh (architecture, literature, local history) are also guided by John Skinner for groups and individuals on request, including 'In the footsteps of Robert Louis Stevenson' and 'Stevenson and Conan Doyle's times at Edinburgh University'.

The Edinburgh Literary Pub Tour

This tour has been in existence now for over a decade. Its ingredients are simple – pubs, laughs and literature – so be prepared to be hilariously entertained, glass in hand, by this two-man romp through 300 years of Edinburgh's literary history. Actors 'Clart' and 'McBrain' lead the tour and bounce off each other in a duel of wits from The Beehive up to the Jolly Judge off the Royal Mile, then downhill to the Doric Tavern in Market Street, ending up outside Milnes and the Abbotsford in Rose Street. En route, via a few wynds and courtyards, the duo recreate the life and times of Edinburgh's literati. Observe Robert Burns's seduction techniques with his beloved Clarinda, while Clart sings 'Ae Fond Kiss' and recites his erotic

Clart and McBrain in a duel of wits.

verse. Other characters brought to life include the Ettrick Shepherd James Hogg, the Wizard of the North Walter Scott and the man who all his life had a love–hate relationship with Edinburgh, Robert Louis Stevenson.

FURTHER INFORMATION: The tour departs from the Beehive Inn, 18 Grassmarket, and lasts approximately two hours. Tour times: May to September, daily at 7.30 p.m.; October, March and April, Thursday to Sunday at 7.30 p.m.; November, December, January and February, every Friday at 7.30 p.m. For prices and bookings contact 0131 226 6665.
Email: info@scot-lit-tour.co.uk.
Website: www.edinburghliterarypubtour.co.uk.

LIBRARIES

**5 Crichton's Close
Scottish Poetry Library**

> For this is the House of Poetry. Here the heart
> finds wholeness; the spirit bursts into song.
> Stewart Conn, from 'Flight of Fancy', on the occasion
> of the Scottish Poetry Library's 21st birthday
> celebration, Friday, 4 February 2005

With its mono-pitch roof slung over a steel frame, and walls of oak and glass, the award-winning building by architect Malcolm Fraser is deceptively simple, relaxing and, most of all, welcoming. Scottish artists were commissioned to contribute pieces, including Liz Ogilvie's glass-panelled balustrade inscribed with lines from Scottish poems, a tapestry by Ian Hamilton Finlay and a 'carpet of leaves' by Mary Bourne. As if this wasn't enough pleasure, the building also houses a collection of 30,000 items, many of which are available to borrow in person or by post (returnable by Freepost). Here you will find the poetry of Scotland in three languages – English, Scots and Gaelic.

Of the library, founded in 1984, former director Tessa Ransford says:

> One of the nicest comments I've heard is that the books can breathe now. The opening up of the space is symbolic of the opening up of poetry, not just physically, but psychologically as well. Poetry has always been related to music, dance, painting and the arts, but in this building I think people will appreciate it more in its own context – taking poetry into the twenty-first century.

FURTHER INFORMATION: Scottish Poetry Library, 5 Crichton's Close, Canongate, Edinburgh EH8 8DT. Tel: 0131 557 2876. Email: inquiries@spl.org.uk. Website: www.spl.org.uk.

Parliament Square
The Signet Library

This library belongs to the Society of Writers to Her Majesty's Signet, the oldest body of lawyers in Scotland. The Signet was the private seal of the early Stuart kings. It was increasingly used in civil litigation, and now all writs initiating civil actions have to be sealed with the Signet, which is held and used under the authority of the keeper of the Signet.

The exterior of the three-storey classical building was built between 1810 and 1812 to the design of the King's architect, Robert Reid. For many years, the building housed one of the finest collections of books in Scotland, totalling over 150,000 volumes by 1950. Since then, the number has been reduced and the library is largely devoted to books on law and books of specific Scottish interest. The library is a private one used by writers to the Signet, mainly in connection with their professional work.

FURTHER INFORMATION: Although private, ready access is always given to researchers. Open days are held during the year. Tel: 0131 225 4923. Email: library@wssociety.co.uk. Website: www.signetlibrary.co.uk.

30 George Square
Edinburgh University Library

The largest university library in Scotland, EUL is spread over 17 sites across the city. The main library, located in George Square, holds three and a half million books, periodicals and pamphlets, 9,000 journals and 30,000 volumes of manuscripts. It was founded in 1580 when Clement Litill, an Edinburgh advocate, died, bequeathing his collection of 276 volumes to the Toun and Kirk of Edinburgh. A year after the founding of the Tounis College, now the University of Edinburgh, in 1583, these books were handed over to the College as a basis for its library. By the beginning of the eighteenth century, the library had acquired other significant collections, one of which had been donated by the poet William Drummond of Hawthornden (1620–30), a graduate of the University. The Laing Collection is the largest single manuscript collection in the EUL. The charters and other papers contained within it are of national importance and are the most distinguished collections of their kind in any Scottish university. The Library's continuous existence since 1580 and its status as a legal deposit library has led to the amassing of a large number of early printed books on many subjects. Tel: 0131 650 3384. Email: special.collections.library@ed.ac.uk.

George IV Bridge
The National Library of Scotland

This is Scotland's largest library and is the world centre for the study of Scotland and the Scots. It also ranks among the largest libraries in the UK, housing 8,000,000 printed books, 120,000 volumes of manuscripts, 2,000,000 maps and over 20,000 newspaper and magazine titles. The online catalogue records 3,500,000 items for public access. The NLS developed from the Advocate's Library of 1682, the legal section of which is still housed in its original premises at Parliament Square. In 1925, its

entire contents, apart from its legal section, were removed to the NLS. The library has the right to receive free of charge a copy of every book published in the United Kingdom and Ireland, based on the Legal Deposit Libraries Act 2003, and before that the Copyright Act 1911. This right has enabled the library to build extensive general collections on all subjects, though it has a special responsibility for the acquisition and preservation of material of Scottish interest. NLS is one of only five libraries in the UK today with copyright status. Since 1925, the NLS has also been collecting literary manuscripts, working papers and correspondence of writers such as Robert Burns, Sir Walter Scott, Edwin Muir, Sydney Goodsir Smith, A.J. Cronin, Lewis Grassic Gibbon, Neil Gunn, Muriel Spark, Hugh MacDiarmid, Naomi Mitchison, Alasdair Gray, Eric Linklater and Robert Louis Stevenson. The NLS also holds frequent public exhibitions of its collections and has a small gift shop.

FURTHER INFORMATION: Tel: 0131 226 4531.

Website: www.nls.uk.

George IV Bridge
The Central Library

Visited by half a million people and lending out 300,000 books annually, the Central Library was founded by the Scots philanthropist Andrew Carnegie (1835–1919). Opened in 1890, and built in the French François I style, its foundations are rooted several storeys below George IV Bridge in the Cowgate. As well as being a general lending library, it houses important collections of Scottish and Edinburgh-related material. Collections in the Edinburgh Room and Scottish Library hold extensive

information about the city and Scotland.

FURTHER INFORMATION: Opening hours: Monday to Thursday 10 a.m.–8 p.m; Friday 10 a.m.–5 p.m; Saturday 9 a.m.–1 p.m. General enquires: 0131 242 8000.

The Scottish Library: 0131 242 8070.

The Edinburgh Room: 0131 242 8030.

Email: central.scottish.library@edinburgh.gov.uk.

Email: edinburgh.room@edinburgh.gov.uk.

Edinburgh City Libraries

Central	George IV Bridge, EH1 1EG (0131 242 8000)
Balerno	1 Main Street, EH14 7EQ (0131 529 5500)
Balgreen	173 Balgreen Road, EH11 3AT (0131 529 5585)
Blackhall	56 Hillhouse Road, EH4 5EG (0131 529 5595)
Colinton	14 Thorburn Road, EH13 OBQ (0131 529 5603)
Corstorphine	12 Kirk Loan, EH12 7HD (0131 529 5506)
Craigmillar	7 Niddrie Marischal Gardens, EH16 4LX (0131 529 5597)
Currie	210 Lanark Road West, EH14 5NN (0131 529 5609)
Fountainbridge	137 Dundee Street, EH11 1BG (0131 529 5616)
Gilmerton	13 Newtoft Street, EH17 8RG (0131 529 5628)
Granton	29 Wardieburn Terrace, EH5 2DA (0131 529 5630)
Kirkliston	Station Road, Kirkliston, EH29 9BE (0131 529 5510)
Leith	28–30 Ferry Road, EH6 4AE (0131 529 5517)
McDonald Road	2 McDonald Road, EH7 4LU (0131 529 5636)
Moredun	92 Moredun Park Road, EH17 7HL (0131 529 5652)
Morningside	184 Morningside Road, EH10 4PU (0131 529 5654)
Muirhouse	15 Pennywell Court, EH4 4TZ (0131 529 5528)
Newington	17–21 Fountainhall Road, EH9 2LN (0131 529 5536)
Oxgangs	343 Oxgangs Road North, EH13 9LY (0131 529 5549)
Piershill	30 Piersfield Terrace, EH8 7BQ (0131 529 5685)
Portobello	14 Rosefield Avenue, EH15 1AU (0131 529 5558)
Ratho	6 School Wynd, EH28 8TT (0131 333 5297)
Sighthill	6 Sighthill Wynd, EH11 4BL (0131 529 5569)
South Queensferry	9 Shore Road, EH30 9RD (0131 529 5576)
Stockbridge	Hamilton Place, EH3 5BA (0131 529 5665)
Wester Hailes	1 West Side Plaza, EH14 2FT (0131 529 5667)

Library opening hours

Central, Blackhall, Corstorphine, Leith, Morningside and Piershill libraries:

> Monday, Tuesday, Wednesday, Thursday: 10 a.m.–8 p.m.
> Friday: 10 a.m.–5 p.m.
> Saturday: 9 a.m.–1 p.m.

Muirhouse, Newington, Oxgangs, Portobello and Wester Hailes libraries:

> Weekdays: as above.
> Saturday: 9 a.m.–5 p.m.
> Sunday: 1 p.m.–5 p.m.

Balerno, Balgreen, Central Children's, Colinton, Craigmillar, Currie, Fountainbridge, Gilmerton, Granton, Kirkliston, Moredun, Ratho, Sighthill, South Queensferry and Stockbridge libraries:

> Monday, Wednesday: 1 p.m.–8 p.m.
> Tuesday, Thursday, Friday: 10 a.m.–5 p.m.
> Saturday: 9 a.m.–1 p.m.

McDonald Road library:

> Weekdays: as above.
> Saturday: 9 a.m.–5 p.m.
> Sunday: 1 p.m.–5 p.m.

BOOK FESTIVALS

Edinburgh International Book Festival

Established in 1983 as a biennial festival, and becoming an annual celebration in 1997, this event is now the largest of its kind in the world. A mere 30 writers were hosted at the first festival, but today it holds hundreds of events, including debates, discussions, workshops and book signings, and has a vibrant children's programme. Located in Charlotte Square during August, when the Edinburgh International Festival and its satellite festivals are in full swing, the Book Festival becomes a place of sanctuary to recharge, reflect, relax and even read – an island in the stream when Edinburgh goes stark-raving bonkers.

FURTHER INFORMATION: Available from the Edinburgh International Book Festival, Scottish Book Centre, 137 Dundee Street, Edinburgh EH11 1BG.
Tel: 0131 228 5444. Website: www.edbookfest.co.uk.

Edinburgh Independent Radical Book Fair

This event takes place annually in May at the Assembly Rooms, George Street, Edinburgh. Attend workshops, listen to some great music and hear writers read excerpts from their books. Past guests have included A.L. Kennedy, Alasdair Gray and James Kelman. Website: www.word-power.co.uk.

The Debut Festival

The Traverse Theatre in Cambridge Street, Edinburgh, runs a debut authors' festival in early June, which is the first festival dedicated to new writers. Introducing an exciting range of writers from Britain and beyond, the festival includes writers from a range of backgrounds, ages and styles. It focuses on how the writers chose what to write about, how they approached it and how they found an agent and got published. Email: pru@authortalks.org. Website: www.traverse.co.uk.

The Scottish International Storytelling Festival

A ten-day celebration during October of live oral storytelling when Scottish and international storytellers join forces to share an exciting array of myths, legends, folk tales and fairy tales. Events are held in various venues, including bookshops, restaurants, libraries and visitor attractions like the Castle and the Zoo. Further information from The Scottish Storytelling Centre, 43–5 High Street, Edinburgh EH1 1SR.
Tel: 0131 556 9579/557 5724.
Website: www.scottishstorytellingcentre.co.uk.

The Festival of Scottish Writing

Hosted by Edinburgh City Libraries and Information Services, this festival stages a variety of events and workshops at city libraries during the last two weeks of May. The focus is on Scottish writing and most events are free. Tel: 0131 242 8000.

LITERARY EVENTS

Shore Poets

Shore Poets exists to promote new poets and to provide them with a platform to read alongside the more established names on the Scottish scene. Shore Poets' monthly events take place in the cellar-bar atmosphere of the Canon's Gait pub, 232 Canongate (0131 556 4481). All events start at 7.45 p.m. and run until approximately 10.30 p.m. Admission to events is £2 (concessions £1). Each poet reads for 15 to 20 minutes and there are three 10-minute music spots during the evening. Email: info@shorepoets.org.uk.

Big Word Performance Poetry

Fortnightly cabaret at The Tron Bar (0131 226 0931) every second Thursday, 9 Hunter Square, Royal Mile. Doors 8.30 p.m. Show 9 p.m.–11 p.m. MCs Jem Rollins and Jenny Linsey. Entry: £3 (concessions £2).
Email: jemrolls@bigword.fsnet.co.uk.

Kin

Fortnightly open-mike sessions at the Waverley, the Forest and the Café Royal (where Kin currently resides) have provided servings of acoustic soup for Edinburgh crowds since January 2001. Kin's ingredients are simple: gently simmer a freshly picked crop of locally grown poets, singers, players and story-sayers on a warm stage; add generous servings from the bar; garnish with the warmest audience in Edinburgh; repeat fortnightly. Kin is at the Café Royal Bistro Bar (0131 557 4792), 1st floor, West Register Street, Edinburgh, 9 p.m.–11 p.m. £1 entrance (performers free). To join the Kin mailing list send an email to: info@kinhead.net.

Out Loud

Monthly open-mike nights run by the Phoenix Writers' Group, first Thursday of the month at 'The Diggers' pub' (Athletic Arms), 1–3 Angle Park Terrace, Edinburgh EH11 2JX, from 7.30 p.m. Entry: £1 donation. Tel: 0131 337 3822. Email Julie Clark at words@outloud.org.uk.

School of Poets

A group of poets who meet at the Scottish Poetry Library once a month to read their poems to each other and receive feedback and criticism.

Contact: Scottish Poetry Library, 5 Crichton's Close, Canongate, Edinburgh EH8 8DT. Tel: 0131 557 2876.

Email: inquiries@spl.org.uk. Website: www.spl.org.uk.

Christian Aid Book Sale

Christian Aid's largest single fundraising event in the UK, this annual book sale, begun in 1974, raises thousands of pounds for charity at St Andrew's and St George's Church, 13 George Street,

Edinburgh, during one week every May. Books of all sorts, particularly antiquarian and Scottish, are displayed on 150 tables, accompanied by scores of helpers. Tel: 07714 186 754. Website: www.standrewsandstgeorges.org.uk.

LITERARY SOCIETIES

The Edinburgh Friends of William McGonagall

When Lord Provost Eric Milligan was unveiling the Robert Louis Stevenson paving stone in Edinburgh's Makars' Court, the Edinburgh city archivist Richard Hunter suggested to Bob Watt

Bob Watt.

that there might be a place for McGonagall's name on one of the paving stones. From that day, Bob decided to focus attention and interest on McGonagall and, together with his wife Pat, formed the Edinburgh Friends of William McGonagall in 1999. At the time of writing, a case is being prepared to have McGonagall's stone placed in the Makars' Court. If this is rejected, an American who owns the flat above the close has agreed to hang a pair of red long johns from his window pulley with 'William McGonagall' printed across the back!

Bob and Pat raised money for a plaque in Greyfriars Kirkyard by running a McGonagall dinner at their home, and so the McGonagall East of Scotland Dinner was invented. At the dinner, each guest was asked to compose and read four lines of verse in the style of McGonagall. Bob was the sole judge of these efforts. One enthusiast had written nine pages with ten verses on each page, but Bob's judgement was not purely poetry based – Mrs Lind came third because she was Bob's sister. A bardic crown (a 'See you, Jimmy' hat) was placed on the head of the winning makar. The evening generated over £700 and the plaque was ordered up.

FURTHER INFORMATION: Tel: 0131 441 2580.

The Robert Louis Stevenson Club

Robert Louis Stevenson is synonymous with Edinburgh but with both feet firmly placed on the world's literary stage. He has bridged the centuries better than many other writers and his works are regularly filmed, televised, broadcast and republished. Stevenson himself continues to fascinate and on average two books are published every year about the author. The Robert Louis Stevenson Club must also take credit for keeping the RLS flag flying so high. Its membership spans the globe.

From 1926 to 1963, the club's headquarters and museum were located in Stevenson's birthplace at 8 Howard Place. The

RLS Club's main objective is to foster interest in Stevenson's life and works. Since 1920, when the club was formed, it has passionately carried out this remit by lectures, presentations, literary lunches, awards, and visits to Stevenson-related locations as far-flung as Samoa, California, the Cévennes and even to David Balfour's islet of Erraid, off Mull.

The RLS Club visiting 17 Heriot Row.

In 1985, on the centenary of *A Child's Garden of Verses*, the RLS Club launched an international appeal with two aims: to erect a memorial to RLS and to create and endow the RLS Memorial Trust to help children with respiratory diseases. The resulting memorial, designed by the Scottish artist-poet Ian Hamilton Finlay, was inaugurated in 1989, consisting of a small stone column surrounded by a coppice of birch trees, and can be seen in West Princes Street Gardens.

The Robert Louis Stevenson Club works closely with the Writers' Museum, home to the club's collection of Stevenson artefacts and papers, which remains one of the largest in the world. The annual luncheon in November is the main social occasion of the year, when friends meet, socialise and listen to outstanding speakers on RLS, who have included Walter de la Mare, John Buchan and J.B. Priestly. The RLS Club warmly welcomes new members, whether Stevenson first-timers or seasoned and serious readers of his works.

FURTHER INFORMATION: Website: www.rlsclub.org.uk.

The Edinburgh Walter Scott Club

> I can think of no higher compliment to the movie than that it awakened in me a desire to read Scott's novel, although when I failed to find it on my shelves, I was able to live with the disappointment.
>
> Roger Ebert reviewing the 1995
> film adaptation of *Rob Roy*

Roger Ebert's put-down is fairly typical of the way many people react to Scott today. 'Nobody reads Scott any more,' one hears people say, and they're probably right, but Scott's impact on literature was revolutionary, and there are still many rewards to be gained from reading this founding father of the European Romantic movement.

The Edinburgh Sir Walter Scott Club has been in existence for over 100 years, and celebrated its centenary in 1994. It has a membership of over 400, most of whom live in Edinburgh. The object of the club is to foster the name of Sir Walter Scott through meetings, lectures, publications and excursions. In March each year, the club holds an annual dinner and a public lecture is regularly held jointly with the University of

Edinburgh. Members also enjoy regular visits to Abbotsford and trips to other parts of Scotland associated with Sir Walter. The lectures and addresses are published in an annual bulletin, which also includes other articles of interest on Scott, his work and contemporaries.

FURTHER INFORMATION: Email: murfra@btinternet.com.

The Dorothy Dunnett Readers' Association

A highly regarded writer of very well-researched historical fiction, Dorothy Dunnett (1923–2001) has been described by *The Times* as 'the best writer of the genre since Walter Scott'. The Dorothy Dunnett Readers' Association was created in 2000 with the aim of studying and discussing her works, and their relation to the history, politics, culture and religion of the fifteenth and sixteenth centuries. The DDRA has a yearly

'gathering' in Edinburgh, where her works are discussed, speakers are invited and members taken to sites of historical interest. There have also been large gatherings in Oxford, Carlisle, Philadelphia, New Orleans, Dublin and Malta. Members receive a quarterly

Members of the DDRA visiting the Dunnett archive at the National Library of Scotland. (© Olive Millward)

magazine, *Whispering Gallery*, which contains articles on the international politics, music, medicine, dress, etc. of the times in which the novels are set. The DDRA is sponsoring a commemorative stone to Dorothy Dunnett in the Makars' Court of the Writers' Museum, and the stone will be laid on 22 April 2006. Dorothy Dunnett took a close interest in the DDRA and she expressed a wish that 'it would live forever!'.

FURTHER INFORMATION: The Dorothy Dunnett Readers' Association, Anne McMillan (secretary), Rowanlea, 41 Ottoline Drive, Troon KA10 7AN. Tel: 01292 311 245.

The Edinburgh & District Burns Clubs Association

On 7 January 1925, a meeting was held at 129 Princes Street to consider what steps ought to be taken to form an association of Edinburgh Burns Clubs. The minute book, which is still in existence, records that the association was formed that evening. The objects of the association were to strengthen and consolidate by district affiliation the bond of fellowship existing among the members of Burns clubs in the area.

In 1927, at the third annual general meeting, a proposal was made and carried out for a scheme of schoolchildren's competitions, all related to Burns, confined at first to children under the Edinburgh Education Authority. Prizes of up to £10 were awarded – a very large sum of money in those days. Schools taking part in that first competition included

Stockbridge, Niddrie, Tollcross and Balerno, some of which regularly take part to this day. The first competition held in the individual schools attracted 1,727 entrants. Those organising the event considered this to be highly satisfactory. The following year, 3,240 pupils took part! The competition has continued ever since, held annually, even during the Second World War, gradually evolving into its present form. Winners take part in the National Festival for Scottish Schools.

In addition to the competition, the association holds its annual wreath-laying ceremony at the Flaxman Statue of Burns situated within the National Portrait Gallery, Queen Street, Edinburgh, at 3 p.m. on the Sunday closest to 25 January each year. The association presently represents around a dozen clubs within its district and holds quarterly meetings.

FURTHER INFORMATION: Gordon Innes WS (secretary, The Edinburgh & District Burns Clubs), Messrs Gillespie MacAndrew, 31 Melville Street, Edinburgh. Website: www.robertburnsfederation.co.uk.

The John Buchan Society

The John Buchan Society was founded in Edinburgh in 1979 by a core of enthusiasts who took an Edinburgh University evening class tutored by Dr Eileen Stewart, whose Ph.D. thesis was the first written on John Buchan and his work. Initially, the society's activities were largely based in and around Edinburgh but now the membership of about 500 is spread worldwide and events reflect this. The annual general meeting and annual dinner are held alternately in Scotland and England. Other events have been located in Kent, Canada, South Africa,

John Buchan's granddaughter, Lady Stewartby, sitting beside her grandfather's stone inscription in The Makars' Court, outside the Writers' Museum.

London, Edinburgh, New England and the Scottish Borders: in other words, wherever a group of members want to get together. The society, now a charity, publishes *The John Buchan Journal*, which appears twice a year. Contributions range through scholarly articles, personal reminiscences about the Buchan family and discussions on his fiction, to notes and queries, which cover questions asked and points made by readers.

FURTHER INFORMATION: The Secretary, Greenmantle, Main Street, Kings Newton, Melbourne, Derbyshire DE73 8BX. Website: www.johnbuchansociety.co.uk.

The Muriel Spark Society

The MSS at the annual Muriel Spark Birthday Lunch.

Founded in March 2001, with Dame Muriel's personal approval and blessing, the Muriel Spark Society offers a varied programme of events, including talks by eminent speakers, an annual lunch on Dame Muriel's birthday on 1 February, guided walks around relevant parts of Edinburgh, and meetings in the National Library where the Muriel Spark archive is held.

FURTHER INFORMATION: Gail Wylie, 13 Bangholm Bower Avenue, Edinburgh EH5 3NS. Email: gewylie@btinternet.com.

The Saltire Society

Not strictly a literary society, but an organisation which saw the need in the 1930s to interest Scots in their own culture and preserve all that is best in Scottish tradition. Literature is a big part of that tradition, and the annual Saltire Literary Awards reflect this. The name 'saltire' is taken from the heraldic name of the Cross of St Andrew.

FURTHER INFORMATION: The Saltire Society, 9 Fountains Close, 22 High Street, Edinburgh EH1 1TF. Tel: 0131 556 1836.
Email: saltire@saltiresociety.org.uk.
Website: www.saltiresociety.org.uk.

The Carlyle Society, Edinburgh

This society was founded in 1929 to examine the lives of Thomas Carlyle and his wife, Jane, their writings, contemporaries and influences. Meetings are held about six times a year and occasional papers are published annually.

FURTHER INFORMATION: The President, The Carlyle Society, Dept of English Literature, The University of Edinburgh, David Hume Tower, George Square, Edinburgh EH8 9JX. Email: ian.campbell@ed.ac.uk.

LITERARY MAGAZINES

Anon
A poetry magazine that doesn't care who you aren't.
Editor: Mike Stocks
67 Learmonth Grove
Edinburgh
EH4 1BL

Cencrastus
The magazine for Scottish and international literature, arts and affairs.
Editor: Raymond Ross
Unit One, Abbeymount Techbase
Abbeyhill
Edinburgh
EH8 8EJ
Tel: 0131 661 5687
Email: cencrastus1@hotmail.com
Quarterly

Chanticleer
Editor: Richard Livermore
1 Alva Street (2FL)
Edinburgh
EH2 4PH

Chapman
Scotland's quality literary magazine.
Editor: Joy Hendry
4 Broughton Place
Edinburgh
EH1 3RX
Tel: 0131 557 2207
Email: chapman-pub@blueyonder.co.uk
Website: www.chapman-pub.co.uk
Thrice yearly

Edinburgh Review
Scotland's leading biannual journal of ideas, the *Edinburgh Review* publishes essays, short fiction, poetry and reviews aimed at an educated reading public with an interest in critical thought.
Editor: Ronald Turnbull
22a Buccleuch Place
Edinburgh
EH8 9LN
Tel: 0131 651 1415
Email: edinburgh.review@ed.ac.uk
Website: www.edinburghreview.org.uk

Folio
Collections, research, events at the National Library of Scotland.
Editor: Jennie Renton
National Library of Scotland
George IV Bridge
Edinburgh
EH1 1EW
Website: www.nls.uk

Gath
An iris Ghàidhlig.
Editors: Dòmhnall E. Meek, Jò NicDhòmhnaill
27 Ceàrnag Sheòras/George Square
Dùn Eideann/Edinburgh
EH8 9LD
Email: d.e.meek@ed.ac.uk
Quarterly

Green Shoots
An occasional magazine of poetry, verse and prose by the people of Edinburgh. Available in hard copy from Edinburgh City Libraries and Information Services. If you are interested in contributing, contact community.information@edinburgh.gov.uk or 0131 242 8110. For further information, visit the Green Shoots webpage on the Edinburgh libraries website: www.edinburgh.gov.uk/libraries.
Community Information Service
Central Library
George IV Bridge
Edinburgh
EH1 1EG

island
A biannual literary magazine providing a distinctive space for new writing inspired by nature and exploring our place within the natural world. Hand-bound, with a gentle use of colour and texture and an uncluttered design approaching that of an artist's book, it combines a spare beauty with perceptive content, publishing poetry and prose poems, concrete poetry, essays and non-fiction fragments in themed issues. It is published by Essence Press.
Editor: Julie Johnstone
8 Craiglea Drive
Edinburgh
EH10 5PA
Website: www.essencepress.co.uk
Email: jaj@essencepress.co.uk

One O'Clock Gun
'First in, best dressed; original and still the best.' A double-sided broadsheet with 'cunning folds', published by:
Top Slot Publications
Edinburgh
Tel: 07969 463 232
Email: paxedina@yahoo.co.uk

Quarto

Newsletter of the National Library of Scotland.
National Library of Scotland
George IV Bridge
Edinburgh
EH1 1EW
Website: www.nls.uk

Scottish Review of Books

Editor: Alan Taylor
The Sunday Herald
9/10 St Andrew Square
Edinburgh
EH2 2AF
Quarterly

Scottish Studies

School of Scottish Studies
University of Edinburgh
27 George Square
Edinburgh
EH8 9LD
Tel: 0131 650 4156
Fax: 0131 650 4163
Email: ScottishStudies@ed.ac.uk
Annual

textualities: online literary magazine

An online literary and book-collecting magazine with a Scottish flavour, this ever-growing literary resource offers a range of interviews with authors, including Louise Welsh, Yann Martell and Philip Pullman, alongside creative writing, reviews and profiles. For collectors, the website focuses on rare and out-of-print books, typography, publishing history and special library collections. Here you will find articles on subjects as diverse as collecting Lewis Carroll first editions and Robert Louis Stevenson's library in Samoa. It also has an interesting section of profiles of second-hand booksellers, many from Edinburgh. There is a growing selection of articles of Gaelic and Highland interest, and a section devoted to book illustrators such as

Jennie Renton.

Jessie M. King. Hundreds of articles from the *Scottish Book Collector* archive are gradually being displayed here. Among the archive audio files is the very first SBC interview, with Norman MacCaig, made in 1987. As a service to the writing community, *textualities* offers free Web space to authors whose names appear on the Scottish Book Trust Writers' Register.

Email: the.editor@textualities.net or phone Jennie Renton: 0131 228 4837. A print version of *textualities* appears annually. Both website and magazine are based at:

Main Point Books
8 Lauriston Street
Edinburgh
EH3 9DJ
Website: www.textualities.net

Tocher
Editor: Morag MacLeod
School of Scottish Studies
27 George Square
Edinburgh
EH8 9LD
Tel: 0131 650 3056

Understanding
Editor: Denise Smith
Dionysia Press
20A Montgomery Street
Edinburgh
EH7 5JS
Tel: 0131 478 2572

(LITERARY SERVICES)

UNESCO City of Literature

I feel part of a tradition which is as vibrant now as ever before. Edinburgh remains a city of the mind, a writer's city.

Ian Rankin

When Edinburgh became the first UNESCO City of Literature in 2004, UNESCO's assistant director general for culture, Mounir Bouchenaki, expressed the opinion that by sharing its entrepreneurial and creative know-how, Edinburgh has the potential to achieve a truly global impact.

Edinburgh already is a world city of literature. Its great heritage of the book and its contemporary literary life define it as a cultural capital for the ages. The idea of a formal designation came about because it was thought that Edinburgh, and indeed Scotland, should take on responsibility for the future development of a literary culture that has distinguished and enlightened our country's past, as well as sharing the literary culture of Edinburgh with the world. The idea is not about competition but about aspiration and partnership.

FURTHER INFORMATION: Edinburgh City of Literature, 137 Dundee Street, Edinburgh EH11 1BG. Tel: 0131 229 9498.
Email: edinburgh@cityofliterature.com
Website: www.cityofliterature.com

Scottish Book Trust

Founded in 1956, Scottish Book Trust is an independent educational charity which exists to promote literature in all its forms as central to the cultural life of Scotland, ensuring that everyone has access to good books and to related resources and opportunities. They do this in various ways: by representing literature in Scotland on a national and international platform, by connecting writers and readers, by supporting professional practice in Scottish writing and by providing training to writers and educationalists; by providing direct financial support, and creative and organisational advice for live literature events throughout Scotland, by operating readership development initiatives, by operating an educational outreach programme of events and projects across Scotland, focusing on areas of deprivation and/or geographical remoteness; by providing impartial, independent information on books, writers and reading, by representing the peoples of Scotland through campaigning for the continued greater development of provision in literature nationwide and by acting as a coordinating collaborative umbrella organisation for literature initiatives and opportunities in Scotland.

FURTHER INFORMATION: Scottish Book Trust, Sandeman House, Trunk's Close, 55 High Street, Edinburgh EH1 1SR. Tel: 0131 524 0166.

Website: www.scottishbooktrust.com

Scottish PEN

In May 1927, Hugh MacDiarmid wrote to the leading writers of his day in Scotland and invited them to join him in establishing a Scottish Centre of International PEN. PEN originally stood for 'poets, essayists and novelists' and International PEN was founded in 1921. Neil Gunn, Edwin and Willa Muir, Naomi Mitchison and R.B. Cunninghame-Graham, among others, responded and Scottish PEN was born. Since then, it has vigorously promoted the founding principles of International PEN, campaigning consistently for the writers' freedom of expression above all, but also for internationalism, for the centrality of literature in world culture, for imprisoned writers and other important causes. Today, with 130 centres throughout the world, PEN is international in scope and, in addition, recognised by UNESCO as the voice of the worldwide community of writers.

FURTHER INFORMATION: Email: info@scottishpen.org. Website: www.scottishpen.org.

The Scottish Storytelling Centre

The Scottish Storytelling Forum is Scotland's national charity for storytelling. It was founded in 1992 to encourage and support the telling and sharing of stories across all ages and all sectors of society, in particular those who, for reasons of poverty or disability, are excluded from artistic experiences.

The Centre trains and supports professional storytellers and volunteer storytellers who use storytelling in their professional or community lives. It also stimulates and supports local festivals, storytelling clubs and community projects in association with voluntary groups, studies older storytelling traditions, arranges a programme of events including the annual Scottish International Storytelling Festival and provides information and advice on all aspects of storytelling, including storytellers.

The new home of the Scottish Storytelling Centre is rising steadily from the ashes of the old Netherbow in Edinburgh's Royal Mile and is due to be operational by the beginning of 2006. The George Mackay Brown Storytelling Library will be a focus of the new building and there will be regular storytelling events taking place and a fun, interactive story-wall where people can engage with Scottish stories.

FURTHER INFORMATION: The Scottish Storytelling Centre, 43–5 High Street, Edinburgh EH1 1SR. Tel: 0131 556 9579. Website: www.scottishstorytellingcentre.co.uk.

The Poetry Association of Scotland

This was founded in 1924 to promote public readings of the best poetry from all over the world. Annual membership gives you entry to all meetings, puts you on the mailing list and gives you voting rights. Tel: 0131 443 6874. Email: dmr.lit@fsmail.net.

(WRITERS' GROUPS)

ALP Writers' Workshop

184 Dalry Road
Edinburgh
Tel: 0131 337 5442
Website: www.alpedinburgh.com
Meets on the first and third Tuesdays every month,
7.30 p.m–9.30 p.m.

Bo'ness and Linlithgow Writers' Workshop

Community Education Base
North Street
Bo'ness
Tuesdays fortnightly at 7 p.m., September to May
Tel: 01506 843 581

The Bosachs Writing Group

Wednesdays at 7 p.m. in Causewayside. Contact bosachs@yahoo.co.uk for more information or visit the Bosachs Club webpage at the address below.
Website: www.edinburgh.gov.uk/libraries

Chancers Creative

2nd Chance to Learn
The Old Fire Station
27 East Norton Place
London Road
Edinburgh
Tel: 0131 661 1788

Craigmount Writers' Group
Craigmount Community Education Office
Craigs Road
Edinburgh
Tel: 0131 339 8278
Fridays 10 a.m.–12 p.m. during school terms

The Diggers' Writers
c/o The Athletic Arms
1 Henderson Terrace
Edinburgh
Tel: 0131 225 7772

Edinburgh Writers' Club
Osborne Hotel
53–9 York Place
Edinburgh
Tel: 0131 228 3651
Alternate Mondays, September to May, 7.30 p.m.

East Lothian Literary Society
Mrs Gavin
22 Edgehead Road
Pathhead
Midlothian

Fountainbridge Writers' Group
Fountainbridge Library
Meets every Wednesday, 6.30 p.m.–7.45 p.m.
Tel: 0131 447 4784

Kersiebank Writers
Anne Hayward
KC Projects
Oxgangs Road
Grangemouth
FK3 9EF

Leith Writers' Workshop
Jimmy Spence
Kirkgate Community Centre
Kirkgate
Leith
Edinburgh
Tel: 0131 661 1920

Pentland Writers
5 Bridge Road
Balerno
Edinburgh
Tel: 0131 449 6655
Meets weekly at Balerno High School

West Lothian Writers' Club
Kathleen Ross-Hale
43 Ivanhoe Rise
Dedridge
Livingston
EH45 6JA

Words Women's Writing Group
ALP
184 Dalry Road
Edinburgh
Tel: 0131 337 5442
Meets at St Colm's Church, 2 p.m.–3 p.m. on the last Sunday of
the month

Workers' Educational Association
34b Thistle Street North-West Lane
Edinburgh
Tel: 0131 225 7772

Writers Against Writing
c/o Centurion Bar
243 St John's Road
Edinburgh
EH12 7XD
Tel: 0131 334 7687
Contact writersagainstwriting@yahoo.co.uk
or visit www.freewebs.com/writersagainstwriting

WHAT THEY SAID ABOUT EDINBURGH

A dirty, cold, wet, run-down slum; a city of dull, black
tenements and crass concrete housing schemes which
were populated by scruffs, but the town still somehow
being run by snobs.

Irvine Welsh, *Marabou Stork Nightmares* (1995)

There is no street in Europe more spectacular than
Princes Street; it is absolutely operatic.

Henry James

It is quite lovely, bits of it.

Oscar Wilde

But I must add (the more's the pity)
that though in fair Dunedin's city
Scotland's taste is quite delightful,
the smaller Scottish towns are frightful.

Sir Arthur Conan Doyle, from *Songs of the Road* (1911)

But Edinburgh pays cruelly for her high seat in one of the vilest climates under heaven. She is liable to be beaten upon by all the winds that blow, to be drenched with rain, to be buried in cold sea fogs out of the east, and powdered with the snow as it comes flying southward from the Highland hills. The weather is raw and boisterous in winter, shifty and ungenial in summer, and a downright meteorological purgatory in the spring. The delicate die early, and I, as a survivor, among bleak winds and plumping rain, have sometimes been tempted to envy them their fate.

> Robert Louis Stevenson, *Edinburgh: Picturesque Notes* (1878)

This accursed, stinking, reeky mass of stones and lime and dung.

> Thomas Carlyle, letter to his brother John, February (1821)

Edinburgh is looking at its best, which is I think the best in the world, for it must be about the most romantic city on earth. But it strikes cold on me nowadays, for the familiar faces have long been gone and there are only buildings left.

> J.M. Barrie, 1909

What a wonderful City Edinburgh is! What alternation of Height & Depth! – a city looked at in the polish'd back of a Brobdingnag Spoon, held lengthways – so enormously stretched-up are the Houses.

> Samuel Taylor Coleridge

The city stands upon two hills, and the bottom between them; and, with all its defects, may very well pass for the capital of a moderate kingdom.

> Tobias Smollett, *The Expedition of Humphry Clinker* (1771)

Tho' many cities have more people in them, yet, I believe, this may be said with truth that in no city in the world do so many people live in so little room as at Edinburgh.

> Daniel Defoe

It seems like a city built on precipices, a perilous city. Great roads rush down hill like rivers in spate. Great buildings rush up like rockets.

> G.K. Chesterton, 1905

Edinburgh alone is splendid in its situation and buildings and would have even a more imposing and delightful effect if Arthur's Seat were crowned with thick woods and if the Pentland Hills could be converted into green pastures, if the Scotch people were French and Leith Walk planted with vineyards.

> William Hazlitt, 1826

It is the peculiar boast of Edinburgh, the circumstances on which its marvellous beauty so essentially depends, that its architecture is its landscape; that nature has done everything, has laid every foundation, and disposed of every line of its rocks and its hills, as if she had designed it for the display of architecture.

Edinburgh Review, 1838

Arrived at Edinburgh a little before sunset. As we approached, the Castle rock resembling that of Stirling – in the same manner appearing to rise from a plain of cultivated ground, the Firth of Forth being on the other side, and not visible . . . The Old Town, with its irregular houses, stage above stage, seen as we saw it, in the obscurity of a rainy day, hardly resembles the work of men. It is more like a piling up of rocks and I cannot attempt to describe what we saw so imperfectly, but must say that, high as my expectations had been raised, the city of Edinburgh far surpassed all expectations.

Dorothy Wordsworth, *Recollections of a Tour Made in Scotland, AD 1803*

Well may Edinburgh be called Auld Reekie! The houses stand so one above another that none of the smoke wastes itself upon the desert air before the inhabitants have derived all the advantages of its odour and its smuts. You might smoke bacon by hanging it out of the window.

Robert Southey, 1819

So Edinburgh is what a city ought to be, somewhere to live and walk about in.

Sir John Betjeman

I am not sorry to have seen the most picturesque (at a distance) and nastiest (when near) of all capital cities.

Thomas Gray, 1765

Far set in fields and woods, the town I see
Spring gallant from the shadows of her smoke,
Cragged, spired and turreted, her virgin fort beflagged.

Robert Louis Stevenson

It would make a good prison in England.

Dr Johnson on Edinburgh Castle

This braw hie heapit toun.

Lewis Spence, 'The Prows o' Reekie'

Six, seven, eight storeys high were the houses; storey piled above storey, as children build with cards.

Charles Dickens

Piled deep and massy, close and high
Mine own romantic town.

Sir Walter Scott, *Marmion* (1808)

This (the Royal Mile) is, perhaps, the largest, longest,
and finest street for buildings and number of
inhabitants not in Britain only, but in the World.

Daniel Defoe, *A Tour Through the Whole Island of
Great Britain* (1724–27)

What horrible alleys on each side of the High Street,
especially downwards like passes of quarries of dark
stone. I ventured down one, and hastened back to
escape from the spitting of two children who were
leaning out of an upper window.

Dorothy Wordsworth, 1822

The wynds down which an English eye may look but
into which no English nose would willingly venture for
stinks older than the Union are to be found there.

Robert Southey, 1819

The main side streets are narrow, filthy and with six storey
houses; one has to think of the great buildings in the dirty
towns of Italy; poverty and misery seem to peep out of the
open hatches which normally serve as windows.

Hans Christian Andersen, 1847

No smells were ever equal to Scotch smells. It is the
School of Physic; walk the streets and you would imagine
that every medical man had been administering
cathartics to every man, woman and child in town. Yet the
place is uncommonly beautiful and I am in constant
balance between admiration and trepidation.

Sydney Smith, 1798

As far as I am acquainted with modern architecture, I
am aware of no streets which, in simplicity and
manliness of style, or general breadth and brightness of
effect, equal those of the New Town of Edinburgh.

John Ruskin, *Letters on Architecture and Painting*
(1854)

Fareweel, Edinburgh, where happy we hae been,
Fareweel, Edinburgh, Caledonia's Queen!
Auld Reekie, fare-ye-weel, and Reekie New beside,
Ye're like a chieftain grim and gray, wi' a young bonny
bride.

Baroness Carolina Nairne, 'Fareweel Edinburgh'

Beneath, the Old Town reared its dark brow, and the
New one stretched its golden lines, while, all around,
the varied charms of nature lay scattered in that
profusion, which nature's hand alone can bestow.

Susan Ferrier, *Marriage* (1818)

We rode to Edinburgh; one of the dirtiest cities I have ever seen not excepting Cologne in Germany.

John Wesley, 1751

My dear Sir, do not think that I blaspheme when I tell you that your great London, as compared to Dun-Edin, 'mine own romantic town', is as prose compared to poetry, or as a great rumbling, rambling, heavy Epic compared to a Lyric, brief, bright, clear, and vital as a flash of lightning.

Charlotte Brontë, 1850

The spectacle of the Old Town, seen from the New, is inspiring and splendid, and places Edinburgh, from the artistic point of view, on a level with Constantinople and Stockholm.

John Ruskin

Except Naples [Edinburgh] is I think, the most picturesque place I have ever seen.

Washington Irving, 1811

Glasgow plays the part of Chicago to Edinburgh's Boston. Glasgow is a city of the glad hand and the smack on the back; Edinburgh is a city of silence until birth or brains open the social circle.

H.V. Morton

Edinburgh is a hot bed of genius.

Tobias Smollett, *The Expedition of Humphry Clinker* (1771)

Edina! Scotia's darling seat!

Robert Burns, *Address to Edinburgh* (1786)

The cook was too filthy an object to be described; only another English gentleman whispered me and said, he believed, if the fellow was to be thrown against a wall, he would stick to it.

Edmund Burt, on an Edinburgh eating-house, *Letters from the North of Scotland* (1728–37)

The most beautiful of all the capitals of Europe.

Sir John Betjeman, *First and Last Loves* (1952)

When I looked out in the morning it is as if I had waked in Utopia.

George Eliot

This profusion of eccentricities, this dream in masonry and living rock is not a drop scene in a theatre, but a city in the world of reality.

Robert Louis Stevenson

A setting for an opera nobody performs nowadays an opera called 'Scottish History'.

Alasdair Gray, *1982, Janine* (1984)

And I forgot the clouded Forth
The gloom that saddens Heaven and Earth
The bitter east, the misty summer
And gray metropolis of the North

Alfred, Lord Tennyson

Enchanting. It will make a delightful summer capital when we invade Britain.

Dr Joseph Goebbels, 1938

Who indeed that has once seen Edinburgh, but must see it again in dreams waking or sleeping?

Charlotte Brontë, 1850

Edinburgh is a mad god's dream.

Hugh MacDiarmid, *The Complete Poems* (1978)

A city too well known to admit description.

Dr Johnson

As long as sixteen or seventeen years ago, the first great public recognition and encouragement I ever received was bestowed on me in this generous and magnificent city – in this city so distinguished in literature and the arts . . . coming back to Edinburgh is to me like coming home.

Charles Dickens, 1858

Of all the cities in the British Islands, Edinburgh is the one which presents most advantages for the display of a noble building; and which, on the other hand, sustains most injury in the erection of a commonplace or unworthy one.

John Ruskin, 1853

It seemed as if the rock and castle assumed a new aspect every time I looked at them; and Arthur's Seat was perfect witchcraft, I don't wonder that anyone residing in Edinburgh should write poetically.

Washington Irving, 1817

Edinburgh . . . a disappointed spinster with a hare-lip and inhibitions.

Lewis Grassic Gibbon, *Scottish Scene* (1934)

I do wonder that so brave a prince as King James should be born in so stinking a town as Edinburgh in lousy Scotland.

Sir Anthony Weldon, *A Perfect Guide to the People and Country of Scotland* (1617)

When I was lately in Scotland I went to visit some poor inhabitants of the Old Town of Edinburgh. In a close wynd – a most picturesque place – (picturesque and typhus synonymous) I saw more poverty and sickness than I ever saw before. In one wretched dwelling I saw a poor sick child cradled in an egg-box, which his mother had begged from a shop and that little wan child with his fevered face, his wasted hand and his bright watchful eyes, I have ever before my sight. I can still see him and seem to hear him say, 'Why am I lying here, shut in from the light of day and from the play of other children?'

Charles Dickens, 1858

Athenians, indeed! where is your theatre? who among you has written a comedy? where is your Attic salt? which of you can tell who was Jupiter's great-grandfather? . . . you know nothing that the Athenians thought worth knowing, and dare not show your faces before the civilised world in the practice of any one art in which they were excellent.

Thomas Love Peacock on the
pretensions of Edinburgh as the 'Athens
of the North', in Crotchet Castle (1831)

Reikie, fareweel! I ne'er cou'd part
Wi' thee but wi' a dowy heart.

Robert Fergusson, Auld Reikie (1773)

I saw rain falling and the rainbow drawn
On Lammermuir. Hearkening I heard again
In my precipitous city beaten bells
Winnow the keen sea wind. And here afar
Intent on my own race and place I wrote.

Robert Louis Stevenson

Index